Early
Childbearing

Volume 192 Sage Library of Social Research

RECENT VOLUMES IN . . .
SAGE LIBRARY OF SOCIAL RESEARCH

 84 Gelles **Family Violence, 2nd Edition**
150 Frey **Survey Research by Telephone, 2nd Edition**
155 Russell **Sexual Exploitation**
163 Markides/Mindel **Aging and Ethnicity**
166 Steinmetz **Duty Bound**
167 Teune **Growth**
168 Blakely **Planning Local Economic Development**
169 Mathews **Strategic Intervention in Organizations**
170 Scanzoni/Polonko/Teachman/Thompson **The Sexual Bond**
171 Prus **Pursuing Customers**
172 Prus **Making Sales**
173 Mayer **Redefining Comparative Politics**
174 Vannoy-Hiller/Philliber **Equal Partners**
175 Brewer/Hunter **Multimethod Research**
176 Chafetz **Gender Equity**
177 Peterson **Political Behavior**
178 So **Social Change and Development**
179 Gomes-Schwartz/Horowitz/Cardarelli **Child Sexual Abuse**
180 Evan **Social Structure and Law**
181 Turner/Turner **The Impossible Science**
182 McCollum **The Trauma of Moving**
183 Cohen/Adoni/Bantz **Social Conflict and
        Television News**
184 Gruter **Law and the Mind**
185 Koss/Harvey **The Rape Victim**
186 Cicirelli **Family Caregiving**
187 Caves **Land Use Planning**
188 Blalock **Understanding Social Inequality**
189 Gubrium **Out of Control**
190 Albrecht **The Disability Business**
191 Alter/Hage **Organizations Working Together**
192 Freeman/Rickels **Early Childbearing**
193 Burr **Managing Family Stress**
194 McGrath/Hollingshead **Groups Interacting With Technology**

Early Childbearing

*Perspectives of Black
Adolescents on Pregnancy,
Abortion, and Contraception*

Ellen W. Freeman
Karl Rickels

Sage Library of Social Research 192

SAGE Publications
International Educational and Professional Publisher
Newbury Park   London   New Delhi

For information address:

SAGE Publications, Inc.
2455 Teller Road
Newbury Park, California 91320

SAGE Publications Ltd.
6 Bonhill Street
London EC2A 4PU
United Kingdom

SAGE Publications India Pvt. Ltd.
M-32 Market
Greater Kailash I
New Delhi 110 048 India

Printed in the United States of America

Library of Congress Cataloging-in-Publication Data

Freeman, Ellen W.
  Early childbearing: Perspectives of black adolescents on pregnancy,
    abortion, and contraception/
Ellen W. Freeman, Karl Rickels.
      p. cm.—(Sage library of social research: v. 192)
    Includes bibliographical references and index.
    ISBN 0-8039-5282-1.—ISBN 0-8039-5283-X (pbk.)
    1. Teenage mothers—United States. 2. Abortion—United States.
  3. Childbirth—United States. 4. Teenagers—United States—
  Attitudes. I. Rickels, Karl, 1924- . II. Title. III. Series.
  HQ759.4.F74   1993
  306.7'0835—dc20   93-21682

93 94 95 96 10 9 8 7 6 5 4 3 2 1

Sage Production Editor: Diane S. Foster

Contents

List of Tables   vii
List of Figures   viii
List of Appendixes   x
Foreword   xi
   EMILY HARTSHORNE MUDD

Acknowledgments   xv

1. Studying the Problem of Teenage Pregnancy   1
    Introduction   1
    The Penn Study of Teenage Pregnancy   6
    Overview of Chapters   15

2. Risking Pregnancy: Avoidance, Ignorance, and Delay
    of Contraceptive Use   20
    Introduction   20
    The Penn Study   23
    Chapter Summary   35

3. Wanting Pregnancy: Teenagers' Attitudes, Goals,
    and Perceived Support   40
    Introduction   40
    The Penn Study   43
    Chapter Summary   57

4. Choosing Abortion or Delivery: Influences and
    Outcomes   60
    Introduction   60
    Influences on the Pregnancy Decision   62
    Outcomes of the Pregnancy Decision   72
    Chapter Summary   83

5. Avoiding Childbearing: Teenagers Who Terminated a
   First Pregnancy Compared to Never-Pregnant Peers   86
   Introduction   86
   Characteristics at Study Enrollment   88
   Characteristics Two Years Later   94
   Chapter Summary   99

6. Pregnancies After Study Enrollment: "Pregnant
   Because They Are Different or Different Because
   They Are Pregnant?"   102
   Introduction   102
   Pregnancies After Study Enrollment   103
   Chapter Summary   116

7. Family Involvement: Preventing Early Teenage
   Childbearing   119
   Introduction   119
   The Family Involvement Project   121
   Results of the Family Involvement Project   124
   Results of the Group Meetings   130
   Results at the 1-Year Follow-up   131
   Chapter Summary   135

8. Male Teenagers and Contraception   138
   Introduction   138
   Male Teenagers in High School Classes   140
   Male Partners of Teenagers in the Penn Study   144
   Male Teenagers in the Family Involvement Project   148
   Chapter Summary   151

9. Conclusions and Recommendations   153
   A Glimpse 10 Years Later   153
   Conclusions   155
   Recommendations   161

   Appendixes   164
   Bibliography   195
   Index   207
   About the Authors   216

List of Tables

Table 1.1 Pregnancy Status at the Beginning and End
of the Study for Participants and Dropouts   10

Table 2.1 Sexual Information and Attitudes of Female
Teenagers at Study Enrollment   30

Table 3.1 Attitudes Toward Pregnancy:
Distributions at Enrollment   49

Table 3.2 Goals of the Teenagers:
Education, Work, Maternity   51

Table 3.3 Mean Scores for Support of Early Childbearing 55

Table 4.1 Mother's Support for Abortion and Delivery
Reported by Teenagers at Study Enrollment   69

Table 6.1 Incidence of Pregnancy During the Study by
Enrollment Status   104

Table 6.2 Contraceptive Use at First and Second Year
Follow-up by Initial Study Status and
Subsequent Pregnancy Groups   107

Table 6.3 School Status at 2-Year Follow-up by Initial Study
Status and Subsequent Pregnancy Groups   109

Table 7.1 Talking About Sexual Topics as Reported by
Mothers and Teenagers at Project Enrollment   129

Table 7.2 Percent of Teenagers Reporting Sex Before
and 1 Year After Project Participation   134

List of Figures

Figure 3.1. Teenagers' Ratings on 100 mm Analog Scales at 3 Time Points of How Much Pregnancy Was "Wanted"   45

Figure 3.2. Teenagers' Ratings on 100 mm Analog Scales at 3 Time Points of How Much Pregnancy Was "Planned"   47

Figure 4.1. Teenagers' Ratings at Study Enrollment of How Happy Their Parents and Friends Were About the Teenagers' Having a Baby   66

Figure 4.2. Percent of Abortion- and Delivery-Group Teenagers Who Reported Very Strong Support for Childbearing From Mother and Grandmother   67

Figure 4.3. Percent With Worsened Educational Status at 2-Year Follow-up in the Abortion and Delivery Groups   73

Figure 4.4. Mean Scores on 3 Self-Esteem Dimensions at Baseline, 1-Year, and 2-Year Follow-ups for the Abortion and Delivery Groups:
Self-Acceptance   77
Family Relations   78
Assertiveness   79

Figure 4.5. Percent Reporting "Life Better" at Present Time Compared to Baseline Pregnancy Time in Abortion and Delivery Groups   82

Figure 6.1. Reports of "Always" Use Contraception at the
First- and Second-Year Follow-ups in the
3 Original Study Groups   106

Figure 6.2. Educational Status Variables at 2-Year
Follow-up Compared Between Teenagers
With Pregnancies or With No Pregnancies
After Study Enrollment   108

Figure 7.1. Comparison of Post-Group Responses
by Mothers and Teenagers   131

Figure 7.2. Comparison of 1-Year Follow-up Responses:
Mothers Versus Controls, Teenagers
Versus Controls   133

List of Appendixes

A. Measurement Instruments and Assessment Points in
    the Study   164

B. Statistical Procedures Used   165

C. Summary of Theoretical Framework With
    Main Variables Analysis   166

D. Background Characteristics of the Sample
    at Enrollment   168

E. Additional Statistical Tables   172

F. Initial Interview Questionnaire for the Teenagers   178

Foreword

Authorities report that an exploding world population, which today (1992) stands at 5.5 billion, will more than double in the next 40 years, overwhelming all natural and human resources—and no one can predict what will happen thereafter. Teenage pregnancies in the United States and around the world are one aspect of this dilemma and add their own specific problems of inadequately cared-for children. Pregnancy in the teenage years has been the norm throughout history, but two particular problems characterize teenage pregnancies in the United States today. More teenagers are becoming pregnant at younger ages: 16, 15, 14, and even younger. And many more unmarried teenagers are starting families as single mothers, often with no means of economic support, with uncompleted high school education, and with increasing evidence that their children have developmental difficulties associated with their mothers' immaturity as well as poverty.

Early Childbearing shows that many teenagers who are sexually active and from disadvantaged circumstances can and do avoid early teenage childbearing. When we see that this is so and contrast these young people to other teenagers from the same circumstances who begin childbearing early, we can recognize the complexity of the pregnancy problem "that does not go away."

Early Childbearing is based on the perceptions of urban, poor, African-American adolescents who described their decisions about having or not having babies in the context of their goals and the attitudes of their families and peers. The study was conducted during the first half of the 1980s, a time when abortions were available to poor women, and these teenagers could choose between delivery or termination of an unwanted pregnancy. Their feelings about pregnancy, the decisions they made, and the subsequent pathways of these adolescents who lived in disadvantaged circumstances are the substance of this study.

What justifies a study of these teenagers? In the late 1970s, after family planning services expanded and births to teenagers, many of whom were unmarried with unintended pregnancies, accounted for about 20% of the births in the United States, questions were raised about whether these pregnancies were in fact "wanted" rather than "unwanted." If teenagers did not want to have a pregnancy, then it followed that they would use contraception, if they could obtain it easily at low or no cost. This study shows us that even in this disadvantaged population, not many teenagers strongly "wanted" pregnancy. But although they did not want pregnancy, they were not concerned with preventing pregnancy for various reasons. Like many teenagers, they did not get around to obtaining contraception, and they believed that pregnancy, because it had not yet happened, would not occur to them. More important, many of these disadvantaged teenagers *did not believe that the consequences of pregnancy would negatively affect their lives. Although they did not "want" pregnancy, they had no strong motivation to avoid it, because they had no understanding that their lives would be any different.*

How to prevent unplanned teenage pregnancy is now an essential question in my long professional career in educating and counseling women and their families. My first involvement was making contraception available to all women, so they could have the families they wanted and avoid the misery of unwanted pregnancies. We developed marriage counseling to strengthen family life. I worked with Kinsey and with Masters and Johnson, whose research was to enable our understanding of healthy sexuality in family life. The governor of Pennsylvania appointed me the cochairperson of the Pennsylvania Commission for the Study of Abortion Law. In this capacity I heard testimony from pediatricians, who reported horrifying treatment of unwanted children, and from many young women who themselves had experienced unwanted pregnancies and their aftermath. As unintended teenage pregnancies increased, providing sex education and sensitive, caring reproductive health-care services for adolescents seemed paramount. It is my belief that all women of all ages and backgrounds should be able to control their bodies to ensure healthy families and a strong society.

The study of Freeman and Rickels is grounded in a long history of medical, counseling, and other support services for pregnant minority women at the Hospital of the University of Pennsylvania. In 1967, Dr. Helen Dickens, associate dean for minority students in the School of Medicine, established one of the first teen programs in the country for the prenatal care and delivery of pregnant adolescents. Although initially the Teen Clinic groups fared better in terms of returning to school and using contraception, after several years, most had repeated pregnancies. *The challenge was—and still is—to reach teenagers before unintended pregnancy occurred.* Furthermore, we know now what we did not know at the beginning: that social conditions in the United States are appalling for unmarried teenagers to both earn a living and care for a child.

Dr. Dickens and I then organized educational programs in nearby high schools, along with informal counseling, "rap sessions," and referral to family planning services at Penn. We were amazed to find that as we worked with the teenagers, many of their *mothers* made appointments in the family planning program, about which they had no former knowledge. In one of the first outreach projects to the male partners of teenage mothers, we found that many of the young men were involved with their partners and wanted to avoid further unplanned pregnancies. In 1973 we initiated one of the first family planning programs for teenagers who had not had pregnancies. Our report stated our conviction that "as these young women learn in a constructive way that pregnancy is a *choice* for them, they will be able to move into a future responsible relationship with the ability to handle adequately and with dignity, desired and planned motherhood."

The message of the present study is that many teenagers could and did learn that pregnancy is a *choice*, that their own behavior affected their lives. The chance that these teenagers had to terminate unwanted pregnancies allowed them not to become mired in too-early motherhood; many continued to avoid another pregnancy and were still childless when contacted nearly a decade later. They had finished high school, were employed, and were not receiving welfare. To reduce abortions, clinicians, teachers, mothers, and teenagers must understand these issues sooner, before pregnancy occurs.

Communication has been the theme throughout my career. Women initially needed to be given a voice and heard in order to enjoy marital relations and to have access to reproductive health care. Counseling services were instrumental, for better reproductive health care and for better family life. Counseling and educational services then were extended to unmarried teenagers, whose needs for communication are amply described in this book. But communication has no magic alone. It must be grounded in support and caring at all levels. Opportunities must be possible for the disadvantaged. And communication must be aimed at helping all young people mobilize themselves as active directors of their health.

Emily Hartshorne Mudd, Ph.D.
Professor Emeritus of Family Study in Psychiatry
University of Pennsylvania
School of Medicine
Philadelphia, PA

Acknowledgments

Support for the study of Unwanted Pregnancy in Adolescents was provided by the National Institute of Child Health and Human Behavior (RO1 HD 13630). Additional support for data analysis was generously provided by the William T. Grant Foundation. The Family Involvement Project was funded by a grant from the Pew Memorial Trust. The generous support from the Emily Hartshorne Mudd Research Fund made the preparation of this book possible. To each of these, we express our deep appreciation.

Many people were involved in these projects, and we owe them our thanks. The study of Unwanted Pregnancy in Adolescents was originally based on the programs for pregnant and sexually active teenagers in the Department of Obstetrics and Gynecology at the University of Pennsylvania. Dr. Helen O. Dickens directed the Teen Obstetrical Program; Dr. George R. Huggins, and later Dr. Steven J. Sondheimer, directed Family Planning Services; and Jacqueline Logan conducted the Family Life course in nearby high schools and forged a remarkable link between the school-based classes and the hospital-based family planning services. Dr. Celso-Ramon Garcia gave generous guidance to the development of the project, and Dr. Luigi Mastroianni, Jr., chairman of the department at that time, was instrumental in ensuring that reproductive health-care services were available to the teenagers.

The willingness of the teenagers to participate in the study and the unusually high retention rate of 96% of the teens at the 2-year follow-up were due in large measure to the study coordinator, Paula Sanders Goldberg, and to the sensitive and skillful interviews conducted by her and others: Carol Busacca, Susan Carson, Deborah Toogood, and Julie Zucker. Gloria Rowan, who handled the Teen Clinic appointments and tracked the missing teenagers, helped us keep in touch with the study participants.

The interviews with the male partners were conducted and reported by Dr. Judith A. Shea. The 9-year follow-up study of the teens was conducted by Dr. Roberta R. Iverson, in partial fulfillment of the requirements for the Ph.D. at Bryn Mawr College.

The Family Involvement Project was led by Dr. Catherine Higgins. The community-based discussion groups were organized and directed by Edna L. Smalls, whose skills in family therapy contributed uniquely to the success of the project. She was ably assisted by additional group leaders: Patricia G. Branham, Cynthia Howard, Horace E. Means, Brenda Ross, and Deborah Wright.

Research assistance was provided by Barbara Altimari, Lula Hendrix, and Leslie Kelley. Computer file management and programming were conducted by Leslie Koo, Tahmina Ferdousi, Beatriz Garcia, and Pradip Muhuri. We also express our appreciation for the less visible but essential contributions of the hard-working support staff: data coders Marcia Carpentier, Robert Faucher, and Gus Faucher and the administrative assistants who typed numerous tables, figures, and many drafts of the reports—Theresa Alcorn, Emanda Tall-Beckham, and Cheryl Irving. Finally, we thank all others who contributed to the success of these projects, most of all the teenagers and the mothers of teenagers who shared their perceptions and feelings about teenage pregnancy, abortion, and contraception.

ONE

Studying the Problem of
Teenage Pregnancy

INTRODUCTION

Teenage childbearing is normative in many societies and conditions. Teenage pregnancy emerged as a social problem in the United States only around 1970. Although overall birthrates were declining, teenage birthrates increased as the new generation of the postwar baby boomers converged with increased sexual activity at younger ages and greater acceptance of unmarried childbearing.

When the baby boomers became teenagers (and mothers), their sheer numbers drew widespread attention. In the preceding decades, from 1940 to 1960, teenage mothers accounted for about 12% of all births. By 1970 the percentage of births to teenagers rose to 18%. It remained at this level as the rest of the baby boomers passed through their early reproductive years, and then declined to its former level (12.5%) by 1985.

Nevertheless, more than 1 million teenagers become pregnant each year in the United States, and about half of them give birth. About 11,500 of these births in 1989 were to girls age 14 or younger (National Center for Health Statistics, 1991). Two thirds of the total births to teenagers in 1989 were to unmarried teenagers—about 190,000 whites, 140,000 blacks, and 10,500 individuals from other racial backgrounds (National Center for Health Statistics, 1991).

More problematic than numbers alone is the increase in births to *unmarried* teenagers, particularly because many have no means of economic support. In 1940, 1950, and 1960, about 15% of all teenage births were to single women. By 1970 the percentage had climbed to 30%, and by 1989 it had escalated to 67% (National Center for Health Statistics, 1991). In 1989, 37% of the births to white teenagers and 92% of the births to black teenagers were to unmarried young women. As increasing numbers of unmarried teenagers became parents, problems related to inadequate economic and social resources multiplied: delivery of low-birth-weight infants; interrupted education, particularly before completing high school; lowered job potential; and reliance on public support for essentials such as food and shelter (Hayes, 1987).

Increasing numbers of births to unmarried teenagers also reflected the disintegration of the once strong social pressure to marry when pregnancy occurred (Cutright, 1972). Whether pregnant or not, fewer teenagers married. The median age of women at first marriage gradually increased, from 20.3 years in 1960 to 20.8 years in 1970, 22.0 years in 1980, and 23.6 years in 1988 (U.S. Bureau of the Census, 1989). In 1988, 60% of women from age 20 to 24 were unmarried, compared to only 36% in 1970 (U.S. Bureau of the Census, 1989).

The public cost of teenage childbearing has risen steadily, paralleling the number of births to teenagers with no means of economic support. Every year, more than half of the federal welfare budget goes to women who were teenagers when they gave birth for the first time. In 1990, the estimated cost was over $25 billion for Aid to Families With Dependent Children, Medicaid, and food stamps to families started by a teenage birth (Center for Population Options, 1992). Approximately one third of teenage mothers receive public assistance at some time (Center for Population Options, 1989).

The economic costs of too-early childbearing imply that teenage pregnancy causes these effects, but this ignores other complex socioeconomic factors that play a role in teenage births. Single teenage mothers disproportionately come from disadvantaged backgrounds. Poverty and lack of job skills are strongly associated with early childbearing. For example, among teenagers (ages 15 to 19) who gave birth in 1985, 90% of the blacks, 52% of the Hispanics, and 45% of the whites were unmarried (Children's Defense Fund's Adolescent Prevention Clearinghouse, 1988), but in all groups low family incomes and below-average basic job skills figured prominently. When economic status was controlled in the analysis, racial and ethnic differences were minimal.

There is no political consensus in the United States on how to reduce the problems associated with births to unmarried teenagers, but the public generally concurs that something should be done to reduce these pregnancies, which often are described as unintended (Zelnik & Kantner, 1980). To this end, the National Research Council established a blue-ribbon panel to study adolescent pregnancy and childbearing. The panel examined existing research and programs, recommended approaches for future programs and policies, and identified the following primary goals:

1. Reduce the rate and incidence of unintended pregnancy among adolescents, especially among school-age teenagers
2. Provide alternatives to adolescent childbearing and parenting
3. Promote positive social, economic, health, and developmental outcomes for adolescent parents and their children (National Academy of Sciences, 1987)

The panel's report particularly recognized the moral, religious, and political questions that surrounded decisions about teenage pregnancies, and noted that these pregnancies involved young women who would be considered children in any other context (National Research Council, 1987). Moreover, the report emphasized the relationship of social circumstances to teenage pregnancy and childbearing.

> Youth unemployment, poverty, poor education, single-parent families, television content—all these and more are accompaniments and very likely determinants of the high rates of adolescent pregnancy in the United States. The hope for a solution to the problem of teenage pregnancy is illusory without simultaneous amelioration of some of these contributing factors. (National Research Council, 1987, p. xiv)

Millions of teenagers risk pregnancy by engaging in sexual intercourse. The 1990 Youth Risk Behavior Survey, conducted by the Public Health Service, found that more than half of all high school students reported having had sexual intercourse (Centers for Disease Control, 1992). Male students were more likely than female students to have had intercourse (61% and 48%, respectively), and blacks were more likely than whites to report intercourse experience (72% and 53%, respectively) (Centers for Disease Control, 1992).

More disturbing is the downward trend in age, with more teenagers becoming sexually active at younger ages. Twenty-six percent of females reported having had intercourse before age 15 (Centers for Disease Control, 1991b). These are the young women identified in the National Research Council Report "who would be considered children in any other context."

Experience of sexual intercourse in the teen years is similar throughout Western developed countries. A survey by the Alan Guttmacher Institute reviewed data from 35 developed countries, and closely studied data from 5 countries that were culturally similar to the United States: Canada, Britain, France, the Netherlands, and Sweden (Jones et al., 1985, 1986). The study found great similarities in the age at initial intercourse and the frequency of subsequent intercourse among teenagers in industrialized nations. In contrast to the similarities in age at initial intercourse, the study found strong differences in the successful use of contraception: The teenage pregnancy rate in the United States was more than two times higher than in Canada, England, and France; three times higher than in Sweden; and seven times higher than in the Netherlands (Jones et al., 1985).

The researchers speculated that inadequate contraceptive use by U.S. teenagers was partly due to the cultural double standard that glorifies sexuality, yet expects teenagers (particularly females) to avoid sexual intercourse. "Movies, music, radio, and television tell [teenagers] that sex is romantic, exciting, titillating. . . . yet, at the same time, . . . almost nothing that they see or hear about sex informs them about contraception or the importance of avoiding pregnancy" (Jones et al., 1985). The diversity of the U.S. population and the greater disparities in socioeconomic conditions also may affect contraceptive use in ways that are neither simple nor well understood.

Another study conducted at around the same time examined the effects of the cultural milieu on contraceptive use (Whitley & Schofield, 1986). In an analysis of 134 studies of teenage contraceptive use, the researchers concluded that contraceptive use by teenage girls depends on three factors. The first and second factors in particular are influenced by the adolescent's family, a context that varies greatly in the attitudes toward early childbearing:

1. Psychosexual maturity. Before the teenager will use contraception, she must accept herself as a sexual being and view herself as responsible for sexual activity and contraception.
2. Ability to weigh the alternatives of pregnancy and nonpregnancy. She must be able to analyze the risks and benefits of contraceptive use and nonuse.
3. Circumstances under which intercourse takes place. In contrast to the "spontaneity" or unexpected event of intercourse described by so many teenagers, couples who admit their sexual relationship and recognize the likely result of pregnancy are more likely to use contraception. Persons who are not in an ongoing sexual relationship may not have contraception readily available and become caught in unplanned sexual situations, which puts them at risk of pregnancy.

Although teenage pregnancy cuts across all socioeconomic and racial groups, large differences exist in the birthrates among cultural and socioeconomic groups. For example, the birthrate of black school-age teenagers (ages 15 to 17) is nearly three times that of white school-age teenagers (Children's Defense Fund's Adolescent Prevention Clearinghouse, 1988). Unfortunately these differences have been little studied, in part because of the actual or feared issues of racism. One undeniable difference is the extent of poverty and lack of perceived opportunities that are found disproportionately among blacks. Nevertheless, all racial and ethnic groups can be stratified by socioeconomic status, which strongly affects childbearing. When these groups are stratified, the result is that higher status groups, which usually have more education and perceived opportunities, tend to delay childbearing. Lower socioeconomic groups may not perceive work as "opportunity" and may view early childbearing as acceptable. In her study of black families, Stack (1974) described the heavy dependence on extended family members for economic and social support in lower socioeconomic groups. The extended family also may incorporate additions to the family and provide social support for its young members who begin childbearing.

A survey of teenagers at their first visit to a family planning clinic found the role of family members significant—frequently more important than that of peers. However, it also found that parental approval for contraception was markedly *higher* among black parents than white parents. Black mothers of young teenagers were concerned about possible offspring and were more eager to prevent pregnancy; white mothers were more concerned with the morality of sexual behavior than with its outcome (Nathanson & Becker, 1986). However, in spite of this evidence of parental concern to prevent pregnancy, considerable data show that in the United States, most parents do not discuss specific information about contraception. Three quarters of all unintended teenage pregnancies occur to adolescents who do not use contraception (Westoff, 1988). Another major study of family influences on sexual behavior concluded, "Not many children receive much direct instruction about sexuality, or sexual intercourse, or fertility regulation from their parents" (Fox, 1980).

THE PENN STUDY OF TEENAGE PREGNANCY

The subject of this book, the Penn Study of Teenage Pregnancy, examined teenage pregnancy from the perspective of young adolescents enrolled in family planning and obstetric services. Based on individual interviews, which followed each participant for 2 years in the early 1980s, this clinical study provided details about the teenagers' attitudes, perceptions, and decisions about pregnancy. It also investigated their background characteristics and sexual knowledge and behavior. It examined their feelings about pregnancy—how much pregnancy was wanted or unwanted, planned or unplanned—and how these feelings influenced decisions about pregnancy.

The teenagers in this study were all black and between the ages of 13 and 17 at the outset. None were married, and the study explored the extent to which they considered marriage as a basis for childbearing. When this study was conducted, abortion was available to all of these teenagers, without cost or parental consent. Therefore, we were able to compare teenagers who terminated a first pregnancy to those who delivered the pregnancy, without cost and access to abortion services being a deciding factor. Most important, the study also included never-pregnant teenagers, matched in age and background characteristics to the pregnant ones. This let us determine how never-pregnant teenagers successfully avoided childbearing, rather than focusing solely on those who became pregnant. It also allowed us to identify behavioral, psychological, and social differences between those who gave birth and those who avoided it.

By following each participant for 2 years, we were able to compare the results of the initial pregnancy status (delivery, abortion, or never pregnant) with the occurrence of a pregnancy after study enrollment. We also were able to examine changes in the teenagers' perceptions and behaviors during a 2-year period of their adolescence. The Penn Study of Teenage Pregnancy received primary funding from the National Institute of Child Health and Human Development (NICHD). It received additional funding from the William T. Grant Foundation and the Emily B. H. Mudd Research Fund.

Premises and Assumptions of the Study

In spite of efforts to extend reproductive health care to sexually active teenagers, most teenagers enroll in family planning only after they become pregnant or have a "pregnancy scare." Nevertheless, some sexually active teenagers, even very young ones, enroll in family planning before pregnancy occurs and successfully prevent unwanted pregnancy. The Penn Study sought to learn why. Do these teenagers differ in social, emotional, or psychological factors? Or do they differ only in the timing of their decision to obtain contraception and in their good luck that they obtained it before pregnancy occurred?

This study specifically proposed to examine the extent to which teenage pregnancies were "wanted" or "unwanted," a long-standing debate even among the professionals associated with early childbearing. Some experts believed that if teenagers did not "want" pregnancy, they would use contraception, provided it was easily accessible and cost little or nothing. However, record numbers of teenagers became pregnant and carried their pregnancies to term, even after family planning services were expanded through Title X and even after abortions became legal and—in major metropolitan areas—accessible. Currently more than 40% of all teenage pregnancies end in abortion (Center for Population Options, 1990a), a powerful indication of the extent to which many teenage pregnancies are perceived as unintended and unwanted. Teenagers account for about 25% of abortions in the United States (Centers for Disease Control, 1991b). Whether they decided to terminate or deliver the pregnancy, both white and black teenagers became pregnant at rates that surpassed those of any other developed nation, and their pregnancies could not be explained simply by whether they "wanted" pregnancy or not.

The Penn Study assumed that many pregnancies occurred not because they were "wanted and deliberately intended, but because there were lessened feelings of unwantedness" (Pohlman, 1969). In addition to assuming that most teenagers did not intend to become pregnant, the study also considered that many teenagers denied that pregnancy probably would result from their sexual activity. Moreover, the "wantedness" of pregnancy was expected to be complex, described with ambivalence, and changeable over time. For example, as the political, social, and ethical conflicts that surround abortion increased, the climate of negativity might affect perceptions of pregnancy or prevent "unwanted" pregnancies from being terminated. Teenagers who carried their pregnancies to term might initially describe them as "unwanted" but state they were "wanted" after delivery. Conversely, pregnancies that were "wanted" might become "unwanted" if the child became too burdensome.

Psychological ambivalence is a hallmark of adolescence, and teenagers are ambivalent about many things. They want to separate and individuate from their family, but still need their family's psychological support. Propelled by profound physical and intellectual changes, they typically engage in activities in classrooms, jobs, sports, or peer groups that prepare them for autonomous functioning outside the home. Yet their prolonged economic dependence on the family during education and vocational training postpones their full independence. In this transition from childhood to adulthood, ideas and feelings about pregnancy and motherhood are understandably fluid and changeable.

The Penn Study assumed that preventive efforts modeled on family planning with adults would be ill-suited to teenagers and therefore less likely to be successful. Consistent contraceptive use requires strong feelings of not wanting pregnancy. Even infrequent sexual intercourse eventually will result in pregnancy unless pregnancy is actively and consistently prevented by effective contraceptive use or complete abstinence. Ambivalent feelings and the denial of the likelihood of pregnancy too easily overcome the vigilance needed for effective contraception.

Sample Selection

The sample was composed of urban black teenagers, whose homes were near the Hospital of the University of Pennsylvania, a large teaching hospital that provided primary medical care for them and their families. All study participants were receiving reproductive health-care services in the Obstetrics and Gynecology Department of the hospital when they enrolled in the study. They were drawn from consecutive registration in the service programs and divided into three age-matched study groups according to pregnancy status at enrollment (Table 1.1):

1. Teenagers who were pregnant and planning to deliver a first pregnancy (n = 137 at enrollment)
2. Teenagers who had terminated a first pregnancy (n = 94 at enrollment)
3. Teenagers who had never been pregnant and had been receiving contraceptive services for at least 1 year (n = 110 at enrollment)

Eligibility criteria were ages 13 to 17 and their signed consent for study participation. For the teenagers in the delivery and abortion groups, eligibility criteria also included a first pregnancy. Criteria

Table 1.1 Pregnancy Status at the Beginning and End of the Study for
Participants and Dropouts

Pregnancy Status	At Enrollment	At Endpoint (2-year)	Dropout
Never pregnant	107	84	3
Abortion only	88	81	6
Delivery, 1 baby	131	132	5
Repeat, 2 babies	—	29	—

for the never-pregnant group included at least 1 year of family planning services for contraception. All participants were unmarried students in junior or senior high school. The age distribution in the completed sample was approximately 20% at ages 13 to 14, 25% at age 15, 25% at age 16, and 30% at age 17 in each study group.

Most of the pregnant teenagers (termed the delivery group) were in the second trimester at enrollment. Teenagers who terminated their first pregnancy (termed the abortion group) were enrolled when they returned for scheduled medical follow-up several weeks after the abortion. Never-pregnant teenagers (termed the never-pregnant group) were recruited at a regular family planning visit, which was scheduled every 6 months in the teen clinic.

Study participation involved four interviews in the research offices over 2 years. Participants were paid after each completed follow-up interview for a total of $75 over the entire study.

Data Collection

Data were collected at study enrollment, 6 months after enrollment (adjusted in the delivery group, as needed, to occur *before* childbirth), 1 year after enrollment, and 2 years after enrollment. A semistructured interview questionnaire was used at each of the four assessment points. Trained counselors conducted individual interviews that lasted about 1 hour. After each interview, the interviewers rated their global assessment of the teenager's coping skills, future orientation, affect, and relationships as well as the overall quality of the interview. The interviews provided sufficient information for a second counselor to read and then rate the interviews independently. The interview ratings were then compared and discrepancies resolved by discussion or by using a third rater to reach a consensus.

Other data collection tools supplemented the interviews. At all four assessment visits, the teenagers were asked to complete several analog scales that rated the "wantedness" and "intendedness" of pregnancy; the Symptom Checklist (SCL-90) (Derogatis, 1977), a self-report questionnaire of feelings and behaviors to describe nine dimensions of emotional distress; and self-esteem rating scales by Coopersmith (1967) and Rosenberg (1965). At the first, third, and fourth visits, the teenagers also were asked to complete questionnaires on sex information (Freeman, Rickels, Huggins, Mudd, Garcia, & Dickens, 1980) and sex roles and attitudes (Cvetkovich & Grote, 1980). At the final interview, they were given the Eysenck Personality Inventory (Junior Version, Eysenck & Eysenck, 1975).

Sample Attrition and Changes in Pregnancy Status

The results are reported for the 326 teenagers (out of 341 at enrollment) who completed the 2-year study. These teenagers represented 96% of the original sample. This unusually high retention rate may be due to the fact that the teenagers were generally pleased with the attention they received, and many stated that they benefitted from the interviews, which encouraged them to think about important issues in their lives. This was evident in their remarks at the end of the study when the teens were asked what they had liked and not liked about study participation. As one teen said: "I like being part of the study.... It teaches me things about myself that I wouldn't ordinarily concentrate on. Mainly I like most of the questions—they require thought. Once the results come out, it might help other teenagers."

Not included in this report were the 14 study dropouts and 1 teenager in the delivery group with unusable data. Three other delivery-group teenagers were omitted from some analyses: 1 had a stillbirth, 1 had a child who died, and 1 miscarried after enrollment. Of the study dropouts, 7 left the area or could not be located, 6 refused to continue, and 1 died. There were no apparent differences in the background characteristics or the enrollment data between the dropouts and the remaining sample that completed the study.

By the end of the study, the pregnancy status of some participants had changed. Only 84 remained in the never-pregnant group, 81 had one or more abortions but no delivery, 132 had given birth once, and 29 had given birth twice.

Background Characteristics of Participants

All the participants were black teenagers. They lived in the same urban area; attended the same large, inner-city, public high schools; and received primary medical care from the same hospital. Appendix D lists their background characteristics, which are summarized below.

Age

The mean age of the sample was 15.6 years. The sampling was stratified by age: 46% were ages 13 to 15, and 54% were ages 16 to 17.

Household Composition

Most of these teenagers (53%) lived with their mothers in single-parent, female-headed households. About 21% lived with their biological parents, 13% lived with their mother and stepfather, 2% lived with their father, 8% lived with other relatives, and 3% lived with nonrelatives. Because previous research (Hogan & Kitagawa, 1985) indicated that two-adult households had a lower incidence of teenage pregnancy, and that households with a mother and grandmother were similar to households with two parents, we identified another 5% with two-adult households. This brought the total of all two-adult households to 40%.

Only 21% of the sample lived with their biological father, but another 57% were in contact with him. About 11% had no contact with their father, and another 11% said their father had died.

The average household size was 5.1 people, and the average number of siblings was 3.1. About 28% of the teenagers had sisters who gave birth as teenagers.

Economic Status

At study enrollment, 60% of the teenagers said that their household received welfare, and 63% had Medicaid cards.

Other measures of economic status included the ratios of working adults to all household members and of working adults to all adults in the household. The overall ratio of working adults to all household members was 1 to 5, and the ratio of working adults to all adults in the household was just under 1 to 2.

Social Status

An indicator of social status was constructed using the Hollingshead Two-Factor Index, a weighted calculation of the education and occupation of each teenager's mother (or the higher status of the mother or father if the father was in the household). On a scale of 1 (highest status) to 5 (lowest status), 50% received a rating of 5; 33%, a rating of 4; and 17%, a rating of 1 to 3. These percentages indicate the prevalence of low-income status and low educational achievement among the parents of these teenagers.

Many of the teenagers' mothers were teenagers themselves when they had their first children at an average age of 18.2. More than half (58%) were age 17 or younger—the ages in the Penn Study— when they had their first children. Forty-nine percent of the mothers did not finish high school, 41% were high school graduates, and 10% had technical training or college education beyond high school. During the study, 40% of the mothers were employed.

Location

About 46% of the teenagers said they had moved at least once in the past 5 years. (Just under 20% of the U.S. population moves annually, with negligible racial differences [U.S. Bureau of the Census, 1985].) Approximately 10% had moved three times or more.

However, nearly all of these teenagers (94%) were born in the Philadelphia area. Thus nearly all had remained near their birthplace, and their moves reflected local transience rather than major changes of residence.

Education

Most of the teenagers (87%) were attending high school when they enrolled in the study. The mean school grade was 10, with similar distributions in all four high school grade levels. About two thirds of the teenagers (69%) were at the appropriate grade for their age. Because poor school performance is associated with teenage pregnancy, it is noteworthy that 28% were below their grade level, with the remaining 4% above grade level. Most (83%) reported that their course grades were C or better, 9% had a D average, and 8% were failing.

Religion

The sample was predominantly Protestant (66%). About 12% were Catholic; 9% followed other religions, including Islam; and 13% stated they practiced no religion.

Differences Among Pregnancy Status Groups

The three study groups were selected to have the same age distributions. The groups showed little or no differences in household composition, family size, siblings' ages at first childbirth, residential mobility, school grade, religion, and mother's education. However, the study groups differed significantly in economic status and school performance. Delivery-group teenagers were more likely to live in welfare households (72%) than teenagers in the abortion group (58%) or the never-pregnant group (47%). Also, the ratio of working adults to household members was 1 to 7 in the delivery group compared to 1 to 4 in the abortion and never-pregnant groups. The ratio of working adults to adults in the household was nearly 1 to 3 in the delivery group compared to approximately 1 to 2 in the abortion and never-pregnant groups. The mothers of the delivery-group teenagers were younger when they had their first child (17.4 years compared to 18.7 years in the abortion and never-pregnant groups) and were significantly more likely to be unskilled or unemployed (54% compared to 48% in the abortion group and 40% in the never-pregnant group).

School dropout was significantly greater in the delivery group, in which 17% of the teenagers had dropped out compared to 1% in the abortion group and 2% in the never-pregnant group. These teenagers had already dropped out of school at study enrollment. More delivery-group teenagers were below grade level (36% compared to 28% in the abortion group and 16% in the never-pregnant group) and had grade averages of D or F (26% compared to 9% in the abortion group and 13% in the never-pregnant group).

Representativeness of the Sample

These teenagers had similar background characteristics and were recruited from consecutive enrollments for medical services based on their pregnancy status. Because they were not randomly selected from the adolescent population, the study's results cannot be generalized to all teenagers or even to all black female teenagers. However, the sample may well describe teenagers with similar background characteristics, particularly sexually active teenagers from low-income families.

OVERVIEW OF CHAPTERS

In the following chapters we report what these teenagers said about themselves when they enrolled in the study; what they thought about pregnancy, having a baby, and having sex; what they knew about sex and contraception; and what they said about their sexual behavior, school performance, work experience, and their educational, occupational, and childbearing goals. The analysis particularly focuses on their perceptions of family relationships and support for early childbearing, relationships with boyfriends, and the degree to which they "wanted" and "planned" pregnancy.

Chapter 2, "Risking Pregnancy: Avoidance, Ignorance, and Delay of Contraceptive Use," presents the teenagers' reports of their sexual behavior, how much they knew about sex and contraception, and their attitudes toward having sex. It also compares the psychological measures of self-esteem, emotional distress, and personality factors among the three groups over the 2-year study.

Chapter 3, "Wanting Pregnancy: Teenagers' Attitudes, Goals, and Perceived Support," examines the question, "Is pregnancy really wanted?" It explores the relationship of "wanting" and "planning" of pregnancy and compares the degree of "happiness" to have a baby within and among the three study groups over time. The chapter also investigates factors associated with "wanting" pregnancy, such as school and work experience as well as career, family, and marriage goals—experiences that affect the perceived advantages and disadvantages of having a child. It examines family and peer acceptance of early childbearing within the context of "wanting" pregnancy. Finally, it reviews changes in the "wantedness" of pregnancy and the relationship between "wanting" pregnancy and its occurrence during the 2 years of the study.

Chapter 4, "Choosing Abortion or Delivery: Influences and Outcomes," probes factors that influenced the pregnant teenagers' choice to deliver or abort a first pregnancy. The time during which the study took place provided a unique opportunity to make these comparisons. The study occurred during the brief interval in which a teenager could use her medical assistance card to obtain an abortion without parental consent. Because the study groups all had similar demographic characteristics, the Penn Study could examine the effect of factors other than economics and demographics on the abortion or delivery decision. First we examine the influences on the teenagers' decision to terminate or deliver the pregnancy, including the teenagers' perceived support from their families and boyfriends and their attitudes toward childbearing. Then we investigate outcomes after the decision about the pregnancy, such as repeat pregnancy, changes in educational and occupational goals, relationships with family members and boyfriends, and the teenagers' satisfaction with their decision.

In Chapter 5, "Avoiding Childbearing: Teenagers Who Terminated a First Pregnancy Compared to Never-Pregnant Peers," the teenagers who terminated pregnancy are compared with the never-pregnant, contraceptive users to identify similarities and differences in their attitudes, behaviors, and goals.

Chapter 6, "Pregnancies After Study Enrollment: 'Pregnant Because They Are Different or Different Because They Are Pregnant?' " examines pregnancies that were conceived during the 2-year study period. Although all the study participants obtained family planning services before or immediately after the initial pregnancy of the study, pregnancies did occur in all three study groups. In this chapter we also examine the effects of pregnancy status, age, and contraceptive use in relation to the occurrence of pregnancy. In addition, we describe the effects of repeat pregnancy, especially on education.

Chapter 7, "Family Involvement: Preventing Early Teenage Childbearing," describes a pilot project, the Family Involvement Project (supported by the Pew Memorial Trust), that grew from the results of the Penn Study. In this project, mothers, their young never-pregnant daughters, and other young female teenagers participated in a series of group discussions that were held in their neighborhoods. The project particularly focused on the mothers' views on sexual activity, pregnancy, and childbearing in relation to their children and on mother-daughter communication about sexual issues and behavior.

In Chapter 8, "Male Teenagers and Contraception," we examine responses from male teenagers who were asked many of the same questions about information and attitudes about pregnancy and contraception that we asked the female study participants. The male respondents included a large group of high school students who were in a sex education course in their high school classes; a small group of partners of the Penn Study participants; and a group of very young male teenagers who participated in the Family Involvement Project.

The final chapter, "Conclusions and Recommendations," provides a brief glimpse of a subgroup of the Penn Study teenagers nearly 10 years later. It includes discussion of the major results of the Penn Study, review of the implications, and recommendations for programmatic approaches and interventions to prevent early teenage childbearing.

REFERENCES

Center for Population Options. (1989, September). *Teenage pregnancy and too early childbearing: Public costs, personal consequences.* Washington, DC: Author.

Center for Population Options. (1990a, July). *Adolescents and abortion: Choice in crisis.* Washington, DC: Author.

Center for Population Options. (1990b). *Teenage pregnancy and too early childbearing: Public costs, personal consequences* (5th ed.). Washington, DC: Author.

Center for Population Options. (1992). *Teenage pregnancy and too early childbearing: Public costs, personal consequences* (6th ed.). Washington, DC: Author.

Centers for Disease Control. (1991a, July). Abortion surveillance, United States, 1988. *Morbidity and Mortality Weekly Report, 40*(SS-2), 15-42.

Centers for Disease Control. (1991b). Premarital sexual experience among adolescent women, United States, 1970-1988. *Morbidity and Mortality Weekly Report, 39*(51-52), 929.

Centers for Disease Control. (1992). Sexual behavior amongst high school students, United States 1990. *Morbidity and Mortality Weekly Report, 40*(51-52), 1-8.

Children's Defense Fund's Adolescent Prevention Clearinghouse. (1988). *Teenage pregnancy: An advocate's guide to the numbers.* Washington, DC: Children's Defense Fund.

Chilman, C. (Ed.). (1980). *Adolescent pregnancy and childbearing: Findings from research* (NIH Publication No. 81-2077). Washington, DC: Department of Health and Human Services.

Coopersmith, S. (1967). *The antecedents of self-esteem.* San Francisco: Freeman.

Cutright, P. (1972). The teenage sexual revolution and the myth of an abstinent past. *Family Planning Perspectives, 4*(1), 24-31.

Cvetkovich, G., & Grote, B. (1980). Psychological development and the social problem of teenage illegitimacy. In C. Chilman (Ed.), *Adolescent pregnancy and childbearing: Findings from research* (pp. 15-41) (NIH Publication No. 81-2077). Washington, DC: Department of Health and Human Services.

Derogatis, L. R. (1977). *SCL-90* (rev. ed.). Baltimore, MD: Johns Hopkins University, School of Medicine.

Eysenck, H. J., & Eysenck, S. B. G. (1975). *Manual for the Eysenck Personality Questionnaire (Junior and Adult).* San Diego, CA: Educational and Industrial Testing Service.

Fox, G. L. (1980). *Mother-daughter communications re sexuality* (Final report to the National Institute of Child Health and Human Development). Detroit, MI: Merrill-Palmer Institute.

Freeman, E. W., Rickels, K., Huggins, G., Mudd, E. H., Garcia, C.-R., & Dickens, H. O. (1980). Adolescent contraceptive use: Comparisons of male and female attitudes and information. *American Journal of Public Health, 70*(8), 790-797.

Hayes, C. (Ed.). (1987). *Risking the future: Adolescent sexuality, pregnancy, and childbearing* (Vol. 1) (Report by the National Research Council). Washington, DC: National Academy Press.

Hogan, D. P., & Kitagawa, E. M. (1985). The impact of social status, family structure, and neighborhood on the fertility of black adolescents. *American Journal of Sociology, 90*(4), 825-855.

Jones, E. F., Forrest, J. D., Goldman, N., Henshaw, S. K., Lincoln, R., Rosoff, J. I., Westoff, C. F., & Wulf, D. (1985). Teenage pregnancy in developed countries: Determinants and policy implications. *Family Planning Perspectives, 17*(2), 53-63.

Jones, E. F., Forrest, J. D., Goldman, N., Henshaw, S. K., Lincoln, R., Rosoff, J., Westoff, C. F., & Wulf, D. (1986). *Teenage pregnancy in industrialized countries.* New Haven, CT: Yale University Press.

Nathanson, C. A., & Becker, M. H. (1986). Family and peer influence on obtaining a method of contraception. *Journal of Marriage and Family, 48*(3), 513-525.

National Center for Health Statistics. (1991). Advance report of final natality statistics, 1989. *Monthly Vital Statistics Report, 40*(8 Suppl.). Hyattsville, MD: Public Health Service.

Pohlman, E. H. (1969). *The psychology of birth planning.* Cambridge, MA: Schenkman.

Rosenberg, M. (1965). *Society and the adolescent self-image.* Princeton, NJ: Princeton University Press.

Stack, C. (1974). *All our kin: Strategies for survival in a black community.* New York: Harper & Row.

U.S. Bureau of the Census. (1985). *Statistical abstracts of the United States: 1986* (106th ed.). Washington, DC: Government Printing Office.

U.S. Bureau of the Census. (1989). *Studies in marriage and the family* (Current Population Reports, Series P-23, No. 162). Washington, DC: Government Printing Office.

Westoff, C. F. (1988). Contraceptive paths toward the reduction of unintended pregnancy and abortion. *Family Planning Perspectives, 20*(1), 413.

Whitley, B. E., & Schofield, J. W. (1986). A meta-analysis of research on adolescent contraceptive use. *Population and Environment, 8*(3-4), 173-203.

Zelnik, M., & Kantner, J. F. (1980). Sexual activity, contraceptive use and pregnancy among metropolitan-area teenagers. *Family Planning Perspectives, 12*(5), 230-237.

TWO

Risking Pregnancy: Avoidance, Ignorance, and Delay of Contraceptive Use

INTRODUCTION

Each year in the United States, about 4.5 million female teenagers obtain family planning services (Horn & Mosher, 1984). Although some young women seek these services before or within the same month as initial intercourse, about three fourths delay an average of 23 months after initial intercourse (Mosher & Horn, 1988). For too many teenagers, pregnancy occurs during this interval of delay: more than one third of a teenage sample made their first family planning visit because they thought they were pregnant (Zabin & Clark, 1981). More than one fifth of premarital pregnancies occurred in the first month after initial intercourse, and half occurred within the first 6 months (Zabin, Kantner, & Zelnik, 1979). These facts prompt two questions:

1. Why do teenagers delay obtaining contraceptive services, particularly when they do not want pregnancy?
2. Are there differences in information and attitudes about contraception between teenagers who obtain services before or after pregnancy occurs?

Why female teenagers wait so long to use family planning services is a continuing puzzle. Public family planning programs are widely available (Horn & Mosher, 1984). The length of delay is nearly identical in white and black women, and background variables fail to explain why contraceptive services are not obtained more immediately (Mosher & Horn, 1988). Teenagers say that they do not think they will get pregnant, but even this faulty perception was not among the leading reasons for delaying the first family planning visit. The predominant responses given by teenagers when asked why they did not obtain contraceptive services were "just didn't get around to it," "afraid my family would find out," and "waiting for a closer relationship with my partner" (Zabin & Clark, 1981). These responses suggested simple procrastination, but they also implied psychological issues of ambivalence, guilt, and romantic notions of sex that deny the need to prepare for sex.

The documented delay in obtaining contraception has been difficult to change, particularly among teenagers, for reasons that are not well understood. Although psychological factors might help explain sexual behavior and contraceptive use, they are not readily amenable to programmatic change. Relatively few studies have examined psychological factors, and none has provided strong predictors of contraceptive use or teenage pregnancy.

Cobliner (1974) studied a group of teenagers who had terminated unwanted pregnancy and identified reasons that their intentions to avoid pregnancy had failed. The largest single group (43%) were "risk-takers," whose reasons for not using contraception were "I didn't think I could get pregnant" or "I didn't expect to have sex." The researchers viewed these responses as a probabilistic appraisal of risks, "a protective psychological mechanism . . . that is commonly practiced to make life more bearable" (p. 24). The researchers noted that the explanation was too frequent to be ascribed to emotional difficulty and that it was not correlated with educational level.

Luker (1975) described risk-taking behavior in relation to sex and contraception by weighing the costs of contraception against the benefits of pregnancy. The cost-benefit analysis illustrated that women who took a successful risk then faced the next contraceptive decision with the fact that they had not become pregnant. This weighted subsequent decisions about contraceptive use further toward risk-taking, because they had risked successfully and obtained little new information.

Other psychological studies assessed teenagers' lack of ability to plan ahead or anticipate future events (Keller, Sims, Henry, & Crawford, 1970; MacDonald, 1970; Mindick, Oskamp, & Berger, 1977; Rader, Bekker, Brown, & Richard, 1978; Rovinsky, 1972). A common theme of these studies is that preventing pregnancy is an abstraction that requires a more mature level of cognitive development. Concrete thought and the recognition and processing of directly experienced events characterize young people. Less than 75% of 15-year-olds exhibited the ability to understand abstractions in a study of U.S. teenagers (Dale, 1970). A concrete thinker does not consider an abstract future and does not link future consequences to present events. A concrete thinker is unlikely to weigh the possibilities of alternative behaviors ("If I do this rather than that, then this rather than that will happen"). Researchers generally concluded that teenagers risked pregnancy not because of "any form of pathology, moral or otherwise" but because of normal factors of adolescent development (Cvetkovich & Grote, 1980). They also indicated that pregnant teenagers did not lack intelligence, but lacked reasoning ability to analyze abstract issues realistically (Kreipe, Roghmann, & McAnarney, 1981).

Little evidence suggests that emotional distress or psychopathology are significant in teenage sexual behavior. Intercourse experience even in early adolescence is no longer exceptional. Studies using the Minnesota Multiphasic Personality Inventory (MMPI), a measure to identify neurotic personality concepts, failed to identify differences between pregnant and nonpregnant teens (Brandt, Kane, & Moan, 1978; Gispert & Falk, 1976; Kane, Moan, & Bolling, 1974).

However, the effects of common emotional factors, such as anxiety and depression, and related psychological concepts, such as self-esteem, remain unclear in relation to teenage sexual behavior and pregnancy. Gabrielson, Klerman, Currie, Tyler, and Jekel (1970) identified an increased rate of suicide among pregnant teenagers. Others suggested that depression in teenagers commonly is unrecognized (Inamdar, Siomopoulos, Osborn, & Bianchi, 1979) and consequently its frequency and effects are not evaluated.

Closely related to depression, low self-esteem was associated with sexual behavior and pregnancy of young adolescents (Chilman, 1979), although little data support the hypothesis. The studies of Jessor and Jessor (1975) found that sexually experienced male teenagers, but not female teenagers, had higher self-esteem than their inexperienced counterparts. Teenagers who became mothers before age 16 had reasonably high self-esteem, with black teenagers having more self-esteem than white teenagers (Miller, 1983). Another study found no differences in the self-esteem of teenage mothers compared to childless teenagers (Streetman, 1987). Ladner (1971) observed that pregnancy often validated a teenager's passage into the maternal role and thus increased her self-esteem.

THE PENN STUDY

We assumed that our teenage sample, which had experienced intercourse before study enrollment, was no different from the many other reported samples that showed limited information about contraceptive use and delay in family planning enrollment. This clinical sample, which compared never-pregnant, contraceptive users and pregnant teenagers who chose abortion or delivery of a first pregnancy, would address the following questions:

1. Did the three study groups differ in the levels of contraceptive information, sexual attitudes, and the length of time after first intercourse before obtaining family planning services?
2. Did emotional distress factors and self-esteem differ among the three study groups?

Sexual Behavior

The teenagers in the Penn Study had all started dating: 30% at age 12 or younger, 49% at ages 13 to 14, and 21% at ages 15 to 16. About 40% had been dating their current boyfriend for more than 1 year, nearly 50% had been with their current boyfriend for less than 1 year, and 10% said they had no boyfriend when they entered the study.

The mean age at first sexual intercourse was 14.2 years, nearly identical in all three study groups. About 10% first had sex at age 12 or younger, 74% at ages 13 to 15, and 16% at ages 16 to 17. At study enrollment, nearly one fourth of all the teenagers said they had had sex only a few times, but 72% reported having sex more than five times, an indication that it was more than a "one-time" experience. Nevertheless, sporadic rather than regular sexual activity was characteristic: 42% said they had no sex in the past month, 44% had sex one to five times, and only 14% had sex more than five times in the past month.

Contraceptive Use

At the initial interview, 9% of the abortion group and 63% of the delivery group said they had never used contraception. In contrast, 81% of the never-pregnant teenagers (all of whom were enrolled in family planning) reported using contraception the last time they had had sex. Almost all (89%) of the teenagers who became pregnant (both the abortion and delivery groups) said they were not using contraception when pregnancy occurred. Of those who said they were using contraception when they became pregnant, 2% said they were using oral contraceptives but missed taking some pills, 6% said their method failed, and 3% said they didn't know why pregnancy occurred. Although these latter numbers describe contraceptive failure, most of the teenagers simply said they were not using any method when they became pregnant.

Delay After Initial Intercourse

One fourth of the teenagers said that some contraceptive method was used at the first sexual intercourse, but this was nearly three times more likely in the never-pregnant group (44%) than in the abortion and delivery groups, where only 16% in each group said they used contraception initially ($p < 0.001$). About 20% began using contraception up to 3 months after initial intercourse, 6% began using it 4 to 6 months later, 13% used it 7 to 12 months later, and 8% used it 13 to 48 months later. About 28% had never used any contraceptive method before pregnancy occurred.

Contraceptive Information

Many teenagers have only limited and often incorrect information about reproduction and contraception (Freeman, Rickels, Huggins, Mudd, et al., 1980; Zelnik & Kantner, 1977). This puts them at high risk for pregnancy because they believe they know how to prevent pregnancy when in fact they do not. The teenagers in this study were no exception. At study enrollment the teenagers were asked to identify the most fertile time in the menstrual cycle, a question that is particularly important because many teenagers believe they can avoid pregnancy by having intercourse during their "safe" (nonfertile) time. Only 28% knew the most fertile time in the cycle at their first study interview. More than half (56%) answered incorrectly, and 16% said they did not know.

Two thirds of the teenagers said pregnancy was extremely likely if they had intercourse without using contraception. However, the other one third—including many who already had become pregnant—said pregnancy was *not* a very likely outcome of unprotected intercourse. Perhaps realistically, the teenagers did not express much confidence in their own use of contraception. Only 38% said that if they used contraception, it was "extremely likely" to prevent pregnancy. The rest said it was "somewhat likely" (24%), "not at all likely" (9%), or "didn't know" (29%). Even never-pregnant teenagers who received family planning services were uncertain: Only 61% said that by using contraception they were "extremely likely" to prevent pregnancy, compared to 45% in the abortion group and only 16% in the delivery group ($p < 0.0001$). Although the responses in the pregnant groups may have reflected their experiences of having become pregnant, many of these teenagers also said they had never used contraception at all, and nearly all said they were not using contraception when pregnancy occurred. Rather, many teenagers, including those in family planning services, appeared to lack sufficient information to use contraception effectively.

Contraception to these teenagers almost invariably meant oral contraceptives, or "the pill." Taken daily, the pill's theoretical effectiveness exceeds 99% (Garcia & Rosenfeld, 1977). Nonetheless it failed to prevent pregnancy for many teenage users. Teenage sexual activity often is sporadic, defined by shifting relationships and weekend social activity. Occasional or unpredictable intercourse may make daily pill-taking seem unnecessary and difficult to remember. Missed pills—even just a few in a monthly cycle—increase the risk of pregnancy. At study enrollment, one fourth of the teenagers in the delivery and abortion groups did not know that pregnancy was possible if just a few pills were missed during the cycle. Also, starting the pill after intercourse (a common practice among teenagers) cannot prevent a pregnancy that has already occurred.

The teenagers' knowledge of contraceptive methods other than oral contraceptives was meager. Only 25% had used condoms, 36% knew about them but had never used them, and 39% had no information about them. Only 15% reported ever using spermicidal foam, 33% said they knew about it but had not used it, and 52% had no information about it. Most disturbing of all, fully 29% of these sexually active teenagers—many of them pregnant and expecting to carry to term—said they had never used *any* contraceptive method, including limiting intercourse to their "safe times" and withdrawal, and appeared to have little or no knowledge about contraception.

Access to Contraception

The teenagers' knowledge of where to obtain contraceptives was greater than their reported use. Overall, 88% identified a place that they could obtain oral contraceptives, and 66% knew where to obtain an abortion or counseling for an unwanted pregnancy. (Omitting the abortion group, 63% of the never-pregnant teenagers and 47% of the delivery group knew where they could obtain an abortion—a significant difference [$p < 0.05$].) In addition, a high percentage knew where to obtain condoms (82%), intrauterine devices (78%), and spermicidal foam (79%). These data do not tell us what the teenagers knew before they became pregnant, but even at this time, the never-pregnant and abortion group teenagers had more information about where they could obtain contraceptives, abortions, or counseling for unwanted pregnancy than did those in the delivery group.

Sources of Information

We asked the teenagers who had contraceptive information (71% of the total) where they had first obtained it. The most frequent response was that contraceptive information had been obtained from their mothers (22%) or another family member (23%). The never-pregnant and abortion group teens were more than twice as likely as the delivery group teenagers to have obtained contraceptive information from their mothers ($p < 0.05$). Although mothers were the primary source of contraceptive information, the numbers were small. Less than half the teenagers with any contraceptive information (and less than one third of all the teenagers in the study) had obtained contraceptive information from family members, even though the family is widely viewed as the appropriate source of sex education. Other sources combined—friends (18%); school classes (18%); a clinic or doctor (13%); and books, television, and other media (6%)—were more likely to be the initial source of contraceptive information for these teenagers than were family members.

Because mothers were the single leading source of contraceptive information for these teenagers, we further explored the range of sexual topics that mothers and daughters discussed. At study enrollment, 92% of the teenagers said they had talked about sex with their mothers. (The daughter's pregnancy may have spurred such discussion *after* the pregnancy occurred.) However, the specific topics discussed varied greatly. Menstruation was the most common topic (discussed by 79% of the teenagers and their mothers), followed by contraception (discussed by 64%), pregnancy (discussed by 62%), and body changes (discussed by 59%). The delivery-group teenagers were the *least* likely to have ever talked with their mothers about pregnancy compared to the abortion- and never-pregnant-group teenagers (55%, 63%, and 73%, respectively; $p < 0.05$).

More behaviorally specific topics were discussed even less frequently. Abortion was discussed by about half the sample—predominantly by those who had recently had an abortion (74%), but *least* by the delivery-group teenagers (40%)—again a significant difference ($p < 0.001$). Where to obtain contraceptives (50%), how to use contraceptives (40%), and how to avoid sexually transmitted diseases (37%) were the topics least frequently discussed by the mothers and daughters. Contraceptive use had been discussed more in the never-pregnant and abortion groups than in the delivery group (47%, 45%, and 31%, respectively; $p < 0.05$). The delivery-group teenagers clearly were less likely to have talked with their mothers beyond the most general aspects of these sexual behavior issues.

Although nearly all of the teenagers reported talking with their mothers about sex, the data show the considerable range in the specific topics discussed. Talking about menstruation and body changes clearly is important for a young girl entering puberty, but this information does not provide guidance for preventing pregnancy. Talking about birth control may provide information, but does not necessarily mean that a young teenager adequately understands where to obtain and how to use contraceptive methods. Although these were all sexually active teenagers, only a minority reported any communication with their mothers about contraceptive use and sexually transmitted diseases. The teenagers who were planning to deliver were the least likely to have talked about pregnancy, contraception, and abortion with their mothers.

Sexual Information and Attitudes

In addition to answering interview questions, the teenagers completed a 14-item self-report Sexual Information and Attitudes Questionnaire (SIAQ) that we used in high school classes and in other family planning samples (Freeman, Rickels, Huggins, Mudd, et al., 1980). (See Appendix F for the SIAQ.)

Sexual Information

At study enrollment the SIAQ results indicated that the never-pregnant and abortion-group teenagers had more contraceptive information than the delivery-group teenagers ($p < 0.05$). However, only three items on this questionnaire discriminated among the three study groups with significantly different responses ($p <$ 0.05). More never-pregnant teenagers (89%) than abortion (79%) or delivery (75%) teenagers knew that contraception was needed even with infrequent sex. More never-pregnant teenagers (88%) than abortion (78%) or delivery (73%) teenagers knew that missed pills during the cycle could result in pregnancy. And more never-pregnant (71%) and abortion (78%) compared to delivery teenagers (63%) agreed that it was *not* "showing more love" to risk unprotected sex. Expectedly, the never-pregnant teenagers, who were enrolled in family planning, were more likely to have this information, and the two groups of teenagers who became pregnant had less information.

Although the remaining SIAQ items did not elicit differential responses from the three study groups, some items are noteworthy for responses that described the limited basis these teenagers had for preventing pregnancy. The teenagers' responses overall are shown in Table 2.1.

Only about half could correctly identify the most fertile time in the cycle—a major problem when they think it is a "safe" time to have sex. Their responses to the attitudinal items suggested their ambivalence about contraceptive use. More than half agreed they felt "used" if their boyfriends knew they used contraception. Nearly half thought it was "too much trouble" to prevent pregnancy, and half indicated that boyfriends did not respect girls who used contraception. These ambivalent attitudes about contraceptive use, combined with limited knowledge of the methods, would seem to logically and not surprisingly lead to "user failures" in preventing pregnancy.

The sex information scores as measured by the SIAQ increased significantly over time in all study groups ($p < 0.0001$). At the 1-year follow-up assessment, the delivery-group teenagers still had lower scores than the never-pregnant and abortion-group teenagers ($p < 0.05$). By the 2-year follow-up, however, the three study groups had similar scores with no significant differences. The abortion- and delivery-group teenagers enrolled in family planning after their pregnancies, and all three study groups gradually reached about the same level of contraceptive information.

Table 2.1 Sexual Information and Attitudes of Female Teenagers at Study Enrollment, $n = 326$

	% Agree
1. Pregnancy can occur after unprotected sex even if it did not occur the first time.	87
2. If sex is less than once a week, pregnancy could occur.	80
3. Birth control needs to be used even if sex is infrequent.	80*
4. A girl can get pregnant the first time she has sex.	80
5. Birth control methods (except sterilization) can be stopped when pregnancy is wanted.	79
6. If the pill is missed a few days, a girl can get pregnant.	79*
7. Teenagers do not need parental consent to obtain birth control.	76
8. Sex without birth control does not show more love.	71*
9. Pregnancy can occur without orgasm.	65
10. It is difficult to know when the "safe" time is.	60
11. It is not too much trouble to prevent pregnancy.	56
12. The most fertile time is about 2 weeks before the period begins.	55
13. Boys respect girls who use birth control.	49
14. A girl will not feel "used" if her boyfriend knows she uses birth control.	41

NOTE: *$p<0.05$ in chi-square tests of never-pregnant, abortion, and pregnant groups. All items are stated here to present "agree" as the response supporting contraceptive use and are listed in order of percent agreement. Items were stated on the questionnaire such that both "agree" and "disagree" responses supported contraceptive use.

Sexual Attitudes and Feelings

The teenagers in the three study groups uniformly endorsed a set of attitudes about sex, contraception, and pregnancy, as assessed by the 12-item Sexual Attitudes Questionnaire (SAQ) of Cvetkovich and Grote (1980). The items were not hypothetical to these teenagers, but were directly relevant to their experience, because they all had had sex. The teenagers typically responded in ways consistent with their experience. They agreed with the acceptability of premarital sex with "someone they loved or had good feelings about," but not with someone they didn't "know well." They agreed that "men lie" and women "manipulate" to get sex. Most teenagers agreed that it was "a good idea to experiment sexually before marriage" and did not want to "marry a virgin." They endorsed the male partner's lack of responsibility should pregnancy occur and did not think that marriage was the answer. None of these responses differed among the three study groups.

The above responses can be viewed as expected on the basis that they are consistent with the teenagers' behavior. It was more intriguing to observe that despite their sexual activity, only 37% of the teenagers indicated that it was easy to become sexually excited, and that a majority (63%) indicated that it was difficult to understand their sexual feelings. This suggests that at the emotional level, they were less involved in sexual activity than evidenced by their behavior.

Only two SAQ items had statistically significant differences in responses among the three study groups. First, the abortion-group teenagers (45%) were much more likely than the never-pregnant and delivery-group teenagers (24%) to agree that "having an abortion is a good way to cope with a premarital pregnancy" ($p < 0.001$). Second, the delivery-group teenagers (71%) were the most likely to indicate that it was difficult to understand feelings about sex, compared to never-pregnant (60%) and abortion-group teenagers (56%) ($p < 0.05$).

These sexual attitudes as assessed by the SAQ remained notably stable over the 2-year study. At the 1- and 2-year follow-ups, there were no significant changes in SAQ scores in any study group.

Additional questions were asked at the enrollment interview about what was most important to these teenagers about having sex. About two thirds reported relatively positive reasons: 34% said they engaged in intercourse mainly because they "wanted to experiment," they enjoyed the "excitement," or they "felt sexy"; 27% said they had sex because they were in love or wanted to please their boyfriend. On the negative side, 26% "didn't know" why they had sex, and 13% blamed alcohol, drugs, or loneliness for their sexual activity. Responses did not significantly differ among the three study groups.

Few of these teenagers viewed their initial sexual experience positively. Only 5% said it was pleasurable, 11% said it made them feel closer to their boyfriend, and 12% said it made them feel more grown up. Fully 72% reported no overall satisfaction or pleasure associated with their initial sexual experience: 38% said they felt nothing, 22% said they didn't know what they felt, and 12% said they felt used or cheapened by the experience. When asked to describe their feelings about their most recent sexual experience, more than half (58%) said it was pleasurable, but 33% were still indifferent, 5% disliked it, and 5% had no answer. Again, these responses did not differ significantly among the study groups.

Only one third of these teenagers said they had worried about becoming pregnant, and, interestingly, the never-pregnant group using contraception worried least (26% compared to 35% of the abortion group and 50% of the delivery group, $p < 0.001$). Worry appeared related to unprotected intercourse. When asked what they would do if they became pregnant, 35% said they never thought about it, 24% said they would have an abortion, and 41% said they would have the baby. Forty percent of the delivery group compared to 36% of the abortion group and 28% of the never-pregnant group said they had never thought about what they would do if pregnancy occurred ($p < 0.001$).

As another means of evaluating the teenagers' sexual maturity, after each interview the interviewer rated each teenager's overall degree of comfort in discussing sexual feelings and behaviors. At the initial interview, more than half of the teenagers (58%) had ratings below the midpoint of the rating scale, indicating low levels of comfort discussing the sexual topics or difficulties in talking about abstract feelings or decisions. Typical of these responses is that many of the teenagers stated that they "didn't know" what they thought about having sex or what they would do if they became pregnant.

The ratings became increasingly more positive during the 2 years of the study ($p < 0.001$ for the time effect). A significant interaction between group and time ($p < 0.05$) signified that the delivery-group teenagers, who had the lowest ratings initially, had the greatest improvement during the study. At endpoint there were no differences among the three study groups in these ratings that reflected feelings about discussing sexual issues and behavior.

It is noteworthy that although the mean ratings increased throughout the study, they remained below the midpoint in all study groups. This was consistent with the young ages and mid-adolescent development of these teenagers. Despite their sexual activity, most were not comfortable talking about sex and could not formulate future plans and goals. These global ratings do not detail the complexity of psychological growth and development, but they are descriptive of teenagers who were involved in but not comfortable with sexual activity. Although the teenagers had sex, many indicated little understanding of their feelings or behavior.

Psychological Factors

The Penn Study also examined the teenagers' self-esteem, level of emotional distress, personality dimensions, and future orientation.

Self-Esteem

Self-esteem was assessed at each interview, using two standard self-report questionnaires: the Rosenberg (1965) Scale, which examined the *self-acceptance* dimension of esteem, and the Coopersmith (1967) Inventory, which focused on *family relations* and *assertiveness* dimensions of self-esteem.

There were no significant differences in the self-esteem measures among the three study groups at enrollment. All groups scored above the midpoint on the family relations and assertiveness scales and in the top quartile of the self-acceptance scale. The self-esteem scores on all three measures increased slightly but not significantly in the total sample during the 2-year study. However, there was a significant time by group interaction for the family relations dimension ($p < 0.0001$), which resulted from a *decrease* in esteem in the delivery group, whereas the other two study groups reported increasing esteem in family relations during the 2-year period.

At the end of the study, the three groups showed significant differences in all three self-esteem scales, with the delivery group exhibiting the least self-esteem. After starting with similar ratings of self-esteem at study enrollment, the teenagers in the delivery group fared less well than did teenagers in the abortion and never-pregnant groups, who did not differ from each other. The delivery-group teenagers reported a deterioration in esteem in the family relations dimension, suggesting that childbearing did not continue to enhance their status in the family, but led to more responsibilities and difficulties. This decrease in esteem among the delivery-group teenagers is discussed further in the next chapter, where the decision to deliver or terminate the pregnancy is examined more closely.

Emotional Distress

At each interview we assessed the teenagers' emotional distress level, using the Symptom Checklist (SCL-90, Derogatis, 1977). This self-report questionnaire assessed nine clinically relevant symptom dimensions, including somatization, obsessive-compulsiveness, interpersonal sensitivity, depression, anxiety, hostility, phobic anxiety, paranoid ideation, and psychoticism. The scores for all nine symptom factors and the total score were within normal ranges for all three groups throughout the study. There were no significant differences among the groups at any assessment point. Over the 2 years of the study, the scores for all nine SCL factors *decreased* significantly in all three groups, signifying less emotional distress over time.

Personality Dimensions

Personality dimensions of extroversion-introversion and neuroticism or emotionality were examined at the study endpoint, using the Eysenck Personality Inventory, junior version (JEPI, Eysenck & Eysenck, 1975). The scale is an extension of the widely used measure developed for adults and examines behavioral traits that underlie these two major dimensions of personality. Extroversion is characterized by such things as sociability, activity, optimism, and outgoing or impulsive behavior. Neuroticism is characterized by such qualities as moodiness, restlessness, and rigidity. Individuals are located at all intermediate stages between the extremes, and the statistical distribution on the dimensions is roughly normal (Eysenck & Eysenck, 1975). The JEPI results showed no significant differences in extroversion or neuroticism among the three study groups. The mean scores were similar to those from black school student samples (Eysenck & Eysenck, 1975).

Future Orientation

Teenagers commonly have difficulty making decisions about abstract situations. To most of them, pregnancy and parenthood are mere abstractions. Even those who become pregnant may have no specific plans related to childbearing issues. They may be intelligent but lack the reasoning ability to analyze and process abstract, future-oriented issues realistically.

From this perspective, the interviewer rated how well each teenager appeared to connect her sexual behavior and future goals and to formulate plans for pregnancy, child care, and related issues if pregnancy should occur. These ratings of future orientation significantly differed ($p < 0.0001$) among the three study groups at each assessment. Throughout the study, the never-pregnant and abortion groups had similar ratings, and the delivery group had the lowest ratings. The ratings significantly increased during the 2-year study in all groups ($p < 0.0001$ for the time effect), an expected result of developing with age and experience. However, having a child did not differentially affect this development. All study groups had higher ratings at the end of the 2 years, but the delivery group did not reach the same level of planning for future goals as the teenagers who avoided childbearing.

CHAPTER SUMMARY

The data from these teenagers thus far describe few differences among the three study groups in terms of sexual behavior, information, attitudes, and psychological factors, although the differences that do occur show a consistent pattern that describes the delivery-group teenagers as the least prepared for sexual activity and childbearing.

Did sexual behavior predict pregnancy risk? At study enrollment, the three groups appeared extremely similar in terms of their sexual behavior. The age at first sex (14.2 years), the reported frequency of sex (which typically was sporadic), and the length of the relationship with the current boyfriend (which was less than 1 year) were comparable. However, the never-pregnant teenagers were nearly three times more likely to have used contraception at the first intercourse experience. By sampling definition, the entire never-pregnant group had used contraception, but 63% of the delivery group had never used any contraceptive method. Overall the teenagers shared a similar risk of pregnancy in terms of their sexual activity, but for many pregnancy occurred before they obtained contraceptive services.

Did information and attitudes about contraception differ between the teenagers who did and did not have pregnancies? Lack of information is often cited as a cause of unintended pregnancies, but there is little evidence of relationship between contraceptive knowledge and contraceptive behavior (Chilman, 1979) or between sex education and premarital teenage pregnancy (Marsiglio & Mott, 1986). Among these teenagers, there were initial differences in contraceptive information, but they started from different baselines. The never-pregnant group, which was selected from teenagers enrolled in family planning services, had more correct information than the abortion or delivery groups, many of whom had not used contraception prior to pregnancy. But nearly all pregnancies occurred because the teenagers did not *use* contraception, although many knew generally that contraceptives were available. As would be expected, experience using contraception tended to increase information. At the end of the 2-year study, when all the teenagers had used contraception, there were no differences in contraceptive information among the three original study groups.

Noteworthy differences did appear in communication with the mother. The never-pregnant teenagers were nearly three times more likely than delivery-group teenagers to report that they had learned about contraceptives from their mothers. Furthermore, the never-pregnant teenagers were the most likely to say that they had discussed pregnancy, contraceptive use, and abortion with their mothers. Among these teenagers from similar backgrounds, it appeared that those who had more discussions with their mothers about specific sexual issues and behavior were more successful in preventing pregnancy. This is consistent with a recent analysis of national survey data, which found that the family is effective in encouraging sexually active girls to use contraceptives (Casper, 1990).

What of the teenagers' sexual attitudes? Although excitement or pleasure derived from sexual activity, avoidance of consequences, and lack of concern about pregnancy appeared typical of adolescents, these attitudes did not differentiate the three study groups. Only the global ratings, which evaluated the teenagers' overall ability to answer and be comfortable with questions about sex and pregnancy, showed significant differences among the groups, with the delivery group having the lowest ratings at the outset. However, by the 2-year follow-up, the differences disappeared, and the three groups appeared more similar than different.

Finally, do psychological and emotional factors influence a teenager's risk of pregnancy? The measures of self-esteem, emotional distress, and personality dimensions appeared within normal ranges, with no differences among the three groups at study enrollment. Emotional distress scores decreased during the study, indicating less emotional distress as would be expected for maturing adolescents (or possibly measuring a statistical artifact of regression toward the mean), but clearly not indicating worsening emotional distress in the three study groups.

The self-esteem dimension of assertiveness remained notably stable during the 2-year study, whereas the self-acceptance dimension increased slightly but not significantly for the sample overall. In the delivery group, the family relations dimension of esteem decreased following delivery of the pregnancy. It appeared that early childbearing failed to continue to enhance the family relationships of the teenage mothers. The delivery group also exhibited the least future orientation as rated by the interviewers at every assessment point, whereas the never-pregnant and abortion groups were more likely to recognize that postponing motherhood was important for achieving other educational and career goals.

REFERENCES

Brandt, C. L., Kane, F. J., & Moan, C. A. (1978). Pregnant adolescents: Some psychosocial factors. *Psychosomatics, 19*(12), 790-793.

Casper, L. M. (1990). Does family interaction prevent adolescent pregnancy? *Family Planning Perspectives, 22*(3), 109-114.

Chilman, C. (1979). Teenage pregnancy: A research review. *Social Work, 24*(6), 492-498.

Cobliner, W. G. (1974). Pregnancy in the single adolescent girl: The role of cognitive functions. *Journal of Youth and Adolescence, 3*(1), 17-29.

Coopersmith, S. (1967). *The antecedents of self-esteem.* San Francisco: Freeman.

Cvetkovich, G., & Grote, B. (1980). Psychological development and the social problem of teenage illegitimacy. In C. Chilman (Ed.), *Adolescent pregnancy and childbearing: Findings from research* (pp. 15-41) (NIH Publication No. 81-2077). Washington, DC: Department of Health and Human Services.

Dale, L. G. (1970). The growth of systematic thinking: Replication and analysis of Piaget's first chemical experiment. *Australian Journal of Psychology, 22*(3), 277-286.

Derogatis, L. R. (1977). *SCL-90* (rev. ed.). Baltimore, MD: Johns Hopkins University, School of Medicine.

Eysenck, H. J., & Eysenck, S. B. G. (1975). *Manual for the Eysenck Personality Questionnaire (Junior and Adult).* San Diego, CA: Educational and Industrial Testing Service.

Freeman, E. W., Rickels, K., Huggins, G., Mudd, E. H., Garcia, C.-R., & Dickens, H. O. (1980). Adolescent contraceptive use: Comparisons of male and female attitudes and information. *American Journal of Public Health, 70*(8), 790-797.

Gabrielson, I. W., Klerman, L. V., Currie, J. B., Tyler, N. C., & Jekel, J. F. (1970). Suicide attempts in a population pregnant as teenagers. *American Journal of Public Health, 60*(12), 2289-2301.

Garcia, C.-R., & Rosenfeld, D. L. (1977). *Human fertility: The regulation of reproduction.* Philadelphia: F.A. Davis.

Gispert, M., & Falk, R. (1976). Sexual experimentation and pregnancy in young black adolescents. *American Journal of Obstetrics and Gynecology, 126*(4), 459-466.

Horn, M. C., & Mosher, M. D. (1984). Use of services for family planning and infertility, United States, 1982. *Advance Data From Vital and Health Statistics,* No. 102 (DHHS Publication No. [PHS] 85-1250). Hyattsville, MD: National Center for Health Statistics.

Inamdar, S. C., Siomopoulos, G., Osborn, M., & Bianchi, E. C. (1979). Phenomenology associated with depressed moods in adolescents. *American Journal of Psychiatry, 136*(2), 156-159.

Jessor, S. L., & Jessor, R. (1975). Transition from virginity to non-virginity among youth: A social-psychological study over time. *Developmental Psychology, 11*(4), 473-484.

Kane, F. J., Moan, C. A., & Bolling, B. (1974). Motivational factors in pregnant adolescents. *Diseases of the Nervous System, 35*(3), 131-134.

Keller, R., Sims, J., Henry, W. K., & Crawford, T. J. (1970). Psychological sources of resistance to family planning. *Merrill-Palmer Quarterly, 16*(3), 286-302.

Kreipe, R. E., Roghmann, K. J., & McAnarney, E. R. (1981). Early adolescent childbearing: A changing morbidity. *Journal of Adolescent Health Care, 2*(2), 127-131.

Ladner, J. A. (1971). *Tomorrow's tomorrow: The black woman.* Garden City, NY: Doubleday.

Luker, K. (1975). *Taking chances: Abortion and decision not to contracept.* Berkeley: University of California Press.

MacDonald, A. P. (1970). Internal-external locus of control and the practice of birth control. *Psychological Reports, 27*(1), 206.

Marsiglio, W. K., & Mott, F. L. (1986). The impact of sex education on sexual activity, contraceptive use, and premarital pregnancy among American teenagers. *Family Planning Perspectives, 18*(4), 151-162.

Miller, S. H. (1983). *Children and parents: A final report.* New York: Child Welfare League of America.

Mindick, B., Oskamp, S., & Berger, D. E. (1977). Prediction of success or failure in birth planning: An approach to prevention of individual and family stress. *American Journal of Community Psychology, 5*(4), 447-459.

Mosher, W. D., & Horn, M. C. (1988). First family planning visits by young women. *Family Planning Perspectives, 20*(1), 33-40.

Rader, G. E., Bekker, D., Brown, L., & Richard, T. C. (1978). Psychological correlates of unwanted pregnancy. *Journal of Abnormal Psychology, 87*(3), 373-376.

Rosenberg, M. (1965). *Society and the adolescent self-image.* Princeton, NJ: Princeton University Press.

Rovinsky, J. J. (1972). Abortion recidivism. *Obstetrical Gynecology, 39*(5), 649-659.

Streetman, L. G. (1987). Contrasts in the self-esteem of unwed teenage mothers. *Adolescence, 22*(86), 459-464.

Zabin, L. S., & Clark, S. D. (1981). Why they delay: A study of teenage family planning clinic patients. *Family Planning Perspectives, 13*(5), 205-217.

Zabin, L., Kantner, J., & Zelnik, M. (1979). The risk of adolescent pregnancy in the first months after intercourse. *Family Planning Perspectives, 11*(4), 215-222.

Zelnik, M., & Kantner, J. (1977). Sexual and contraceptive experience of young unmarried women in the United States, 1976 and 1971. *Family Planning Perspectives, 9*(2), 55-71.

Wanting Pregnancy: Teenagers' Attitudes, Goals, and Perceived Support

The absence of the desire for a child does not at the same time imply the rejection of the child; likewise, the failure to apply contraceptives is not identical to desiring a child. It seems that using or not using the methods of family planning has least of all to do with the intentional causation of events or the avoidance of them. (Teichmann, 1984)

INTRODUCTION

For years, experts have hotly debated how much teenagers want pregnancy and have searched for the answers to questions such as these:

- Do teenagers who become pregnant really want to have a baby?
- If teenagers do not want a baby, then why don't they use contraception?
- Does availability of abortion enable teenagers to abort unwanted pregnancies and only carry wanted ones to term?

To date, experts have found little empirical evidence to answer these questions with precision.

The long-standing research and policy interest in the "wanted-ness" of pregnancies stems from the fact that effective contraception requires not only information but also the motivation to intentionally avoid pregnancy. Family planning services assume that unwanted pregnancies result from lack of information, which can be corrected through sex education, and from limited access to reliable contraceptive methods, which can be remedied through increased availability of health-care services. The fact that a number of other developed countries have wide availability of contraceptives and far lower teenage birthrates compared to the United States is used by some as further evidence that teenage birthrates are related to information and availability of effective contraception (Jones et al., 1985).

Issues involving the motivation to prevent pregnancy are less amenable to change by programmatic approaches. These have received relatively little attention in family planning research and policy, with the exception of surveying the extent to which pregnancies were "unwanted." In the 1970s a series of surveys were conducted in U.S. metropolitan areas. They asked unmarried, previously pregnant teenagers from ages 15 to 19 whether they had "wanted" the pregnancy. About three fourths of the respondents in 1971 and 1976, and slightly more in 1979, answered "no" (Zelnik & Kantner, 1980). Although these teenagers did not want to be pregnant, the surveys found that few of them had used contraception, providing further evidence that improved information and access to contraception could prevent large numbers of births to unmarried teenagers.

As family planning services expanded following funding by the federal government in the late 1960s (Forrest, 1988a), teenage pregnancy rates decreased, but did not plummet. As Trussell (1988) pointed out, the teenage pregnancy rate remained high because only a minority of sexually active teenagers consistently used contraceptives and only half of these used the most effective methods. Many of these teenagers still may have lacked information and access to services that would have enabled them to effectively prevent pregnancy. Others may have failed to anticipate intercourse or not used contraception because they thought the risk of pregnancy was low (Zelnik & Kantner, 1979). Still other teenagers may not use contraception because they would not mind having a child, and the extent to which pregnancies among unmarried teenagers are "wanted" or "unwanted" remains poorly understood.

A woman's desire for pregnancy depends on various feelings and conditions that are not easily described or measured. Pohlman (1969) believed that many pregnancies in adults occurred not because they were "wanted and deliberately planned, but because there [were] lessened feelings of unwantedness." This concept addresses the ambivalence of pregnancy and childbearing, and recognizes the presence of advantages and satisfactions as well as disadvantages and problems. At any time, changes in a woman's circumstances may tip the balance in favor of—or against—having a baby (Miller, 1974). In Wilson (1987), Hogan stated that "it is not so much that single motherhood is wanted as it is that it is not sufficiently 'unwanted.' Women of all ages without a strong desire to prevent a birth tend to have limited contraceptive success."

Many factors in women's lives can make each reproductive stage (conception, pregnancy, and motherhood of an infant and then of a child) more or less wanted. Changes in marital status, health problems, or attitudes of significant others are only a few examples that may make a wanted pregnancy unwanted, or vice versa. A pregnancy that is wanted at one time can be completely unwanted at another. "Wantedness" of childbearing is a changing feeling; it is not an immutable condition.

In studies of pregnancy and contraceptive use, several terms have been used to evaluate women's feelings about particular pregnancies. Terms such as *wanted, happy, intended,* and *planned* can each apply to a pregnancy, but may not be interchangeable at the same time. For example, a woman may be "happy" to have a baby in a general sense but not "want" a pregnancy at the present time. Teenagers may indicate at a particular time that they do not "want" a baby, but at the same time indicate they are "happy" to have a baby, perhaps reflecting the acceptability of childbearing among their family and friends (Abrahamse, Morrison, & Waite, 1988) and signaling the lack of strong inhibitors, such as shame or disadvantages of single motherhood. The timing of a pregnancy may be "unwanted," but the child born may become described as "wanted."

Conversely, the pregnancy may be "wanted" at the outset, but later "unwanted" as a result of changed circumstances or problems with the child. Health professionals and researchers often have preferred to inquire whether the pregnancy was "planned" or "intended," rather than interpret the more amorphous terms *wanted* and *happy*. Although *planned* seems to be a less ambiguous term because it describes conscious intention, it fails to describe the desirability of pregnancy, which may not be reflected in intentional behavior. It is important to note that only a minority of women, regardless of age or marital status, state that a pregnancy was "intended": *Less than half of all U.S. pregnancies and only two thirds of all U.S. births reportedly were "intended"* in 1982 (Forrest, 1988b). Even among married women, about one third of births were unintended, and about 30% of the unintended births were unwanted (Williams & Pratt, 1990).

About one fourth of the births to unmarried teenagers (ages 15 to 19) were reported unwanted in the 1982 and 1988 National Surveys of Family Growth (Williams & Pratt, 1990). The proportion of unwanted births was more than three times greater among black teenagers than white teenagers. In these surveys a birth was classified as "unwanted" if the teenager reported that she had not wanted or probably not wanted a(nother) child at the time of conception or at any point in the future.

THE PENN STUDY

A primary aim of the Penn Study of Teenage Pregnancy was to examine the extent to which the teenagers "wanted" pregnancy and the factors that were associated with it. We compared feelings about pregnancy—how much pregnancy was wanted or unwanted, how happy a teenager would be to have a baby, and whether the pregnancy was "planned"—between those who became mothers and those who did not. We also attempted to identify the factors that most influenced these feelings, such as attitudes toward pregnancy, educational and occupational goals, and family and peer support.

Attitudes Toward Pregnancy

To determine the teenagers' attitudes toward pregnancy, we evaluated how much they wanted and planned the pregnancy, how happy they would be to have a baby, and how they perceived the effects of a baby on their lives.

Wanting Pregnancy

At study enrollment we asked the pregnant teenagers and those who had just terminated a pregnancy how "wanted" and "planned" the pregnancy was. We asked the never-pregnant teenagers how wanted and planned a pregnancy would be if they became pregnant now. These questions were repeated at each subsequent assessment during the 2-year study. The teenagers with babies were asked *both* about the babies and how they felt about another pregnancy. The teenagers responded to these questions on a visual analog scale, marking their position on a 10-centimeter line that ranged from 0 (not at all) to 100 (very much) for each perception (Zealley & Aitken, 1969).

Most of the teenagers did not strongly want a pregnancy at any of the assessments in the 2-year period (see Figure 3.1). At study enrollment, even those who were pregnant and expecting to deliver the baby scored barely at the midpoint of the scale, a position that appeared to indicate ambivalence. As Pohlman (1969) described, many of these pregnancies apparently occurred not because they were "wanted and deliberately intended, but because there [were] lessened feelings of unwantedness."

Although the delivery group did not strongly "want" pregnancy, they were more positive about pregnancy than their peers in the never-pregnant and abortion groups at study enrollment ($p < 0.001$). The never-pregnant teenagers were the least likely to "want" pregnancy, and in both the never-pregnant and the abortion groups, a number of teenagers indicated little or no desire for pregnancy.

We had expected that feelings about pregnancy would change over the 2 years of the study as the teenagers grew older, completed high school, had longer relationships with their boyfriends, or had other experiences that might make motherhood more viable and pregnancies more wanted. However, the reports of how

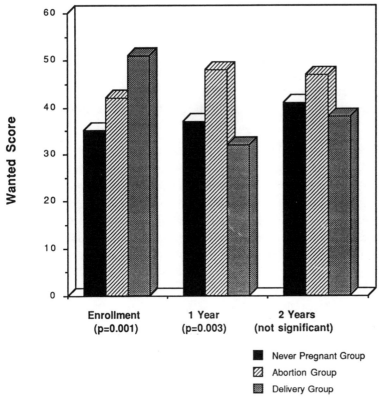

Figure 3.1. Teenagers' ratings on 100 mm analog scales at 3 time points of how much pregnancy was "wanted." Interaction of time by group: $p = 0.0001$; time effect not significant.

much pregnancy was "wanted" remained remarkably stable over the 2-year period. *There was no significant change* in the perceptions of the never-pregnant or abortion groups during the entire study. Only the delivery group demonstrated significant change, in the *negative* direction, a reflection of the feelings of those who clearly did not want another pregnancy in the 2-year interval after giving birth to their first child.

The delivery group's feelings about another pregnancy sharply contrasted with their feelings about the initial pregnancy. It was of particular interest to observe the increasing perception of "wantedness" as the pregnancy progressed. At enrollment, the mean "wanted" score on the visual analog scale for the delivery group was at the midpoint of the scale. By the end of the pregnancy, the mean score had climbed from 51 to 85. At the end of the first year of the study, this score had further increased to a mean of 91. By the end of the second year, it had risen to nearly 94, when all but one teenager in the group described the pregnancy as "wanted."

Planning Pregnancy

Few teenagers said that pregnancy was planned. Figure 3.2 depicts the analog scale scores for how much pregnancy was "planned" at three time points. The great majority indicated that pregnancy was very unplanned when they enrolled in the study, with no significant differences among the study groups. As can be seen in Figure 3.2, there was a modest increase in the intention to have a pregnancy during the 2-year study ($p < 0.004$ for the time effect, which increased from an overall score of 21 at enrollment to 31 at the 2-year endpoint). The slight differences among the study groups were not statistically significant, and it appears more noteworthy that the deliberate intention to plan pregnancy remained low overall. In contrast to "wanting" pregnancy, which discriminated among the study groups, "planning" pregnancy did not.

Correlations of "Wanting" and "Planning" Pregnancy

It was of further interest to observe that the delivery-group teenagers' reports of "planning" pregnancy increased as pregnancy progressed, paralleling their reports of increasingly "wanting" the pregnancy. The average "planned" scores for the delivery group rose from 22 at enrollment to 48 just before childbirth. Although there was almost no correlation between "planned" and "wanted" pregnancy when reported early in pregnancy, the increasing perception as pregnancy progressed that it was "wanted" and "planned" resulted in a high correlation, which was maintained at the 1-year and 2-year follow-ups ($r = 0.64$, $p < 0.0001$).

The correlation between "planned" and "wanted" pregnancy also increased dramatically during the 2-year study among the teenagers who did not give birth ($r = 0.76$, $p < 0.0001$ and $r = 0.71$,

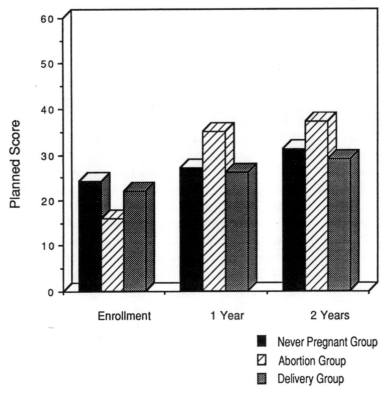

Figure 3.2. Teenagers' ratings on 100 mm analog scales at 3 time points of how much pregnancy was "planned." Time effect: $p < 0.0001$. No significant effect of group; interaction of time by group, $p < 0.05$.

$p < 0.0001$ at endpoint in the never-pregnant and abortion groups, respectively). Initially, only the never-pregnant group showed any meaningful correlation between "wanted" and "planned" variables ($r = .49$, $p < 0.0001$ at enrollment). The abortion group had no correlation ($r = .04$), indicating almost complete absence of relationship between these variables. The desire for and intention to become pregnant became more aligned during the study in all study groups. It may be that the questions about sexual behavior and pregnancy that were part of the study and the teenagers' continued participation in family planning services enabled them to become more aware of the relationship between their feelings and their behavior.

Being Happy to Have a Baby

Responses to other interview questions corroborated the teenagers' ratings of how much they "wanted" pregnancy. When asked in the initial interview how happy they were (or would be) to have a baby now, responses again fell in the middle of the scale. In all three study groups the answers were consistent with the teenagers' reports on the "wanted" scale. Few teenagers in the never-pregnant and abortion groups indicated that they would be happy about having a baby now, just as they had indicated they did not "want" a baby. In contrast, 84% of the pregnant teenagers were "happy" about having a baby—an even higher number than said they "wanted" pregnancy (see Table 3.1).

At the 1-year and 2-year follow-up interviews, the responses to "how happy" they were (or would be) to have a baby at the present time remained similar to the initial responses. The teenagers in the delivery group continued to be happy about having a baby, whereas those in the never-pregnant and abortion groups continued to be unhappy about it. The teenagers in the abortion group were even more unhappy about having a baby at the follow-ups than they were initially, suggesting that their desire to postpone childbearing was maintained for a considerable length of time.

Teenagers' Expectations of Childbearing

At study enrollment we asked the teenagers what effect a baby would have on their lives, and their responses were categorized as "better," "no different," "worse," "ruined," or "don't know." Teenagers in the delivery group were most likely to say that their lives would be better. Although the never-pregnant and abortion-group teenagers were less likely to indicate that a baby would enhance their lives ($p < 0.0001$), it is striking that, overall, the ratings indicated that the teenagers perceived that childbearing would have little impact on their lives. Very few teenagers indicated that a baby would make their lives "worse" or "ruined."

At the 1-year and 2-year follow-up interviews, the responses to "how happy" they were (or would be) to have a baby at the present

Table 3.1 Attitudes Toward Pregnancy: Distributions at Enrollment (percent)

	Never Pregnant	Abortion	Delivery
Planned (≥ 50)[a]	15	6	12
Wanted* (≥ 50)[a]	31	34	45
Happy to have baby now**	22	38	84
Effect of baby on life** (positive, neutral)	32	35	85
Mother happy or "very happy" about baby now**	20	21	62
Girlfriends have babies (yes)*	67	61	78
Expect to have baby before marriage (>50% chance)	56	64	NA
Intend baby in next 2 years (yes, uncertain)	13	13	NA

NOTE: Significant differences among groups (chi-square test):
*$p < 0.05$
**$p < 0.0001$
[a]scale range: 0 (none) to 100 (high).

time remained similar to the initial responses. The teens in the delivery group continued to be happy about having a baby whereas those in the never-pregnant and abortion groups continued to be unhappy about it. The teens in the abortion groups were even more unhappy about having a baby at the follow-ups than they were initially, suggesting that their desire to postpone childbearing was more than short-lived.

The extent to which unmarried childbearing was acceptable to these teenagers was further illustrated by the responses to when they expected to have their first child. More than half of the *nonpregnant* teenagers (56% and 64% of the never-pregnant and abortion groups, respectively) said they expected to have a child before marrying, although only 13% intended to have a child in the next 2 years. These responses bring into sharp focus the prevailing acceptability of single motherhood among these young women.

Summarizing Attitudes Toward Pregnancy

Few teens "planned" or intended pregnancy, and many initially described ambivalence about how much they "wanted" a pregnancy. Only in the delivery group did the perceptions of a "wanted" pregnancy change during the 2 years of the study. Their pregnancies became increasingly "wanted" as time progressed, but they no longer wanted another pregnancy after their child was born. In contrast, the nonpregnant teenagers on average perceived pregnancy as less "wanted" than the delivery-group teenagers, and these perceptions remained stable over the 2-year interval. "Planning" pregnancy overall significantly increased with time and did not differ among the three study groups. The overall number who planned a pregnancy during the study was small.

Goals Competing With Maternity:
Education and Occupation

To better understand the factors that influenced teenagers' desire for—or avoidance of—pregnancy, we examined their educational and occupational goals.

Education

First, we asked teenagers in all groups about their educational goals. Nearly all (91%) expected to graduate from high school, and many (77%) said they would obtain a college education or professional or technical training beyond high school. Only 19% did not cite educational goals beyond high school graduation, and 4% cited no educational goals (see Table 3.2).

We then asked the teenagers about their family's educational goals for them. A much smaller number (54%) indicated that their families expected them to go beyond high school. About 18% said their families had no educational expectations beyond high school, and a large minority (28%) said they did not know what their families' educational expectations were.

We then examined a variable called *opportunity* by combining the teenagers' educational goals with their family's educational ex-

Table 3.2 Goals of the Teenagers: Education, Work, Maternity
(percentage distribution)

	Never Pregnant	Abortion	Delivery
Plan to graduate high school[a]			
Certain, probably	95	95	85
< 50/50, no	5	5	15
Educational goals[b]			
>High school	87	88	62
≤ High school	8	11	33
Don't know	5	1	5
Family's educational goals			
>High school	56	59	48
≤ High school	8	11	31
Don't know, no answer	36	30	21
Number paid jobs[c]			
0	33	39	48
Some	67	61	52
Main occupation at age 30[a]			
Professional (answer 1-3)	47	47	29
Clerical, technical (4-6)	21	20	19
Homemaker (8)	11	11	15
Don't know, no occupation	21	22	37
Work goals[a]			
Professional (1-3)	62	58	47
Clerical, technical (4-6)	28	35	31
Homemaker (8)	1	0	3
None, don't know (0,7,9)	9	7	18
Likelihood of work goals[b]			
High	58	60	37
< 50/50 chance	42	40	63
Baby affects educational goals[d]			
Very much	70	74	20
Some, little, none	30	26	80

NOTE: Significant differences among groups (chi-square test):

[a] $p < 0.01$

[b] $p < 0.001$

[c] $p < 0.05$

[d] $p < 0.0001$

pectations. The results for educational goals beyond high school were similar to those for the family's educational goals: 47% of all the teenagers said that both they and their families perceived educational opportunities beyond high school, and these teenagers were more likely to be in the abortion (57%) or never-pregnant (49%) groups, compared to 38% of the delivery group ($p < 0.05$). Thirty-eight percent of all the teens stated that either they or their families, but not both, had educational goals beyond high school; 15% had no support for opportunities beyond high school, predominantly in the delivery group.

When asked how much having a baby would affect their education, half the teenagers indicated that having a baby would impede or interfere with their education; the other half indicated that a baby would make no difference (see Table 3.2).

Occupation

Sixty percent of the teenagers reported some experience in a paid job; 40% had none. The young ages of these teenagers (ages 13 to 17 at enrollment) made it unlikely that many would have full-time work experience, but any form of paid work—including baby-sitting—was counted here as job experience.

When asked what their main occupation would be at age 30, 40% of the teenagers cited professional employment, 20% cited clerical or technical positions, and 12% said they would be homemakers. Twenty-eight percent could not say what they might do, but none cited unskilled jobs.

When asked what their main occupation would be at a nearer horizon, when they finished school, even more cited professional (55%) or clerical or technical positions (31%), only 2% said they would be homemakers, and 12% could not say what they expected to do.

We then asked the teenagers whether they thought it was likely that they would achieve these occupational goals. Only half of the teenagers believed there was a high likelihood of achieving their work goals, whereas the other half thought the likelihood was low or, at best, a 50/50 chance.

The teenagers who had no occupational goals or described their goals as unachievable generally were the same teenagers who believed a baby would not interfere with their education. The teenagers who said having a baby before completing high school would interfere with their education generally recognized the importance of education in achieving their occupational goals.

Summarizing and Comparing Goals

Nearly all of the teenagers (91%) said they expected to complete high school, and most (86%) could cite a possible occupation. Simply asking what occupation they expected to have tended to produce idealized responses, as revealed when they were asked further about achieving the goals they cited. Only about half the teenagers thought they could achieve the occupations that they cited for themselves. More important, only about half of the teenagers believed that their families expected them to obtain education or training beyond high school, and *that having a baby would seriously interfere with their education or occupational intentions.*

The other half of the teenagers thought they were unlikely to achieve the occupational goals they cited, and most of them said they *did not know what their families thought about their future education or occupation.* These teenagers indicated that a baby would not interfere with their education or occupation. Without clear alternative goals, these teenagers understandably perceived childbearing as enhancing or marking little change in their lives. Particularly revealing was that even among the teenagers who were *not* pregnant, the great majority said they would probably have a baby before they married. Maternity was a status that they could achieve on a near horizon, for themselves.

Comparisons of educational and occupational goals underscored significant differences among the three study groups (see Table 3.2). Compared to the delivery group, teenagers in the never-pregnant and abortion groups were significantly more likely to:

- Believe they would complete high school
- Believe they would obtain education or training beyond high school
- Perceive family support for education beyond high school
- Cite occupational goals
- Perceive a high likelihood of achieving their occupational goals
- Believe that a baby would negatively affect their educational goals

Responses of teenagers who had terminated pregnancy were nearly identical to those of the never-pregnant group. No statistically significant differences existed between responses from these two groups, and each of these groups differed significantly from the delivery group.

Family and Peer Acceptance and Support

The general acceptance of single motherhood by the great majority of these teenagers (even those who were not pregnant and had no need to rationalize a current pregnancy) strongly suggests the extent to which pregnancy reflects familial and social attitudes about teenage and nonmarital childbearing and not simply an adolescent failure to anticipate the consequences of sexual activity.

These teenagers perceived widespread acceptance of early, nonmarital childbearing. Half of them had siblings with babies, and 28% had sisters who had given birth to their first child as teenagers. *Over three fourths* (78%) of the teenagers said their close girlfriends had babies (see Table 3.1). More than half of the nonpregnant teenage respondents said that they, too, would have babies before they were married. Only one quarter of these teenagers thought they would not begin childbearing until after the teen years and after they were married.

To learn more about family attitudes, we asked the teenagers what their mothers thought about them having a baby. More than half of them (53%) said their mothers would be happy or would not mind if they had a baby now. About 45% believed their mothers would be unhappy about early childbearing; only 2% said they did not know what their mothers thought about it. The responses were similar when the teenagers were asked what their fathers would think about them having a baby.

We then asked the same questions in relation to their boyfriends and close girlfriends: How happy would they be if the teenage respondent had a baby now? These teenagers perceived their friends—both their boyfriends and their girlfriends—as "very happy" about having a baby, much more so than their parents. In all three study groups the boyfriends were rated as the most happy among family

Table 3.3 Mean Scores for Support of Early Childbearing[a]

Supportive of Teenager Having a Baby	Never Pregnant	Abortion	Delivery
Mother*	3.2	3.1	4.3
Father	2.1	2.2	2.5
Boyfriend	3.6	4.1	4.0
Girlfriend	3.6	3.8	4.0
Sister	2.8	3.0	3.3
Grandmother	2.2	2.4	2.6
Other	2.0	2.9	3.0
Total support*	19.9	21.4	23.6

[a]The information summarizes the teenagers' ratings of the person's supportiveness of them having a baby. Ratings were made on a scale of 0 to 5, with 5 being most supportive. Total support is the sum of individual support items.
*$p < 0.001$

and friends, with almost no difference between the ratings of the pregnant and nonpregnant teenagers. We then summed the scores for how "happy" the teenagers perceived each of these people to be should they have a baby. The average score was about at the midpoint of the range, one more indication that these teenagers perceived no great opposition to—and considerable acceptance of—early childbearing.

As a way of evaluating the acceptance of early childbearing among the people closest to the teenagers, we asked specifically how *supportive* people would be if they had a baby now. The teenagers indicated considerable supportiveness from others, including family members, boyfriends, and close girlfriends (see Table 3.3). At least two thirds believed that having a baby not only was tolerated, but also that it was strongly supported by three or more people who were important to them.

Most of the teenagers believed that if they had a baby, their families would provide material and emotional support. They thought their mothers would provide money (84%), a home (86%), child care (87%), and advice (94%). About 90% thought the baby's father would provide money, and 83% expected that he would share in child care (although by the study endpoint, these proved to be unrealistic perceptions for many). Two thirds indicated that the baby's father would provide a home for the child, although because few expected to marry the baby's father, this appeared to signify a temporary or visiting arrangement. About two thirds of the teenagers expected that the paternal grandparents would provide money, child care, and advice, although fewer (48%) expected them to provide a home for the baby.

The teenagers' beliefs about terminating pregnancy further reinforced their perceptions of the acceptance of childbearing. Forty percent said they had no support for abortion, in contrast to only 15% who perceived no support for childbearing. One fourth of the teenagers said their mothers and grandmothers *strongly* opposed abortion—twice the number who strongly opposed childbearing. Nearly half (46%) of the teenagers said their boyfriends strongly opposed abortion, but only 4% said their boyfriends opposed childbearing. About 20% believed their girlfriends and sisters opposed abortion, but fewer than 5% believed these women opposed childbearing. Overall, two thirds of the teenagers perceived strong opposition to abortion from at least one person close to them. For these teenagers, abortion not only would be a difficult personal decision, but also could bring strong disapproval or rejection from the people who were most important to them.

Comparing Acceptance and Support of Childbearing

There were no differences among the three study groups in how happy their boyfriends were to have a baby. Most of these teenagers thought their boyfriends would be pleased if pregnancy occurred. Neither were there differences in whether their sisters were teenage mothers or had babies, a standard demographic marker for early teenage childbearing.

In spite of their similar demographic characteristics, the teenagers had clearly different perceptions of the desirability of pregnancy. Delivery-group teenagers were much more likely than those not having babies to indicate that childbearing would make their lives better or make no difference in their lives. Arguably, these responses may have been affected by the existing pregnancy, but consistency of responses to a number of questions about the support of their family and friends set them apart from the teenagers who did not have babies. Delivery-group teenagers were more likely to have girlfriends with babies, a social milieu that not only provided example but also, and more importantly, offered "community with other young women in like circumstances" (An, Haverman, & Wolfe, 1991). They were much more likely to believe that their mothers were happy about them having a baby, in contrast to teenagers in the never-pregnant and abortion groups who were clear that their mothers were *not* happy about early childbearing.

CHAPTER SUMMARY

The findings of this chapter support the hypothesis that pregnancies occurred not because they were "wanted and deliberately intended, but because there [were] lessened feelings of unwantedness" (Pohlman, 1969). At no time during the 2-year study did most of the teenagers strongly "want" a pregnancy. In spite of accurate sexual information and access to contraceptives, the teenagers had pregnancies when pregnancies were not sufficiently "unwanted" to prevent them.

At the same time, it cannot be overemphasized that the teenagers who avoided childbearing were sexually active and had background characteristics and circumstances similar to the teenage mothers, but they indicated more clearly that pregnancy was unwanted.

What makes pregnancy sufficiently unwanted? In these data, primary factors were strong educational and occupational goals and family attitudes that opposed early teenage childbearing. A major difference between teenagers in the delivery group and those in the never-pregnant and abortion groups was the family attitudes perceived by the teenagers. The nonpregnant teens were much more likely to believe that they would obtain—and had family support for—education or training beyond high school, that they would be likely to achieve their chosen occupational goals, and that having a baby would impede these goals. The never-pregnant and abortion groups clearly believed their mothers did not approve of early childbearing. They also were more likely to have friends who did not have babies.

The teenagers who commenced early childbearing had much less support for occupational goals, and many did not know what their families thought about educational goals and future occupations. Nearly two thirds of the teenagers having babies thought their mothers were happy about this event. This perception of mother's approval was three times higher in the delivery group than in the never-pregnant or abortion groups, where relatively few thought their mothers would be pleased if they had a baby. The great majority of delivery-group teenagers said their friends had babies. They were in a social milieu that accepted early teenage pregnancy; they would become members of a community of young mothers.

REFERENCES

Abrahamse, A. F., Morrison, P. A., & Waite, L. J. (1988). *Beyond stereotypes: Who becomes a single teenage mother?* Santa Monica, CA: Rand.

An, C. B., Haverman, R., & Wolfe, B. (1991). Teen out-of-wedlock births and welfare receipt: The role of childhood events and economic circumstances. *Review of Economics and Statistics.* Manuscript submitted for publication.

Forrest, J. D. (1988a). The delivery of family planning services in the United States. *Family Planning Perspectives, 20*(2), 88-95, 98.

Forrest, J. D. (1988b). Unintended pregnancy among American women. In S. K. Henshaw & J. Van Vort (Eds.), *Abortion services in the United States, each state and metropolitan area, 1984-1985.* New York: Alan Guttmacher Institute.

Jones, E. F., Forrest, J. D., Goldman, N., Henshaw, S. K., Lincoln, R., Rosoff, J. I., Westoff, C. F., & Wulf, D. (1985). Teenage pregnancy in developed countries: Determinants and policy implications. *Family Planning Perspectives, 17*(2), 53-63.

Miller, W. B. (1974). Relationships between the intendedness of conception and the wantedness of pregnancy. *Journal of Nervous and Mental Disease, 159*(6), 396-406.

Pohlman, E. H. (1969). *The psychology of birth planning.* Cambridge, MA: Schenkman.

Teichmann, A. T. (1984). The meanings of the notion "desire for a child." Some considerations based on an empirical study of 400 patients applying for legal abortion. *Journal of Psychosomatic Obstetrics and Gynecology, 3,* 215-222.

Trussell, J. (1988). Teenage pregnancy in the U.S. *Family Planning Perspectives, 20*(6), 262-272.

Williams, L. B., & Pratt, W. F. (1990). Wanted and unwanted childbearing in the United States: 1973-1988. *Advance Data From Vital and Health Statistics*, No. 189. Hyattsville, MD: National Center for Health Statistics.

Wilson, W. J. (1987). *The truly disadvantaged: The inner city, the underclass, and public policy.* Chicago: University of Chicago Press.

Zealley, A. K., & Aitken, R. C. B. (1969). Measurement of mood. *Proceedings of the Royal Society of Medicine, 62*(10), 993-996.

Zelnik, M., & Kantner, J. F. (1979). Reasons for nonuse of contraception by sexually active women aged 15-19. *Family Planning Perspectives, 11*(5), 289-296.

Zelnik, M., & Kantner, J. F. (1980). Sexual activity, contraceptive use, and pregnancy among metropolitan-area teenagers. *Family Planning Perspectives, 12*(5), 230-237.

FOUR

Choosing Abortion or Delivery: Influences and Outcomes

INTRODUCTION

Deciding whether to bear a child or have an abortion can be an overwhelming decision. Amidst the divisiveness of the political and religious controversies surrounding abortion, women may experience many conflicting emotions as they struggle with an unintended pregnancy and the personal consequences of childbearing. The conflicts may be even greater for pregnant teenagers, who have never made a fundamental decision in their lives, but must decide within a few weeks whether to give birth or terminate a pregnancy.

Each year about half a million U.S. teenagers have abortions. Teenagers have about 25% of all legal abortions in the United States (Henshaw & Van Vort, 1989). More than 40% of white and non-white teenagers terminate their pregnancies (Alan Guttmacher Institute, 1989). Of these teenagers, 58% were ages 18 to 19, 39% were ages 15 to 17, and 3% were age 14 or younger (Alan Guttmacher Institute, 1992).

The problematic outcomes of teenage childbearing are well known. Teenage mothers are more likely than their nonpregnant peers to have dropped out of school, to be unemployed or sporadically employed, and to obtain welfare support. Although the school dropout rate for teenage parents has decreased, teenagers who become parents before age 17 still are less likely to complete high school than their nonparenting peers (Upchurch & McCarthy, 1989), limiting their occupational opportunities and potential earnings. Having little or no means of economic support, teenage families often need public support. Over half of Aid to Families With Dependent Children (AFDC) goes to families that began with a teenage birth (Burt, 1986). The public cost for teenage childbearing in 1989 was $21.55 billion, a conservative estimate that did not include housing subsidies, day care, special education, and foster care—supports that often are needed by single teenage parents (Center for Population Options, 1990b). The Center for Population Options estimated that costs would be reduced 40% if teenage births were delayed until the mothers were in their twenties (Center for Population Options, 1990b).

Teenagers are at greater risk than older women of serious medical complications during pregnancy, such as anemia, toxemia, cervical trauma, and premature delivery (Armstrong & Pascale, 1990). Low-birth-weight infants and infant mortality are more common among teenage mothers than among older mothers, primarily because teenage mothers do not receive good prenatal care. In 1987, 46% of teenage mothers did not receive prenatal care in the first trimester, 9% did not receive care until the third trimester, and 4% received no prenatal care (National Center for Health Statistics, 1989).

Although there is extensive information on the economic and social effects of teenage childbearing, there is little comparable information on the economic and social effects of terminating teenage pregnancies. Studies of abortion have been concerned primarily with the psychological outcomes (Adler, David, Major, Roth, Russo, & Wyatt, 1990; Cvejic, Lipper, Kinch, & Benjamin, 1977; Freeman, 1978; Freeman, Rickels, Huggins, Garcia, & Polin, 1980) or subsequent fertility (Hogue, Cates, & Tietze, 1983). A recent study of teenagers who obtained abortions compared with peers who gave birth and peers who had negative pregnancy tests found no detrimental psychosocial effects in the abortion group (Zabin, Hirsch, & Emerson, 1989). At a 2-year follow-up, the teenagers who had had abortions were more likely to have advanced educationally, were less likely to have a subsequent pregnancy, and were no more likely to show psychological problems than teenagers in the other two study groups.

This study was conducted at a unique time when economically disadvantaged teenagers could obtain abortions. This made it possible to compare teenagers from similar backgrounds who decided to terminate pregnancy or carry the pregnancy to term. What influenced their choices, and how did these choices affect their lives? Greater understanding of what influenced their decisions might illuminate differences in paths chosen to initiate or delay early motherhood.

In this chapter we examine the decisions of unmarried teenagers about their first pregnancy. The decision to terminate or carry a pregnancy to term is studied here through the teenagers' attitudes and perceptions of childbearing, their educational and occupational goals, the support for childbearing in their personal networks, and assessments of psychological factors that have been associated with teenage pregnancy. Because the teenagers lived with their families and depended on them for emotional and financial support, we particularly explored the teenagers' perceptions of family attitudes toward childbearing and abortion that may have affected their decisions about pregnancy.

We first interviewed delivery-group teenagers in early to midpregnancy and abortion-group teenagers shortly after pregnancy termination. We then followed the two groups for 2 years, comparing their:

- Educational status
- Education and employment goals
- Relationships with parents, other family members, boyfriends, and girlfriends
- Self-esteem and emotional distress
- Satisfaction with the decision about the pregnancy
- Incidence of subsequent pregnancy

INFLUENCES ON THE PREGNANCY DECISION

To examine factors that influenced the decision to deliver or terminate a pregnancy, the Penn Study first compared the teenagers' background characteristics (other than age, race, and socioeconomic status, which were matched or homogeneous in the sample), and then examined educational and occupational goals, feelings about pregnancy, family and peer support, and the teenagers' perceptions of the mother's and boyfriend's role in making the decision.

Background Characteristics

The abortion and delivery groups came from similar backgrounds. (For details, see Chapter 1.) They ranged from age 13 to 17, and the two groups had an identical mean age of 15.6. No significant differences existed between the teenagers' households based on number of parents, persons, or adults in the household; number of siblings; whether they had sisters who were teenage mothers; place of birth; frequency of moving; social class; or religion.

The abortion group, however, did appear to have significantly more employment. The ratio of working adults to adults in the household was about 1 to 2 in the abortion group, compared to 1 to 3 in the delivery group. Also, the ratio of working adults to household members was about 1 to 3 in the abortion group, but 1 to 7 in the delivery group. According to the teenagers' reports, 58% of abortion-group households but 78% of delivery-group households received welfare ($p < 0.01$).

Another difference between the two groups was the age of the teenagers' mothers at first childbirth. Half of the abortion-group mothers, but two thirds of the delivery-group mothers, were age 17 or younger at the birth of their first child ($p < 0.01$). Among these young mothers, half in both groups were age 15 or younger when their first child was born.

Educational and Occupational Goals

Although nearly all the teenagers expected to complete high school, there were differences in educational performance between the abortion and delivery groups at study enrollment. In the abortion group 98% were in school, compared to only 83% of the delivery group ($p < 0.0001$). School performance as reflected by course grades was better in the abortion group. Only 8% of the abortion group reported a grade average below C, compared to 26% of the delivery group ($p < 0.01$).

Not surprisingly in light of better school performance, abortion-group teenagers were more likely to have educational goals beyond high school. (For details, see Chapter 3.) More in the abortion group than in the delivery group expected to have education or technical training beyond high school ($p < 0.001$) and saw these goals as consistent with their families' expectations of educational attainment ($p < 0.01$). Nearly 75% of the abortion group (compared to only 20% of the delivery group) thought a baby would considerably alter their educational goals ($p < 0.0001$).

Teenagers in the abortion group also were significantly more likely to have vocational goals. They aspired to specific occupations outside the home and were more likely to believe that they would be employed in these occupations ($p < 0.01$). Also, 60% of the abortion group thought they had a very high likelihood of achieving their work goals, compared to only 37% in the delivery group ($p < 0.01$). It appeared that there were differences at the outset when the teenagers made their pregnancy choices: the abortion-group teenagers clearly evidenced more belief in their opportunities, both educational and occupational.

Teenagers' Feelings About Pregnancy

At the initial interview the teenagers gave expected responses to questions about how happy they were to have a baby: Abortion-group teenagers said they were unhappy about having a baby, whereas delivery-group teenagers said they were very happy. (For details, see Chapter 3.) However, the teenagers' responses to the question of how much the pregnancy was wanted (using analog scales ranging from 0 to 100, with 100 being the most wanted) fell in the midrange in both groups, indicating considerable ambivalence or uncertainty, rather than clearly "wanting" or "not wanting" the pregnancy. On the average, the "wanted" scores in the delivery group were at the midpoint (51) and in the abortion group were only slightly lower (42), an insignificant difference. These teenagers were not certain they "wanted" a baby, but neither were they clear that they did not want a baby at this point in their lives. Nearly all of the teenagers clearly indicated the pregnancy was "unplanned." There was little difference in the analog scale scores (ranging from 0 to 100 with 100 being the most planned): 22 in the delivery group and 16 in the abortion group, which reflected the teenagers' reports that pregnancy was very unplanned.

Family and Peer Support for Childbearing

Teenagers who terminated the pregnancy had support for the decision. In particular, they had family members and friends who did not approve of early teenage childbearing. Each of the following factors differed significantly between the abortion- and delivery-group teenagers. The majority of the abortion group (59%) thought their mothers were unhappy about them having a baby, compared to only 23% in the delivery group. Fifty-one percent of the abortion group compared to 17% of the delivery group believed their fathers were very unhappy about them having a baby. Almost half (45%) of the abortion group had at least one family member who previously had terminated a pregnancy, compared to only 27% in the delivery group. More teenagers in the abortion group (39%) than in the delivery group (22%) had friends who did not have babies. The abortion-group teenagers were less likely to think that their girlfriends approved of having a baby. Summing the perceived approval for childbearing, there were clear differences between the abortion and delivery groups, with the abortion group reporting much less acceptance of teenage maternity ($p < 0.0001$) and having examples in their families of women who had had abortions.

Figure 4.1 represents the approval that teenagers in the abortion and delivery groups perceived, as constructed from summing the teenagers' ratings of how happy their mother, father, boyfriend, and girlfriend were about them having a baby. Delivery-group teenagers were clearly at the happy end of the scale, whereas many more abortion-group teenagers indicated that these people were unhappy about them having a baby ($p < 0.0001$).

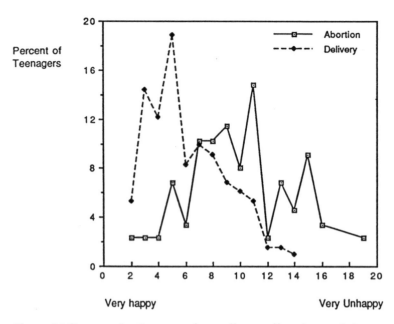

Figure 4.1. Teenagers' ratings at study enrollment of how happy their parents and friends were about the teenagers' having a baby. Scores are the sum of the teenagers' ratings for mother, father, boyfriend, and girlfriend and range from 1 (very happy) to 20 (very unhappy).

When asked where they perceived support for having a baby, the teenagers in both groups indicated that the *most* supportive persons were their boyfriends. Nearly two thirds of all the teenagers in the abortion and delivery groups indicated that their boyfriends strongly supported childbearing. About half indicated that their girlfriends and sisters would strongly support having a baby, and this, in contrast to being happy about having a baby, did not differ between the abortion and delivery groups. These perceptions that their friends and peers supported childbearing reflected an environment where many young teenagers had babies. But these teenagers knew little about childbearing other than its emotional satisfactions. They did not have realistic perceptions of parenting in the long term and did not understand even the immediate social and economic effects of a baby in their lives.

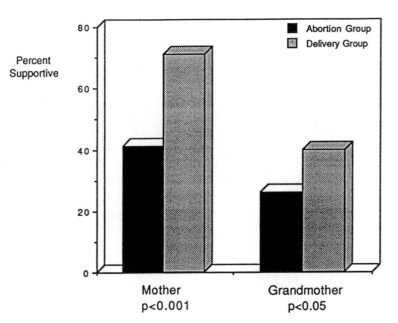

Figure 4.2. Percent of abortion- and delivery-group teenagers who re-ported very strong support for childbearing from mother and grand-mother.

The greatest difference between the abortion and delivery groups was in the support for childbearing from the teenagers' mothers. Forty-one percent of the abortion group but 71% of the delivery group believed that their mothers were very supportive of early childbearing ($p < 0.001$) (see Figure 4.2). The groups also differed in their grandmothers' support for early childbearing, with 26% of the abortion group but 40% of the delivery group in-dicating that their grandmothers strongly supported this ($p < 0.05$). The majority of teenagers indicated that their boyfriends provided strong support for having a baby, with no difference between the abortion (64%) and delivery (61%) groups. Support for having a baby from girlfriends, sisters, and fathers also did not differ be-tween the two study groups: 48% of the teenagers said their girlfriends strongly supported having a baby; 45% said this of their sisters; and 24% said this of their fathers. Summing the support perceived from their mothers, grandmothers, sisters, fathers, boy-friends, and girlfriends, the total support for childbearing remained significantly greater in the delivery group than in the abortion group ($p < 0.05$).

We also asked the teenagers whether they perceived opposition to having a baby. The abortion group reported more objection to childbearing from both parents (33% of both fathers and mothers). In the delivery group only 4% said their mothers and 7% said their fathers opposed early childbearing ($p < 0.0001$). Almost none believed their boyfriends strongly objected to having a baby, and few in either group thought their girlfriends, sisters, or others strongly opposed childbearing. Once again, summing responses for each group of the teenagers, 81% of the delivery group, in contrast to 45% of the abortion group, indicated that no one close to them objected to their having a baby ($p < 0.0001$).

Family and Peer Support for Abortion

Support for terminating pregnancy differed strongly and significantly between the abortion and delivery groups. About 73% of the abortion group and 23% of the delivery group indicated that their mothers were very supportive of this option ($p < 0.0001$). Conversely, almost none in the abortion group believed their mothers strongly opposed abortion, compared to nearly half in the delivery group (5% and 43%, respectively; $p < 0.0001$). Only 41% of the boyfriends in the abortion group supported abortion, but almost none (11%) of the boyfriends in the delivery group did so. ($p < 0.0001$). Fathers, sisters, girlfriends, grandmothers, and others offered little support for abortion. Summing the support for abortion perceived by the teenagers, 84% of the abortion group, compared to 43% of the delivery group, had someone close to them who supported the abortion decision ($p < 0.0001$).

Mother's Influence on the Pregnancy Decision

Less than 5% of these teenagers chose a pregnancy outcome that contradicted their mother's views. The abortion-group teenagers

Table 4.1 Mother's Support for Abortion and Delivery Reported by Teenagers at Study Enrollment (percentage distribution)

Mother's Support	Abortion	Delivery
Strong for baby	6	54
Strong for abortion	42	10
Strong for either	31	13
Other*	21	23

NOTE: *"Other" includes all ratings below "strong" plus "don't know." Teenagers rated support on a scale of 1 to 5; "strong" support is a rating of 5. Chi-square test $p < 0.0001$.

had their mother's support for abortion, and the delivery-group teenagers had their mother's support for having a baby. We then linked each teenager's report of how much her mother supported having the baby with how much she supported terminating the pregnancy to further examine maternal support for the pregnancy outcome. More than half of the delivery group, but only 6% of the abortion group, indicated that their mothers were *very* supportive of having the baby (depicted in Table 4.1).

In contrast, 42% of the abortion group, compared to only 10% of the delivery group, believed their mothers were *very* supportive of the abortion decision. Some teenagers said their mothers strongly supported either decision, but this was much more likely in the abortion group (31%) than in the delivery group (13%). When the teenagers who said their mothers supported either decision were included with the strong support groups, 73% of the abortion group and 67% of the delivery group had very strong support from their mothers for their decision (see Table 4.1).

Most of the teenagers (81%) said they had talked with their mothers about the outcome of their pregnancy. However, less than half in each study group indicated that they talked about the pregnancy outcome *mainly* with their mothers. More than half said friends were the primary confidants—girlfriends as well as boyfriends. Only one teenager in the study indicated that she had talked about the pregnancy decision primarily with a professional outside the circle of family and friends.

Mothers of the abortion-group teenagers clearly appeared to provide more support for abortion than did mothers of the delivery-group teenagers. Less than half of the delivery group had ever talked about abortion with their mothers, and only a small proportion of these believed their mothers supported abortion. Merely 11% of the delivery group knew where to obtain an abortion. Although the abortion-group teenagers may not have talked with their mothers until they needed to make a decision about their pregnancy, the ensuing discussion supported abortion. This was not true for delivery-group teenagers, many of whom received neither support nor correct information about abortion from their mothers.

Differences in maternal involvement also were evident in the teenagers' statements about who made the decision about the pregnancy outcome. Although three fourths of the teenagers in both groups said they themselves made the decision to continue or terminate the pregnancy, among those who did not make their own decision, it was the mother who was usually involved. Rosen (1980) previously observed that the mother's influence was particularly important for black teenagers who chose abortion. Among those who did not make the pregnancy decision themselves, twice as many in the abortion group as in the delivery group said the decision was mainly made by their mother ($p < 0.05$). These results contrast with previous studies that found that teenagers who chose abortion were more independent and more likely to make their own decisions, and that teenagers who delivered pregnancy were strongly influenced by others (Blum & Resnick, 1982; Bracken, Klerman, & Bracken, 1978; Fischman, 1977; Morin-Gunthier & Lortie, 1984). Here we observe that the great majority of teenagers believed they made their own decision, yet both outcome groups were strongly influenced by their families and friends. When the teenagers did not make their own decisions, the mothers' involvement was more influential in the abortion choice than in the delivery choice. The teenagers who chose abortion did not appear to be more independent; rather, their families did not accept early unmarried childbearing.

Boyfriend's Influence on the Pregnancy Decision

The majority of these teenagers had talked with their boyfriends about the pregnancy, but this was even more likely in the delivery group than in the abortion group (81% and 60%, respectively; $p < 0.01$). Most of the teenagers believed their boyfriends were happy about the pregnancy and having a baby. Few of the teenagers believed their boyfriends supported pregnancy termination, although abortion-group teenagers had more support for abortion from their boyfriends than delivery-group teenagers (41% and 11%, respectively; $p < 0.0001$).

The boyfriend's involvement in deciding the pregnancy outcome appeared quite limited. Only one third of all the teenagers said they talked *most* with their boyfriend about the pregnancy decision. Not surprisingly, this was more likely to occur in the delivery group (42% compared to 26%, $p < 0.05$). Although more than three fourths of the delivery group said they alone made the decision to continue the pregnancy, 8% percent said their boyfriend made the decision to carry the pregnancy to term, and another 9% said their decision was made to please their boyfriend. In contrast, no one in the abortion group said their boyfriend made the decision to terminate the pregnancy, and only 2% said the decision was made to please their boyfriend.

The teenagers had relationships with their boyfriends averaging slightly more than 1 year, and generally indicated that they felt the relationship was very close. There were no differences between the two study groups in the closeness or the length of the relationship. Of particular interest, however, was the contrast between the closeness of the relationship with their boyfriends compared to the relationship with their mothers. Delivery-group teenagers overall rated themselves significantly closer to their mothers than to their boyfriends (80 for mothers and 70 for boyfriends on the 0-to-100 analog scales, $p < 0.001$). In contrast, abortion-group teenagers rated closeness to their mothers and their boyfriends nearly identically. It appeared that the mothers—not the boyfriends—were still the most important persons in the lives of the young teenagers who were beginning childbearing.

Only one third of the teenagers indicated that they had substantive discussions with their boyfriends about the pregnancy, and boyfriends appeared peripheral to the pregnancy decision. Neither marriage nor economic support were realistic options for these teenagers. None were married or had any specific plans for marriage at the initial interview. Most had not considered marriage: Seventy-six percent of the abortion group and 55% of the delivery group said they never gave it a thought. More delivery-group teenagers than abortion-group teenagers said they had seriously considered marriage (20% and 3%, respectively; $p < 0.01$), but marriage would not have provided a self-supporting economic base for most of them. Their boyfriends generally were unemployed. Even when the boyfriends were employed, marriage was seldom considered an option. Only one quarter of the teenagers whose boyfriends had full-time employment said they had considered marriage. Few of these teenagers recognized marriage as integral to childbearing.

OUTCOMES OF THE PREGNANCY DECISION

We reinterviewed the teenagers 1 and 2 years after study enrollment. These interviews provided information about whether the decision to terminate or deliver the pregnancy affected the teenagers':

- Educational status
- Educational and occupational goals
- Economic status
- Relationships with their families and boyfriends
- Psychological status
- Satisfaction with the decision they or others had made about the pregnancy
- Occurrence of a subsequent pregnancy during the 2-year study

Educational Status

Two years after study enrollment the abortion group still was doing better in school, and the differences increased between the

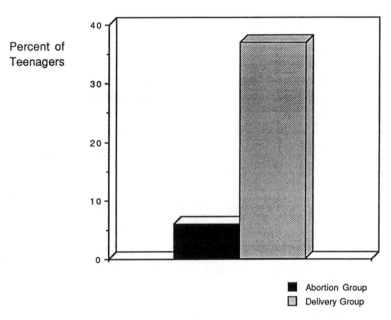

Figure 4.3. Percent with worsened educational status at 2-year follow-up in the abortion and delivery groups ($p < 0.0001$). Worsened status indicates school dropout before completing high school or failure to advance 1 grade in 2 years.

two study groups after the pregnancy decision (see Figure 4.3). At the 2-year follow-up, 93% of the abortion group were in school or had completed high school, compared to only 69% of the delivery group ($p < 0.0001$). More than twice as many in the delivery group had failed one or more school years, compared to the abortion group ($p < 0.001$). Seven times more teenagers in the delivery group had dropped out of high school (34% and 5%, respectively; $p < 0.0001$). Figure 4.3 depicts the change in school status between study enrollment and the 2-year follow-up. In the interval since the pregnancy decision, 37% of the delivery group, compared to only 6% of the abortion group, had either dropped out of school or failed to advance a grade in school ($p < 0.0001$).

Educational and Occupational Goals

Two years after study enrollment the educational goals of the teenagers remained unchanged. The abortion group was more likely at both times to have educational goals beyond high school (88% of the abortion group, compared to about 66% of the delivery group).

Identifying an occupational goal, which the abortion-group teenagers were significantly more likely to do at the beginning of the study, no longer differed between the abortion and delivery groups. Although the great majority of teenagers had not changed their occupational goals at the 2-year follow-up, about 15% overall had lowered their goals or said they didn't know what their occupational goals were, and 10% had raised their goals, with no significant difference between the two study groups.

More teenagers in the abortion group than in the delivery group still expected they would achieve their occupational goals, but the differences had narrowed in the 2-year interval and were no longer significant. *Changes* in perceptions of the likelihood of achieving occupational goals were nearly identical in the two study groups. About one third of the teenagers were unchanged in their ideas of whether they would actually enter the occupation they cited. Nearly half gave a more positive appraisal compared to 2 years earlier, and just under one third gave a more negative appraisal of the likelihood of their employment goals. Clearly, among these teenagers, the changes in goals over the 2 years after the pregnancy decision were not associated with that decision.

Economic Status

At the 2-year follow-up only a few teenagers in either group had full-time employment. The abortion-group teenagers were more likely to have had part-time employment, including summer jobs, during the study (52% and 37%, respectively; $p < 0.05$).

The welfare status of the teenagers' households changed little during the 2 years. At the beginning of the study delivery-group teenagers (78%) were significantly more likely to be in welfare households than abortion-group teenagers (58%) ($p < 0.01$). The welfare status remained unchanged over the 2-year period for about three fourths of the teenagers, with the remaining fourth shifting in and out of welfare status. In the delivery group, the percentages in welfare households were 86% at 1 year and 81% at 2 years. In the abortion group, the percentages were 48% at 1 year and 46% at 2 years.

Relationships With Parents and Boyfriends

Teenagers in the abortion and delivery groups continued to describe positive relationships with their parents, and the ratings of closeness to their parents did not change significantly in the 2 years after the pregnancy decision. At the beginning of the study, abortion-group and delivery-group teenagers indicated that their mothers supported their decisions about the pregnancy. This support did not change over the 2 years of the study.

Closeness to boyfriends significantly increased at the 2-year follow-up in both study groups. Whereas initially many of the teenagers felt closest to their mothers, particularly in the delivery group, attachments to boyfriends increased during the 2 years to where the boyfriends were as close or closer to the teenagers than the mothers. This suggests that the great majority of the teenagers were experiencing the expected development of attachments in the mid-adolescent years. However, less than half of the teenagers still had the same boyfriend as at the time of pregnancy 2 years earlier (39% of the abortion group and 44% of the delivery group). Only three teenagers had married. The three married teenagers were in the delivery group and had married the father of their child.

Initially the abortion group had felt that their boyfriends did not support their decision to terminate the pregnancy, whereas the delivery group had perceived great support from their boyfriends for carrying the pregnancy to term ($p < 0.0001$). Two years later there was no longer any difference in the teenagers' reports of how supportive their boyfriends were about the pregnancy decision. By that time the abortion-group teenagers felt *more* support, and the delivery-group teenagers reported *less* support from their boyfriends in relation to the pregnancy decision they had made. In general, the teenagers indicated that their boyfriends' supportiveness ranged from somewhat supportive to indifferent about the pregnancy decision.

The total support perceived by the teenagers from their family and friends continued to favor the delivery-group teenagers ($p < 0.0001$). Of greater interest is that 2 years later, *both* study groups reported a significant decrease in the overall *total* support from family and friends for the pregnancy decision they had made ($p < 0.0001$).

Psychological Assessments

At the time of the pregnancy decision there were no differences in self-esteem dimensions between abortion-group and delivery-group teenagers. The average self-acceptance scores (Rosenberg, 1965) were in the top quartile of the range, the assertiveness scores (Coopersmith, 1967) were midrange, and the family relations scores (Coopersmith, 1967) were slightly above the midrange of the scales. Although these brief measures have shown high reliability, self-esteem clearly is a complex, multidimensional phenomenon that may not be captured in specific measures. The most important indication of these self-esteem scores is that the two study groups did not differ from each other at the time they made their decisions about the pregnancy outcome.

When reassessed 1 and 2 years later, there were no significant changes in the assertiveness dimension, which was notably stable over the 2-year study. The self-acceptance scores increased modestly in the abortion group, but not the delivery group, and were significantly higher compared to the delivery group at the 2-year follow-up ($p < 0.005$). The family relations dimension changed during the 2-year interval, with a significant interaction between the two study groups over time ($p < 0.001$) (see Figure 4.4). The abortion-group teenagers indicated increased esteem on the family relations measure over the 2-year period; delivery-group teenagers indicated deterioration in their family esteem. The delivery-group teenagers indicated that they felt unimportant and misunderstood

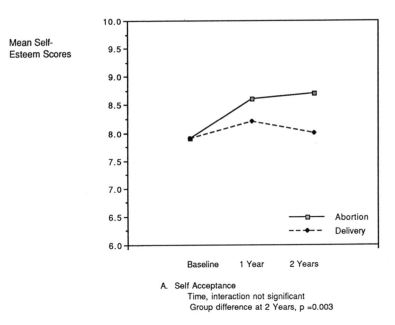

Mean Self-
Esteem Scores

A. Self Acceptance
Time, interaction not significant
Group difference at 2 Years, p =0.003

Figure 4.4a. Mean scores on 3 self-esteem dimensions at baseline, 1-year, and 2-year follow-ups for the abortion and delivery groups: A. Self-Acceptance.

and that too much was expected of them. Although initially at the time of pregnancy they may have received more attention and felt esteemed in their family circles, the teenagers with babies appeared to have less esteem as they dealt with the difficulties and responsibilities of child rearing.

There were no differences between the abortion and delivery groups in emotional distress scores as assessed by the SCL-90 (Derogatis, 1977) at any time in the study. The emotional distress scores decreased significantly at the 2-year follow-up in both groups. We previously found that in normal adolescent populations, the teenagers in higher school grades scored lower (i.e., less distress) than those in the younger school grades (Freeman, Rickels, Mudd, Huggins, & Garcia, 1982), suggesting that in non-clinical groups the symptom ratings decreased with age in the teenage years. More important, in the present study the total symptom scores and all factor scores (which included depression,

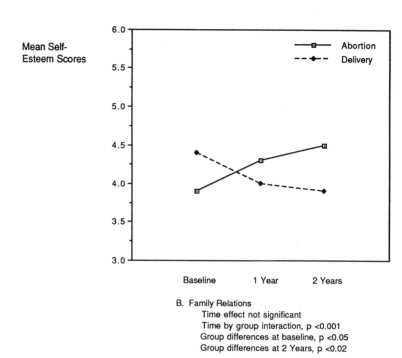

Figure 4.4b. Mean scores on 3 self-esteem dimensions at baseline, 1-year, and 2-year follow-ups for the abortion and delivery groups: B. Family Relations.

anxiety, and others) were within normal ranges at all assessment points. The data gave no evidence that teenagers in the abortion or the delivery group had any increased emotional distress in the 2 years after the pregnancy decision.

Additional assessment at follow-up using the Eysenck Personality Inventory (described in Chapter 2) further buttressed these data. The average scores were in the normal range in both study groups, indicating that the teenagers were no different in these measured personality characteristics, compared to other nonclinical adolescent groups. The extroversion scores of the two study groups were nearly identical. The neuroticism scores also were similar, with no statistically significant difference, although there were more cases of higher neuroticism scores in the delivery group.

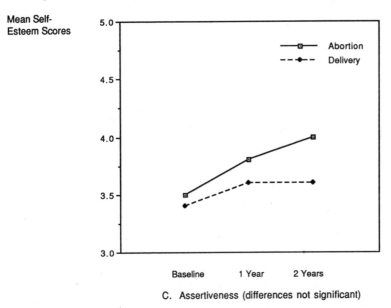

Mean Self-Esteem Scores

C. Assertiveness (differences not significant)

Figure 4.4c. Mean scores on 3 self-esteem dimensions at baseline, 1-year, and 2-year follow-ups for the abortion and delivery groups: C. Assertiveness.

Satisfaction With the Pregnancy Decision

Satisfaction with a decision can be a marker of acceptance or guilt—feelings that emerge from major choices in life. We asked the teenagers at each interview how satisfied they were with the decision made about the pregnancy. Approximately 6 months after the pregnancy outcome decision (or before delivery for those having a baby), nearly all teenagers were satisfied with their decision as rated on a 5-point scale. A year after the pregnancy outcome decision, satisfaction levels remained at nearly identical levels. Although abortion-group teenagers were satisfied, delivery-group teenagers were even more satisfied, as indicated by their choices on the scale ($p < 0.005$). Over time the abortion-group teenagers' satisfaction increased further. By the 2-year follow-up, the satisfaction ratings were nearly identical in the two study groups and indicated a very high level of satisfaction with the decision made. Two years after the decision, there was no significant difference between the two study groups: Eighty-eight percent of the teenagers in the abortion group and 95% of those in the delivery group were satisfied with their respective decisions about the pregnancy outcome. Notably similar levels of satisfaction with the decision to deliver or terminate pregnancy were reported in another sample of urban black teenagers (Zabin, Hirsch, Emerson, & Raymond, 1992), in which 88% were satisfied with their pregnancy outcome.

In the early months after the pregnancy decision the teenagers' satisfaction seemed to be related to who made the decision. Although three fourths of the teenagers said they made their own decision about the pregnancy outcome, there was greater uncertainty or less satisfaction among those who felt they did not make the decision themselves. At the 6-month interviews, 88% of the teenagers who made the decision themselves were satisfied, whereas only 65% of those who believed others had made the decision were satisfied ($p < 0.001$), regardless of whether the decision was to terminate or deliver the pregnancy.

Over time the teenagers' satisfaction with the pregnancy decision increased, and differences between the two study groups disappeared. By the 1-year point there was no longer any difference in satisfaction based on who made the decision. After 2 years satisfaction about the pregnancy decision was nearly identical, regardless of whether the teenager or someone else had chosen the outcome.

Because it might be assumed that satisfaction with the decision about the pregnancy was associated with whether the pregnancy was "wanted," we examined this relationship further. Only in the delivery group and only at the 6-month follow-up was any relationship found. Not surprisingly, delivery-group teenagers who said they "wanted" the pregnancy were more likely to be very satisfied, and those who were dissatisfied with the decision to carry to pregnancy to term were less likely to have "wanted" the pregnancy. However, this relationship was not maintained at the 1- and 2-year follow-ups: As the delivery-group teenagers who had "not wanted" the pregnancy became more satisfied with their decision, there was no relationship between "wanting" the pregnancy and satisfaction with the decision.

At no time was there any significant relationship in the abortion group between satisfaction with the decision to terminate the pregnancy and how much the pregnancy was "wanted" or "unwanted." Although only about 40% of the abortion-group teenagers said the pregnancy was clearly "unwanted," the great majority were satisfied with their decision to terminate the pregnancy.

Effects of the Pregnancy Decision

At each follow-up interview the teenagers were asked to compare their current lives to their lives before the pregnancy. The abortion group appeared to be happier than the delivery group at the 6-month follow-up, but the delivery group had not yet had their babies at this time. At the 1-year follow-up, 46% of the abortion-group teenagers, compared to only 29% of the delivery-group teenagers, said their lives were "better," a highly significant difference ($p < 0.01$) (see Figure 4.5). These ratings remained nearly identical at the 2-year follow-up. In multivariate analysis of these reports over the 2-year study period, abortion-group teenagers were much more likely than delivery-group teenagers to indicate that their lives were better ($p < 0.001$) (see Figure 4.5).

Very few teenagers in either study group said their lives were worse as a result of their pregnancy decision (approximately 6% at each follow-up point from 6 months to 2 years), but it is of interest that these respondents were largely in the delivery group and not in the abortion group. The greatest number of teenagers in both study groups said their lives were "no different" as a result of the pregnancy decision.

Only 13 teenagers in the study, primarily in the delivery group, said their lives were worse after their decision to terminate or deliver the pregnancy. However, when asked a different question about whether they regretted the decision they made about the pregnancy, more teenagers expressed regret about the decision than said their lives were worse. At each interview a consistent 18% of the teenagers who had babies strongly wished they did not have a baby. Ten percent of the abortion group said each time that having the abortion was a "mistake."

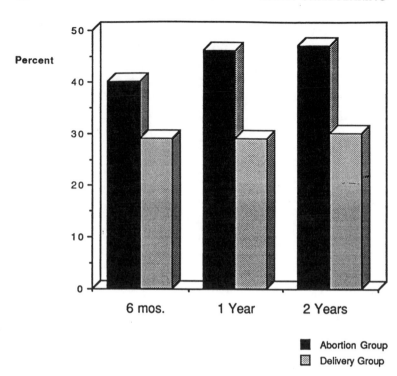

Figure 4.5. Percent reporting "life better" at present time compared to baseline pregnancy time in abortion and delivery groups. Main effect of groups: $p < 0.001$. (Effect of time and interaction not significant.)

The most noteworthy aspect of the teenagers' responses concerning the effect of their pregnancy decisions on their lives was its *stability*. Overall, the teenagers' responses did not change during the 2-year interval. There was no evidence that regret about abortion increased after pregnancy termination. Neither was there any evidence of changed perceptions among the teenagers who had babies. In both study groups the small changes that were observed were in the direction of greater satisfaction. Some delivery-group teenagers expressed dissatisfaction with the decision to carry the pregnancy to term at the outset, and although some of these eventually became more satisfied with the outcome, a few (about 5%) continued to be unhappy about their decision throughout the 2 years of the study.

Subsequent Pregnancy

Whether and for how long teenagers delay a second pregnancy, particularly those who terminate pregnancy, has been a long-standing question of clinicians and others concerned with unintended teenage childbearing. All the teenagers in these two study groups enrolled in family planning after the termination or delivery of their pregnancy and had the same access to contraceptive methods and services for the remainder of the study. During that time the incidence of pregnancy was nearly identical in the two study groups, and was similar to the rate of repeated childbearing reported for adolescents in national survey data (Mott, 1986).

Approximately one quarter of the teenagers in each study group had a subsequent pregnancy during the 2-year study. Of these pregnancies, half were terminated in the abortion group, and nearly one third were terminated in the delivery group, an insignificant difference. In summary, 14% of the abortion group and 19% of the delivery group had a pregnancy that was delivered or being carried to term at the 2-year follow-up. These comparisons between the abortion and delivery groups were made after equalizing the risk of exposure to pregnancy during a 17-month period: the first 17 months of the study for the abortion group and the last 17 months of the study (after the babies were born) for the delivery group. Further comparisons using the entire 2 years of the study (which gave additional exposure to the abortion group) did not alter the results. Subsequent pregnancy and its relationships with other study factors are discussed further in Chapter 6.

CHAPTER SUMMARY

Two broad conclusions can be drawn from these comparisons of teenagers who decided to terminate or deliver a first pregnancy. First, the teenagers who terminated pregnancy had more educational and occupational aspirations and had families who were not supportive of early teenage childbearing. Second, there were few significant changes in psychosocial factors in the 2 years after the pregnancy decision, but those that did occur favored the abortion group.

At the time of the pregnancy decision, the strongest differences between abortion-group and delivery-group teenagers were the mothers' attitudes about childbearing as perceived by the teenagers. The teenagers who continued the pregnancy believed their mothers were happy about this; those who terminated the pregnancy were clear that their mothers were unhappy and did not support early childbearing. (This variable alone explained 25% of the variance between the two groups in multivariate analyses. See Appendix E.) Abortion-group teenagers had their mothers' support to terminate the pregnancy and they had fewer friends with babies. Finally, at the time the pregnancy decision was made, abortion-group teenagers were more likely to be in school, whereas a number of the delivery-group teenagers of the same age had dropped out of school.

Two years later differences in educational performance were even greater, with many more teenagers in the delivery group having dropped out before completing high school. The abortion-group teenagers were more likely to have had some work experience, such as paid summer employment, in the 2 years since the pregnancy decision. Self-esteem increased in the abortion group. The family relations dimension of esteem worsened in the delivery group, where more teenagers felt that they were ignored and misunderstood in their households. Many more teenagers who terminated the pregnancy compared to those who had babies indicated that their lives were better at the 2-year follow-up.

REFERENCES

Adler, N. E., David, H. P., Major, B. N., Roth, S. H., Russo, N. F., & Wyatt, G. E. (1990). Psychological responses after abortion. *Science, 248*(4951), 41-44.

Alan Guttmacher Institute. (1989). *Teenage pregnancy in the United States: The scope of the problem and state responses.* New York: Author.

Alan Guttmacher Institute. (1992). *Abortion factbook, 1992 edition: Readings, trends, and state and local data to 1988.* New York: Author.

Armstrong, E., & Pascale, A. (1990). *Fact sheet: Adolescent sexuality, pregnancy, and parenthood.* Washington, DC: Center for Population Options.

Blum, R. W., & Resnick, M. D. (1982). Adolescent sexual decision-making: Contraception, pregnancy, abortion, motherhood. *Pediatric Annals, 11*(10), 797-805.

Bracken, M. B., Klerman, L. B., & Bracken, M. (1978). Abortion, adoption, or motherhood: An empirical study of decision-making during pregnancy. *American Journal of Obstetrics and Gynecology, 130*(3), 251-262.

Burt, M. R. (1986). *Estimates of public costs for teenage childbearing.* Washington, DC: Center for Population Options.

Center for Population Options. (1990). *Teenage pregnancy and too early childbearing: Public costs, personal consequences* (5th ed.). Washington, DC: Author.

Coopersmith, S. (1967). *The antecedents of self-esteem.* San Francisco: Freeman.

Cvejic, H., Lipper, I., Kinch, R. A., & Benjamin, P. (1977). Follow-up of 50 adolescent girls two years after abortion. *Canadian Medical Association Journal, 116*(1), 44-46.

Derogatis, L. R. (1977). *SCL-90* (rev. ed.). Baltimore, MD: Johns Hopkins University, School of Medicine.

Fischman, S. H. (1977). Delivery or abortion in inner-city adolescents. *American Journal of Orthopsychiatry, 47*(1), 127-133.

Freeman, E. W. (1978). Abortion: Subjective attitudes and feelings. *Family Planning Perspectives, 10*(3), 150-155.

Freeman, E. W., Rickels, K., Huggins, G. R., Garcia, C.-R., & Polin, J. (1980). Emotional distress patterns among women having first or repeat abortions. *Obstetrics and Gynecology, 55*(5), 630-636.

Freeman, E. W., Rickels, K., Mudd, E. B. H., Huggins, G. R., & Garcia, C.-R. (1982). Self-reports of emotional distress in a sample of urban black high school students. *Psychological Medicine, 12,* 809-817.

Henshaw, S. K., & Van Vort, J. (1989). Teenage abortion, birth, and pregnancy statistics: An update. *Family Planning Perspectives, 21*(2), 85-88.

Henshaw, S. K., & Van Vort, J. (Eds.). (1992). *Abortion factbook 1992 edition: Readings, trends, and state and local data to 1988.* New York: Alan Guttmacher Institute.

Hogue, C. J. R., Cates, W., Jr., & Tietze, C. (1983). Impact of vacuum aspiration abortion on future childbearing: A review. *Family Planning Perspectives, 15*(3), 119-126.

Morin-Gunthier, M., & Lortie, G. (1984). The significance of pregnancy among adolescents choosing abortion as compared to those continuing pregnancy. *The Journal of Reproductive Medicine, 29*(4), 255-259.

Mott, F. L. (1986). The pace of repeated childbearing among young American mothers. *Family Planning Perspectives, 18*(1), 5-12.

National Center for Health Statistics. (1989, June). Advance report of final natality statistics, 1987. *Monthly Vital Statistics Report, 38*(3 Suppl.). Hyattsville, MD: Public Health Service.

Rosen, R. H. (1980). Adolescent pregnancy decision-making: Are parents important? *Adolescence, 15*(57), 43-54.

Rosenberg, M. (1965). *Society and the adolescent self-image.* Princeton, NJ: Princeton University Press.

Upchurch, D. M., & McCarthy, J. (1989). Adolescent childbearing and high school completion in the 1980s: Have things changed? *Family Planning Perspectives, 21*(5), 199-202.

Zabin, L. S., Hirsch, M. B., & Emerson, M. R. (1989). When urban adolescents choose abortion: Effects on education, psychological status, and subsequent pregnancy. *Family Planning Perspectives, 21*(6), 245-255.

Zabin, L. S., Hirsch, M. B., Emerson, E. R., & Raymond, E. (1992). To whom do inner city minors talk about their pregnancies? Adolescents' communication with parents and parent surrogates. *Family Planning Perspectives, 24*(4), 148-154.

Avoiding Childbearing: Teenagers Who Terminated a First Pregnancy Compared to Never-Pregnant Peers

INTRODUCTION

Pregnant teenagers and teenage mothers have been studied extensively, but sexually active teenagers who avoid childbearing have been given little attention. In ignoring those who successfully avoid early teenage motherhood, opportunities are missed to understand what leads to contraceptive effectiveness and motivation to delay childbearing. Do teenagers who avoid pregnancy know more about contraception? Do they have less ambivalence about pregnancy? Do they perform well in school and have educational and occupational goals that they truly expect to achieve? What do we know about their relationships with others? Is early childbearing an acceptable choice among those close to them?

In the previous chapter we looked at these questions and compared teenagers who terminated first pregnancies with teenagers who became single mothers. We found that those who avoided motherhood perceived greater educational and occupational opportunities compared to those who gave birth. Conditions including the teenagers' school performance, beliefs about a child's effect on their educational and occupational goals, and perceptions of family support for childbearing (particularly whether the teenagers' mothers supported having a baby) strongly influenced whether these teenagers decided to terminate or carry the pregnancy to term.

In this chapter we examine the same questions but compare the teenagers who terminated the first pregnancy with never-pregnant teenagers who used contraception prescribed in family planning services for at least 1 year before the study. By deciding to have an abortion, it appeared that teenagers who terminated a first pregnancy did not want a child, and we therefore assumed that they would be similar to the never-pregnant group in their characteristics and attitudes about childbearing.

There are other assumptions about teenagers who choose to terminate pregnancy, but there is little empirical information to either support or refute them. One common assumption is that teenagers who have an abortion become pregnant again in a short time, either because they wanted a child or because they relied on abortion as a contraceptive method. Another assumption is that teenagers who have abortions do not want pregnancy, but have inadequate information about contraception, resulting in pregnancies that were unintended and unwanted. Alternatively, they may have had contraceptive information, but failed to initiate contraceptive use.

There are many assumptions about negative sequelae of abortion, particularly emotional factors such as depression and guilt. Evidence from numerous clinical studies consistently shows that negative psychological outcomes have been limited to a small minority and that those that did occur were related to preexisting psychological characteristics (Adler, 1975; Freeman, 1977; Osofsky & Osofsky, 1972). However, few studies focused on teenagers, leaving unanswered questions about whether their experiences differ from the reported studies that are dominated by young women in their early twenties. One recent report, based on a sample of teenagers similar to those in the Penn Study, showed that teenagers who had abortions fared as well as or better than the teenagers who delivered pregnancies on the educational, economic, and psychological variables of the study (Zabin, Hirsch, & Emerson, 1989). On measures of self-esteem, anxiety, and locus of control taken in a 2-year period after abortion, the amount of change was no different in the abortion group compared to the delivery group (Zabin et al., 1989).

In the Penn Study, teenagers in the never-pregnant and abortion groups were from similar backgrounds and were age-matched. We first interviewed abortion-group teenagers within several weeks after the abortion and the never-pregnant teenagers about 1 year after they had obtained family planning services. (This was done to ensure that the teenagers were in fact contraceptive users, and to avoid including in this group teenagers who became pregnant shortly after family planning enrollment.) We then followed the teenagers for 2 years, which made it possible to examine their subsequent attitudes, feelings, and behavior relating to the areas of the study and to determine whether there were *changes* after the abortion. Paralleling the previous comparisons that we have described, the major variables included the following:

- Educational status
- Education and employment goals
- Feelings about pregnancy
- Contraceptive information
- Relationships with parents, family, boyfriends, and girlfriends
- Self-esteem and emotional distress
- Support for childbearing
- Incidence of pregnancy after study enrollment

CHARACTERISTICS AT STUDY ENROLLMENT

As described in Chapter 1, the demographic background characteristics of teenagers in the abortion and never-pregnant groups were similar and showed no statistically significant differences. At the beginning of the study the average age in both groups was 15. The majority of the teenagers were from single-female-headed households. They had an average of three siblings, and about 30% had sisters who were teenage mothers. Their mothers began childbearing at an average age of 18. Half the teenagers' mothers had not completed high school. Based on the Hollingshead index, about 50% of the teenagers were in the lowest socioeconomic group, about 30% were in the next-lowest group, and the remaining 20% were in higher groups, usually because the mother was a teacher or a nurse.

Economic Factors

There were no differences at study enrollment between the abortion and never-pregnant groups on the economic measures of the study. Just over half of the teenagers in the never-pregnant and abortion groups lived in welfare households at study enrollment. Sixty-five percent had part-time or summer paid work experience. Within the next 5 years, 91% expected to be employed, 1 teenager expected to be a homemaker, and 8% did not answer the question.

Educational Status

At study enrollment nearly all of the teenagers were attending high school, and nearly all said they expected to graduate from high school. The academic performance of teenagers in the never-pregnant and abortion groups was average or better. Only 10% reported grade averages of less than "C." None of these educational factors significantly differed between the two groups.

Based on three factors (female-headed household, social class, and school performance), we constructed a composite variable called the parenthood risk factor. A similar composite was used previously to predict single teenage mothers in panel survey data of high school students (Abrahamse, Morrison, & Waite, 1988). In the Penn Study the factor scores indicated a high risk of becoming a single teenage mother for most of the sample, including the teenagers in the never-pregnant and abortion groups, who had nearly identical scores that indicated a high risk of single motherhood.

Educational and Occupational Goals

As detailed in Chapter 3, teenagers in the abortion and never-pregnant groups reported similar educational and occupational goals. Nearly 90% had goals of education or training beyond high school. In both groups, about 50% thought their families had the same expectations for them. Approximately 75% of the teenagers believed a baby would significantly interfere with their educational goals.

About 90% of the teenagers in both groups reported having occupational goals, and nearly 60% indicated a high likelihood of achieving them. Approximately two thirds had paid work experience in summer or part-time jobs when they enrolled in the study.

Attitudes Toward Pregnancy

These nonpregnant teenagers were asked whether they thought they would have a child before marriage. Sixty percent of the never-pregnant and abortion-group teenagers (who were not pregnant and therefore had no need to rationalize their pregnancy status) thought it was more likely than not that they would have one or more children before marriage. This response, from teenagers who already had avoided childbearing, seemed to reflect their perception of marriage as a low-value condition for childbearing. It appeared to be a remarkable indication of the peripheral role of marriage in the attitudes of these teenagers.

How much these teenagers "wanted" pregnancy was detailed in Chapter 3. The analog scale ratings for how much pregnancy was "wanted" at study enrollment were below the midpoint of the scale (an average score of 35 for the never-pregnant group and 42 for the abortion group, with no significant difference), indicating that both groups responded that pregnancy was more unwanted than wanted.

Responding to questions in the initial interview, teenagers in the abortion and never-pregnant groups generally were not happy about having a baby at the time. However, those who had just terminated pregnancy were somewhat more "happy" than the never-pregnant group to "have a baby now" ($p < 0.05$). It is important to underscore that these data do not describe feelings before pregnancy, and they may only reflect the recent pregnancy experience.

Overall, the teenagers indicated no particular desire to have a child at the time, and these feelings did not statistically differ between the abortion and never-pregnant groups. Although they clearly indicated that pregnancy was "unwanted," it is also noteworthy that the average ratings were not at the far "unwanted" end of the scale. Some teenagers in these two groups "wanted" pregnancy, and many others indicated that pregnancy was more unwanted than wanted but did not indicate strong feelings of "unwantedness," based on their analog scale reports.

Contraceptive Information

At study enrollment, contraceptive information, as assessed by the Sexual Information and Attitudes Questionnaire (SIAQ), did not differ between the abortion and never-pregnant groups (as discussed in Chapter 2). These teenagers generally recognized that they were at high risk of pregnancy. At the same time, their interview responses showed that they were not well informed about preventing pregnancy, even though they had positive attitudes about contraception. Only one third of the teenagers in both groups knew when pregnancy was most likely to occur in the menstrual cycle. Many did not know about contraceptive methods other than the pill. One third did not know about condom use and half did not know how to use foam—contraceptive methods that are appropriate for the sporadic and "unplanned" sex that teenagers typically experience. The only significant difference between the abortion and never-pregnant groups was in response to the interview question of what they themselves had to do to ensure effectiveness of their contraceptive method. Expectedly, the never-pregnant teenagers better understood how to use their chosen method ($p < 0.05$) because they had been receiving family planning services for 1 year or more, in contrast with the abortion-group teenagers, many of whom were newly enrolled in family planning after their abortion.

Although both groups were the same ages (average age 15.5 years), had first intercourse experience at the same age (14.2 years), and had similar levels of information about contraception, more abortion-group teenagers delayed using contraception. In the abortion group, contraceptive use was started an average of 8.8 months after first intercourse compared to 3.8 months in the never-pregnant group ($p < 0.001$). Only 16% of the abortion-group teen-agers said they used contraception at first intercourse, compared to 44% of the never-pregnant teenagers ($p < 0.001$). When the abor-tion-group teenagers were asked whether they were using contra-ception when pregnancy occurred, 92% stated they were not, 3% said they had skipped pills in an oral contraceptive regimen, and 5% reported intrauterine device (IUD) failures. Regardless of their contraceptive information, most of the teenagers in the abortion group had not used contraception consistently to prevent preg-nancy.

Relationships With Family and Boyfriend

Teenagers in the abortion and never-pregnant groups were sim-ilar on all measures of the relationships with their parents and boy-friends. They felt their mothers understood them and liked their friends. Many of them indicated that there was not much discus-sion of sensitive subjects with their mothers, but the amount of discussion did not differ between the two study groups. The teen-agers rated how close they felt to each parent and to their boy-friend using 0-to-100 visual analog scales. The ratings of closeness were very high for the mother (74 in the abortion group and 80 in the never-pregnant group), at the scale midpoint for the father (only 20% of the teenagers lived in households with their fathers), and very high for the boyfriend (about 74 in each group). The teen-agers had maintained a relationship with their boyfriend for more than 1 year (1.5 years in the abortion group and 1.3 years in the never-pregnant group), with no significant difference between the two study groups.

Psychological Status

None of the psychological measures differed between the abor-tion and never-pregnant groups when they enrolled in the study. These included the Rosenberg and Coopersmith self-esteem scales and the Symptom Checklist (SCL-90), which were discussed in Chapter 2. The scores on each of these measures were within normal ranges.

Family and Peer Support for Childbearing

Both the abortion and the never-pregnant teenagers believed their families were not supportive of early teenage childbearing. They particularly knew that their mothers would be "unhappy" about them having a baby and that their mothers were not supportive of childbearing if pregnancy occurred. These teenagers also believed that one or more persons close to them strongly opposed early childbearing (55% in the abortion group and 42% in the never-pregnant group, with no significant difference). Fewer teenagers in these study groups had close friends with babies (39% in the abortion group and 33% in the never-pregnant group) than those in the delivery group. None of these factors differed between teenagers in the abortion and never-pregnant groups, but contrasted with those in the delivery group, who perceived much more support for childbearing, as discussed in Chapters 3 and 4.

There were only two differences between the abortion and never-pregnant groups in the relationship factors we explored. First, abortion-group teenagers were more positive that their mothers supported abortion ($p < 0.0001$). This was an expected response for the abortion group because they had just had the experience, and in nearly all cases their mothers were involved with the abortion decision. However, it contrasted with the perceptions of the never-pregnant teenagers, who generally believed their mothers did not support abortion.

Second, these teenagers indicated that their friends were "happy" about childbearing, but there was some difference between the abortion and never-pregnant groups. The primary source of support *for* childbearing in these two groups was their friends. Their boyfriends were "happy" to have a baby, with no significant difference between the study groups. Their girlfriends were similarly "happy" about childbearing, although here the abortion teenagers were somewhat more likely to indicate this than the never-pregnant teenagers ($p < 0.01$). Possibly this difference was influenced by the recent pregnancy experience, where friends' views were filtered through reactions to abortion, or possibly the never-pregnant teenagers were slightly more likely to have friends who wanted to delay childbearing.

Although all of these teenagers had avoided childbearing thus far, they lived in environments where childbearing was sanctioned. Although they had significantly less support for childbearing than the delivery-group teenagers, most also identified someone close to them who was supportive of early childbearing. Generally, their boyfriends were positive about having a baby. About half of these teenagers (45% in the abortion group and 57% in the never-pregnant group, an insignificant difference) said no one close to them *strongly* opposed early childbearing.

CHARACTERISTICS TWO YEARS LATER

We conducted interviews at 1 and 2 years after study enrollment to reassess the study variables and determine whether changes occurred during this time. We particularly wanted to know whether the teenagers who had had abortions fared better or worse over the next 2 years after their abortions and whether the never-pregnant group continued to avoid childbearing. Because there were almost no differences at the outset between the abortion and never-pregnant groups in any areas of the study, we examined whether there were any changes that differed between these two groups in the 2-year interval. In the following sections we describe and compare the teenagers who were initially in the abortion and never-pregnant groups, regardless of pregnancy events during the interval, which are identified in Chapter 6.

Economic Factors

At the 2-year follow-up there continued to be no differences between the abortion and never-pregnant groups on the economic measures of the study. At the end of the study 14% of the teenagers in the never-pregnant and abortion groups had full-time employment, 50% had part-time or summer work experience, and 36% had no paid work experience. These teenagers were still young (ages 15 to 19) and most were in school. Eighty-five percent expected to be employed within the next 5 years, 9% did not answer this question, and the remaining few expected to be still in school or at home caring for children.

The teenagers' reports on the welfare status of their households were nearly identical between the two groups and changed little over the course of the study. At the outset 54% of the abortion and never-pregnant groups lived in households receiving welfare; 2 years later this figure was 46%. Seventy-one percent of the teenagers reported no change in welfare status between study enrollment and endpoint, 10% went on welfare, and 18% went off welfare in the study interval.

Educational Status

At the 2-year follow-up there continued to be no differences between the educational status of the abortion and the never-pregnant teenagers. Only 9% had dropped out of school. Although the number of school dropouts in the abortion group was less than half of that in the never-pregnant group, the small numbers were not statistically significant. Eighteen percent of the teenagers in each group had graduated from high school, and 73% were still in high school. The number of teenagers who had repeated one or more school grades (22% of the abortion and never-pregnant groups) remained unchanged during the 2-year study.

At the 2-year follow-up we calculated the net negative change in school status by combining school dropout and failing to advance at least one grade level during the study. The abortion-group teenagers fared slightly better (only 6% had a negative change in educational status, compared to 11% of the never-pregnant group), but the small numbers were not statistically significant.

Educational and Occupational Goals

There were no differences throughout the study in the educational and occupational goals of the abortion and never-pregnant teenagers. At the end of the study 87% had educational goals beyond high school. These goals were unchanged in the 2-year interval for 83% of the teenagers, were lowered for 10%, and were raised for 7%, with no difference between the two study groups.

At study endpoint 85% of these teenagers cited occupational goals for themselves. The occupational goals remained unchanged in the 2-year interval for 83%, were lowered for 9%, and were raised for 6%, with no differences between the abortion and never-pregnant groups.

The majority of teenagers (62%) continued to believe they would achieve their occupational goals. Forty-one percent of the teenagers did not change this perception during the study, but 21% thought their goals were less likely and 38% thought the goals more likely at the study endpoint. There was more positive and less negative change in the abortion group, but differences compared with the never-pregnant group were not statistically significant.

Attitudes Toward Pregnancy

Teenagers in the abortion and never-pregnant groups indicated throughout the 2-year study that pregnancy was "unwanted" (as rated on 0-to-100 visual analog scales). At the endpoint the "unwanted" scores remained just below the midpoint of the scale: 46 for the abortion group and 41 for the never-pregnant group. These scores were slightly, but not significantly, higher than at study enrollment, and the scores did not significantly differ between the two groups throughout the study.

At the 2-year follow-up it was of interest to observe a significant increase ($p < 0.005$) in intendedness to become pregnant (analog scale scores for "planned" of 37 in the abortion group and 31 in the never-pregnant group). These average scores clearly remained low (on a scale of 0 to 100), but they represented a significant increase from the previous ratings in the study, and suggested that some teenagers in these groups intended to have a pregnancy in the near future.

Contraceptive Information

At study enrollment all the abortion and never-pregnant teenagers were enrolled in the same family planning services. Their information about contraception as measured by the SIAQ significantly increased during the study ($p < 0.001$). The abortion and never-pregnant groups had nearly identical SIAQ scores at the end of the study.

There were no differences in the reports of contraceptive use between the abortion and never-pregnant groups at follow-ups, and there was no significant change in contraceptive use over the 2 study years. At the 1-year follow-up 64% of the abortion group and 59% of the never-pregnant group said they "always" used contraception (nearly all were using the pill). At the 2-year follow-up 61% of the abortion group and 55% of the never-pregnant group said they "always" used contraception.

Relationships With Family and Boyfriend

The teenagers' analog scale ratings of their family relationships did not change significantly during the study. They described positive relationships with their mothers and other family members. There were no significant differences between the abortion and never-pregnant groups at any assessment point.

In peer relationships the ratings of close girlfriends remained stable throughout the study, and closeness to boyfriends increased during the study in the never-pregnant and abortion groups ($p = .05$). This was an expected change for maturing adolescents, and closeness to boyfriends was generally the highest of the relationship ratings at the 2-year follow-up. However, at the end of the study, only a minority (37%) were in a relationship with the same boyfriend they had at the beginning of the study. Forty-six percent had another boyfriend, and 17% had no boyfriend at the time of the interview, again describing the transient nature of early to mid-adolescent relationships.

Psychological Status

The self-esteem ratings increased slightly but not significantly during the study in the abortion and never-pregnant groups. The ratings of the two groups were similar throughout the study, and the abortion-group teenagers showed no diminished self-esteem at the time of the abortion or in the following 2 years, compared to the never-pregnant teenagers.

The emotional distress ratings as assessed by the SCL-90 decreased significantly in both groups during the 2 study years ($p < 0.001$ for the total scores). These ratings indicated less emotional distress at study endpoint compared to enrollment, which again is expected for normal young adolescents. The SCL-90 scores were well within normal range for all factors, with no significant difference between the abortion and never-pregnant groups at any time. The depression factor was specifically noted because of the hypothesized emotional sequelae of abortion. SCL-90 depression scores at endpoint were 0.76 in the abortion group and 0.71 in the never-pregnant group. These scores were well within the normal range as well as notably similar between the two groups.

The Eysenck Personality Inventory, which the teenagers completed at the end of the study, showed no differences between the abortion and never-pregnant groups. The average scores for extroversion and neuroticism were similar to normative data for black secondary school students (Eysenck & Eysenck, 1975).

At the end of the study we asked the teenagers how their lives were now compared to when they entered the study. More teenagers in the abortion group than in the never-pregnant group said their lives were better (60% and 51%, respectively), although the difference was not statistically significant. Most of the remaining teenagers indicated that their lives were the same or "different," but few said their lives were worse. Notably, *none* of the abortion group said their lives were worse, and only 5% of the never-pregnant group gave this response.

Incidence of Pregnancy

There was no difference in the incidence of pregnancy in the abortion and never-pregnant groups during the 2-year study. Twenty-eight percent of the abortion group and 21% of the never-pregnant group had a pregnancy. The average time after study enrollment when these pregnancies occurred was 11.0 months in the abortion group and 11.4 months in the never-pregnant group. Thirty-eight percent of these pregnancies were terminated and 62% carried to term, with nearly identical proportions in each group. Further comparisons of teenagers who chose abortion or delivery outcomes during the study are discussed in Chapter 6.

CHAPTER SUMMARY

Few differences were found between teenagers in the abortion and never-pregnant groups in the areas of this study. The only substantive variations we found were associated with contraceptive use at the beginning of the study. Not surprisingly, because they had become pregnant, abortion-group teenagers were much less likely to have used some method of contraception at their first intercourse experience and had delayed longer after the first experience before using contraception. However, once contraceptive use was initiated, there were no differences between these two groups: About 60% said they always used contraception during the 2 study years.

These data cannot clarify why some teenagers delayed longer than others in obtaining contraceptive services (which resulted in abortions for these teenagers who wanted to delay childbearing), but the differences were *not* in the numerous attitudes, perceptions, and goals that were studied. The abortion and never-pregnant groups shared similar goals for post-high school education and training, part-time work experience, and occupational goals. More of them had families that encouraged educational and occupational goals, and these teenagers thought their families, particularly their mothers, were not supportive of early childbearing. The teenagers described themselves as close to their families and friends and did not have troubled relationships. Psychological measures of self-esteem, emotional distress, and personality dimensions were extremely similar between the abortion and never-pregnant groups, and their scores on standard measures were similar to normative data.

Changes that occurred during the study on average were invariably in a positive direction. There were no significant differences between the abortion and never-pregnant groups in any measured change between baseline and endpoint 2 years later. The only statistically significant changes, which occurred in both groups, were that the teenagers became closer to their boyfriends, gained more contraceptive information, and rated emotional distress symptoms *lower*, the expected direction for maturing adolescents in non-clinical settings. There was an increase at the end of the study in the ratings for "planning" pregnancy, possibly an indication that a few teenagers in both these groups intended pregnancy in the near future.

The numerous other perceptions and behaviors that were assessed at study enrollment and follow-ups were stable. These included contraceptive use, "wanting" pregnancy, closeness to family members, educational and occupational goals, and self-esteem.

There was no evidence of deterioration on any study measure of abortion-group teenagers. They fared as well as or better than the never-pregnant teenagers, although no differences were statistically significant. Abortion-group teenagers increased their contraceptive information (SIAQ) scores, used contraception consistently, became more likely to believe they would achieve their occupational goals, became closer to their boyfriends, had increased self-esteem, and had decreased emotional distress.

The important conclusion from these data is that the teenagers who terminated a first pregnancy were no more likely to have another pregnancy within 2 years than the never-pregnant teenagers, who had used contraceptive services for 1 year or more before their study participation. The small number of abortion-group teenagers who did have another pregnancy in the study interval were even more likely to terminate the pregnancy than pregnant teenagers in the other study groups (although these small numbers were not statistically significant). Their motivation to postpone childbearing stands out, particularly in contrast to many other teenagers in the study, who did not view childbearing as negatively affecting their lives and proceeded to become single teenage parents.

The teenagers in this study who terminated a first pregnancy wanted to delay childbearing, and most continued to do so for at least the 2-year study period by consistently using effective contraception. The question remains as to how these young people could have been enabled to use contraception before the first pregnancy occurred. Although they did not want to commence childbearing, they did not obtain family planning services that were available. Still more must be done to encourage young teenagers to *use* contraception if they have sex, or to postpone sex until they use contraception. This is all the more critical when they are too young to be parents, which was the prevailing perception of the abortion and never-pregnant teenagers.

REFERENCES

Abrahamse, A. F., Morrison, P. A., & Waite, L. J. (1988). *Beyond stereotypes: Who becomes a single teenage mother?* Santa Monica, CA: Rand.

Adler, N. E. (1975). Emotional responses of women following therapeutic abortion. *American Journal of Orthopsychiatry, 45*(3), 446-454.

Eysenck, H. J., & Eysenck, S. B. G. (1975). *Manual for the Eysenck Personality Questionnaire (Junior and Adult).* San Diego, CA: Educational and Industrial Testing Service.

Freeman, E. W. (1977). Influence of personality attributes on abortion experience. *American Journal of Orthopsychiatry, 47*(3), 503-513.

Osofsky, J. D., & Osofsky, H. J. (1972). The psychological reaction of patients to legalized abortion. *American Journal of Orthopsychiatry, 42*(1), 48-60.

Zabin, L. S., Hirsch, M. B., & Emerson, M. R. (1989). When urban adolescents choose abortion: Effects on education, psychological status, and subsequent pregnancy. *Family Planning Perspectives, 21*(6), 245-255.

Pregnancies After Study Enrollment: "Pregnant Because They Are Different or Different Because They Are Pregnant?"

INTRODUCTION

As discussed in Chapter 3 many pregnancies of adults are due to chance, indifference, or error, but they are not valued on the basis of whether they were intended or unintended (Bolton, 1980). Commenting on this, Paulker (1969) concluded that pregnant teenagers were "not pregnant because they were different, but different because they were pregnant." Thus far, the Penn Study lends considerable support to this premise: that many teenagers who became pregnant, particularly those who terminated the pregnancy, were little different from those who avoided pregnancy. The greatest differences were between the teenagers who carried the pregnancy to term and those who avoided childbearing, not between the teenagers who had a pregnancy and those who did not.

Because we followed the teenagers who enrolled in the study for 2 years after their initial interviews, and because all the teenagers obtained the same family planning services in this interval, it provided another view, starting from the same baseline, of teenagers who became pregnant after study enrollment.

- Were the teenagers who became pregnant after study enrollment different from those who did not?
- Were there differences within each of the three study groups between those who became pregnant and those who did not?
- Were differences any greater in the delivery group, where the teenagers already had one child and those who had a repeated pregnancy could have two children?
- Were there differences between the teens who terminated or delivered subsequent pregnancies?
- Were there differences within each original study group between teens who terminated or delivered subsequent pregnancies?

PREGNANCIES AFTER STUDY ENROLLMENT

The 326 teenagers in this study were originally selected in three similar-size, age-matched groups: those who had never been pregnant and were enrolled in family planning services for at least 1 year, those who had just terminated a first pregnancy, and those who were pregnant and intending to deliver a first pregnancy. During the subsequent 2 years of the study, 84 teenagers (26% of the sample) became pregnant again or for the first time in the case of those who were initially in the never-pregnant group. Neither the incidence nor the outcomes of these pregnancies that occurred after study enrollment differed significantly among the three study groups (see Table 6.1). In each study group approximately one third of the teenagers who became pregnant terminated their pregnancies, and two thirds intended to carry the pregnancy to term.

The time when the pregnancies occurred—an average of approximately 1 year after study enrollment—also did not differ among the three study groups. However, because delivery-group teenagers were pregnant when the study began and had approximately 17 months rather than 2 years of exposure to risk of another pregnancy during the study, we also examined the occurrence of pregnancy using a 17-month adjusted period to equalize the risk exposure across the three study groups. In this 17-month period, 78 teenagers (24% of the sample) experienced a pregnancy, and this again did not significantly differ among the three study groups. The outcomes of these pregnancies also remained the same: In

Table 6.1 Incidence of Pregnancy During the Study by Enrollment
Status

| During Study | Enrollment Status | | | |
	NP	TA	DEL	Total
No pregnancy	84 (79)	63 (72)	95 (73)	242 (74)
Baby*	15 (14)	15 (17)	25 (19)	55 (17)
Abortion	8 (7)	10 (11)	11 (8)	29 (9)
Total	107	88	131	326

NOTE: *Includes teenagers pregnant at study endpoint and intending to deliver.
Chi-square tests not significant.

each study group about one third were terminated and two thirds
were delivered or being carried to term at the end of the study.

At first glance it seemed discouraging that teenagers who had
avoided childbearing when they enrolled in the study experienced
the same pregnancy rate as those who had given birth. In fact,
however, the incidence of pregnancy among all the teenagers in
the sample was low (approximately one quarter of the sample became pregnant in the 2-year interval) compared to other studied
groups. In a similar sample of urban black teenagers who were age
17 or younger, 37% of those who had abortions, 47% of those who
gave birth, and 58% of those who initially had negative pregnancy
tests had pregnancies within 18 months after study enrollment
(Zabin, Hirsch, & Emerson, 1989). Another study of economically
disadvantaged teenage mothers showed repeat pregnancy rates of
45% in 2 years (Polit & Kahn, 1986). In a 1979 survey of young
women ages 15 to 19, 20% of teenage mothers experienced a subsequent pregnancy within 12 months of delivery, and 38% within
24 months (Koenig & Zelnik, 1982). Other studies reported repeat
pregnancy rates ranging from 20% to 25% within 12 months after
giving birth (Furstenberg, 1976; Hardy & Zabin, 1991).

Possibly the teenagers in the Penn Study were more effective
contraceptors because they were being studied. All of the teenagers were enrolled in family planning before the end of the first

study year. They were contacted by the study interviewers at yearly intervals, discussed contraception and pregnancy intentions in the study interviews, and received individual attention—all factors that may have encouraged the teenagers to effectively maintain contraceptive use. However, we further examined the data to determine whether the teenagers who had pregnancies after study enrollment differed from those who avoided pregnancy as described by our study variables. Only the variables that suggested any possible differences are described below.

Factors Affecting Pregnancy After Study Enrollment

Various factors seemed to have affected pregnancy after study enrollment, including contraceptive use, age, educational and economic status, "wantedness" of pregnancy, support of family and friends, psychological factors, and demographic factors.

Contraceptive Use

At the 1-year and 2-year follow-up interviews, about two thirds of the teenagers—nearly all of whom were using the pill—said they always used contraception. Multivariate analysis of the responses of the three original study groups at the 1-year and 2-year follow-up interviews showed that contraceptive use did not differ among the three groups, but did deteriorate in the second study year ($p < 0.005$ for the time effect). This deterioration was almost entirely in the original delivery group ($p < 0.05$ for the interaction of group and time) (see Figure 6.1). The decrease in contraceptive use in the original never-pregnant and abortion groups was minimal and not significant.

We then examined the same contraceptive use data, comparing the teenagers who became pregnant during the study with those who did not. Clearly, the teenagers who became pregnant had poorer contraceptive use than those who avoided pregnancy ($p < 0.0001$). (Each subject's report of contraceptive use excluded time periods when they were pregnant.) The results of the multivariate analysis, which was repeated with the addition of the subsequent pregnancy groups, are shown in Table 6.2.

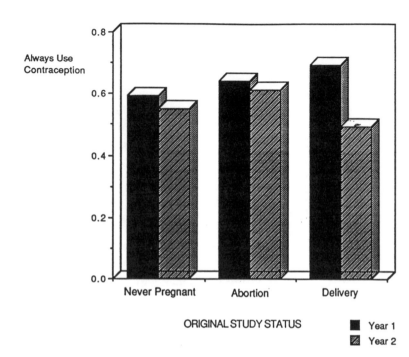

Figure 6.1. Reports of "always" use contraception at the first- and second-year follow-ups in the three original study groups. Responses scored 1 = always, 0 = other, mean scores shown. Results of repeated measures ANOVA: group effect, $p = 0.58$; time effect, $p = 0.004$; group by time interaction, $p = 0.02$.

Age

We examined age to determine whether those who had pregnancies in the 2 years after study enrollment were the older teenagers (ages 18 to 19 at the 2-year follow-up), who had completed high school and were ready to begin families. However, in the overall sample, age had no effect. Those who became pregnant in the 2-year interval were an average age of 15.7, whereas the teenagers who avoided pregnancy were age 15.6. Only when the study groups were examined separately was there slight evidence of a relationship between age and pregnancy in the original never-pregnant group. Teenagers who had not had a previous pregnancy

Table 6.2 Contraceptive Use at First- and Second-Year Follow-up by Initial Study Status and Subsequent Pregnancy Groups

	Initial Study Status					
	NP		TA		DEL	
Follow-up	*Subsequent pregnancy*	*No pregnancy*	*Subsequent pregnancy*	*No pregnancy*	*Subsequent pregnancy*	*No pregnancy*
1st year	.16 (.10)	.69 (.05)	.24 (.10)	.77 (.05)	.49 (.07)	.77 (.05)
2nd year	.42 (.11)	.59 (.05)	.33 (.10)	.71 (.06)	.17 (.08)	.61 (.05)

Repeated measures ANOVA: group effect, $p < 0.73$; subsequent pregnancy effect, $p < 0.0001$; time effect, $p < 0.20$; time * group interaction, $p < 0.0003$; time * group * subsequent pregnancy, $p < 0.008$. Responses scored 1 = always, 0 = other, mean (SE) shown.

but became pregnant during the study were older than those who continued to avoid pregnancy (ages 16.0 and 15.4, respectively; $p < 0.05$), although it is underscored that this "older" age was still only the midteen years. In the original abortion group there was no age difference between those who had another pregnancy and those who did not. In the original delivery group the age trend was in the direction of the *younger* teenagers being the ones who had another pregnancy (age 15.3 compared to 15.7 for nonrepeaters during the study, $p < 0.10$).

Educational Status

Only 69% of all the teenagers who became pregnant after study enrollment were in school or had graduated from high school, compared to 85% of those who did not have a pregnancy after study enrollment ($p < 0.05$). Forty-four percent of the teenagers who had pregnancies were held back one or more grade levels ($p < 0.001$), suggesting that these teenagers fared much more poorly in school than those who avoided pregnancy during the study. They also were less likely to have any educational goals beyond high school, compared to the remaining sample ($p < 0.05$). Half the teenagers who failed to advance one or more school grades after study enrollment became pregnant in the same interval ($p < 0.001$). Figure 6.2 depicts each of these comparisons.

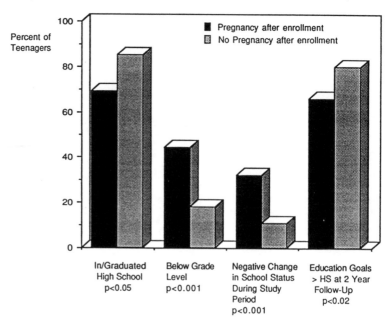

Figure 6.2. Educational status variables at 2-year follow-up compared between teenagers with pregnancies or with no pregnancies after study enrollment.

When we examined pregnancies after study enrollment in each of the original groups, there were within-group differences in these educational status variables. Table 6.3 shows that the teenagers who became pregnant after study enrollment in the original never-pregnant and abortion groups were more likely to have graduated from high school, but the delivery-group teenagers who repeated pregnancy were more likely to have dropped out of high school. Delivery-group teenagers who repeated pregnancy, compared to delivery-group teenagers who avoided further pregnancy, were more likely to be below the school grade level for their age in school ($p < 0.001$), to have failed to advance at least one school grade during the 2-year study ($p < 0.01$), and to have lower educational goals at the end of the study ($p < 0.05$). These differences in school performance and educational goals were *not* found when the same comparisons were made in the original never-pregnant and abortion

Table 6.3 School Status at 2-Year Follow-up by Initial Study Status and Subsequent Pregnancy Groups (percentage distribution)

School Status at 2-Year Follow-up	NP		TA		DEL	
	Subsequent pregnancy	No pregnancy	Subsequent pregnancy	No pregnancy	Subsequent pregnancy	No pregnancy
Graduated high school	48	32	41	36	14	24
In high school	26	59	50	61	39	47
Dropped before high school graduation	26	9	9	3	47	29

NOTE: Chi-square $p < 0.001$. (Within subgroups: never pregnant $p < 0.02$; abortion, not significant; delivery, $p < 0.10$.)

groups, where the differences were not nearly as pronounced and the numbers were small.

Economic Status

Fifty-seven percent of all the teenagers were in households that received welfare support at study enrollment, and this percent remained nearly the same at the 2-year follow-up. Comparing welfare status at the 2-year follow-up to enrollment baseline, 76% of the teenagers had not changed status, 14% were no longer receiving welfare, and 10% who had not initially received welfare were receiving it at the 2-year follow-up—predominantly those who had a pregnancy in this interval ($p < 0.05$).

About half the teenagers overall expected to achieve their occupational goals when asked at study enrollment and at the 2-year follow-up. There were no significant changes in the teenagers' occupational goals or their expectations of achieving them when the 2-year follow-up responses were compared to their initial responses. The teenagers who had pregnancies after study enrollment were no different from the remaining sample in their responses to these questions about occupational goals. Only when each study group was examined separately could differences be observed in the original delivery group. The teenagers who had a child and repeated pregnancy were less likely to believe they would achieve occupational goals ($p < 0.05$).

Other indicators of economic status that were compared between the teenagers who had pregnancies after study enrollment and the remaining sample were the number of working persons and the ratios of working to nonworking persons in each household. These variables showed a consistent pattern of less employment in the households of those who experienced a pregnancy during the study, but the differences compared to the remaining sample were not statistically significant.

Wanting Pregnancy

The teenagers who had a pregnancy after study enrollment were significantly more likely to have indicated they "wanted" a pregnancy when they started the study ($p < 0.05$). This effect was strongest in the never-pregnant group, where the "wanted" scores of the teenagers who subsequently became pregnant were above the midpoint of the scale, indicating that pregnancy was more wanted than unwanted, and contrasted with the larger group who clearly did not "want" pregnancy ($p < 0.05$). At the 2-year follow-up most teenagers who had had pregnancies (before or subsequent to study enrollment) had much lower scores compared to their scores at enrollment, indicating that pregnancy was no longer "wanted." At the study endpoint there was less "wanting" pregnancy across all study groups than was reported at the outset, and the "wanted" scores no longer differed among the original study groups. This suggested that those who had "wanted" pregnancies had had them, and that there were few teenagers who still wanted pregnancy at the end of the study.

Support of Family and Friends

We asked participants to rate how supportive their family members and friends were about having a baby, which indicated the acceptability of childbearing among the people close to them.

Comparing these "support" ratings between the teenagers who became pregnant after enrollment and the remaining sample, the only substantive differences were in the ratings of the boyfriend. The teenagers who had a pregnancy after study enrollment had said at enrollment that their boyfriends were "very supportive" of having a baby, significantly more so than the teens who did not have pregnancies after entering the study ($p < 0.05$). They also rated the closeness to their boyfriend significantly higher at the outset of the study than those who did not experience a pregnancy ($p < 0.005$), although it was of interest that they had not been involved in the relationship any longer than the other study teenagers. This relationship of closeness to the boyfriend was strongest in the delivery group, suggesting that a contributing factor to a second pregnancy among these teenagers was the continued presence of the same boyfriend. Overall, this was unusual at the 2-year follow-up, when more than half of the teenagers, including those in the delivery group, no longer had the boyfriend they had at study enrollment.

During the study there was little change in the teenagers' perceptions of supportiveness for childbearing. Their reports of their mothers' supportiveness were consistent, and most teenagers gave the same responses at the beginning and end of the study. Support from boyfriends significantly decreased over the study, again reflecting the fact that many teenagers no longer had the same boyfriend 2 years later.

Psychological Factors

When the study began we found no significant differences among the three study groups in emotional distress factors as assessed by the Symptom Checklist (SCL-90, Derogatis, 1977). Self-esteem differed among the three groups only in the family relations dimension (Coopersmith, 1967), with the delivery group reporting somewhat better scores at the outset (although these deteriorated over the next 2 years) than the other two groups.

The teenagers who became pregnant after study enrollment had higher emotional distress scores on the SCL-90 at study enrollment than those who did not subsequently have a pregnancy ($p < 0.01$

for the total SCL scores). Inspection of the factor scores on this measure showed that the teenagers who would become pregnant had significantly higher scores on all factors at the outset of the study (before the pregnancies occurred) than those who avoided pregnancy after study enrollment. Further inspection of the SCL scores within each group showed that the differences were in the never-pregnant group, where the teenagers who subsequently became pregnant had significantly higher scores on all factors compared to those who continued to avoid pregnancy. The highest scores in the never-pregnant group were for the factors of obsessive-compulsive performance difficulties, interpersonal sensitivity, and depression. These same teenagers reported increased self-esteem and less emotional distress at the end of the study, after they had a pregnancy, further suggesting that these factors were linked to pregnancy in this subgroup. In multivariate analysis the SCL depression scores were modest predictors of pregnancy in the never-pregnant group, and, together with age and "wanting" pregnancy, explained 19% of the variance between the teenagers who had pregnancies and those who did not.

This evidence of possible depression was *not* found in comparisons of the three main study groups, who overall had normal-range scores. Neither depression nor other emotional distress described the pregnant teenagers at study enrollment, and depression did not differentiate the teenagers with subsequent pregnancies in the delivery and abortion groups at follow-up. Emotional distress overall, and depression specifically, which may engender needs to be close or to have a child, may have contributed to pregnancy for a small number of teenagers, but there was no evidence of it being a significant element in teenage childbearing overall.

When the study began, the teenagers who later experienced pregnancies had lower self-esteem scores than those who did not become pregnant after enrollment, particularly on the assertiveness ($p < 0.005$) and family relationship ($p < 0.05$) scales. The assertiveness effect was strongest in the never-pregnant group, where the teenagers who subsequently became pregnant had significantly lower assertiveness scores (consistent with the higher levels of depression that they also reported) ($p < 0.05$). Self-esteem scores generally increased during the study, and this was found for the teenagers who had subsequent pregnancies as well as for the remaining sample. At the 2-year follow-up the self-esteem scores were nearly identical between the subsequent pregnancy group and those who avoided pregnancy after study enrollment.

Demographic Factors

We examined a number of other demographic factors, including female-headed household, mother's social class (an index of education and employment), mother's age at the birth of her first child, number of people in the household, number of adults in the household, the teenage participant's number of siblings, number of siblings who were teenage parents, sisters who were teenage mothers, ratios of working adults to household size and to the number of adults in the household, and number of times the family had moved. We found no relationship between any of these factors and pregnancy after study enrollment.

The only background variable that exhibited a relationship to pregnancy was the social class index (based on education and employment) when it was calculated for the head of the household (either father or mother, not just for the mother as above). The average level of social class in the sample was class 4 on the Hollingshead (1975) scale, at the low end of the 5-point range, but the teenagers who had subsequent pregnancies had significantly lower social class scores than the remaining sample ($p < 0.01$). This effect was significant in the never-pregnant group, where those who became pregnant had a lower social class index. However, there was no difference in the abortion and delivery groups between those with subsequent pregnancies and those without.

Multivariate Analysis

The variables that were significantly associated with subsequent pregnancy were examined for their individual and combined effects in a series of stepwise discriminant analyses. This procedure selected in a stepwise manner the variables that added the largest independent contribution to discriminating the teenagers who had subsequent pregnancies from those who did not. For the total sample, contraceptive use was the strongest discriminator of the teenagers who had pregnancies after study enrollment and explained 12% of the variance. Within the original abortion and delivery groups, contraceptive use was the *only* significant discriminator of the teenagers who had repeat pregnancies, explaining 22% and 15% of the variance in each group, respectively (see table in Appendix E).

In the original never-pregnant group, variables other than contraceptive use discriminated the teenagers who had pregnancies after they enrolled in the study. In this group the strongest discriminator of those who had pregnancies was the SCL depression factor, which explained 11% of the variance. Three more variables added modest increments to the discrimination function: age (older teens were more likely to have a pregnancy), pregnancy "wanted" at enrollment, and social class index (lower status was more likely to have a pregnancy). Together these variables explained 24% of the variance of the teenagers who had pregnancies and those who did not in the original never-pregnant group (see table in Appendix E).

Repeat Pregnancy Among the Teenagers Who Had Babies

In each of the three original study groups, *the teenagers who avoided pregnancy after study enrollment were more alike than not.* Even in the original delivery group, where a second pregnancy could be viewed as even more problematic for these young unmarried teenagers, the variables at enrollment did not predict which teenagers would have repeated pregnancies in the 2-year study interval.

However, we did find in the original delivery group that the teenagers who had another pregnancy during the study fell further behind in school and were less likely to have occupational goals at the 2-year follow-up. The following variables differed at the 2-year follow-up between the delivery-group teenagers who repeated pregnancy and those who did not:

- The delivery-group repeaters were unlikely to use contraception ($p <$ 0.001). Although they registered in family planning, only 49% said they always used contraception at the 1-year follow-up, and this dropped to 17% at the 2-year follow-up.

- The repeaters were more likely to be younger (ages 13 to 15), although this did not reach statistical significance.
- The repeaters appeared to be the most disadvantaged in school performance and educational goals.
- They were four times more likely to be below their school grade level ($p < 0.001$).
- They were more than twice as likely to have fallen behind in school since study enrollment (47% compared to 20% of those who did not repeat pregnancy, $p < 0.01$).
- They were less likely to have educational goals beyond high school ($p < 0.05$).
- They were nearly three times more likely to have *lowered* their educational goals since study enrollment (trend level $p < 0.10$). These educational differences are shown in Figure 6.2.
- The repeaters were less likely to believe they would achieve occupational goals ($p < 0.05$).
- The repeaters were more likely at the outset of the study to indicate they were very close to their boyfriends ($p < 0.05$).

Factors Associated With Abortion or Delivery of Pregnancies After Enrollment

We focused on subsequent pregnancies that occurred after study enrollment and now briefly summarize the study variables that were associated with the teenagers' decisions to terminate or carry the pregnancy to term. Of the 84 pregnancies that occurred after study enrollment, 29 (35%) were terminated, and the remaining were delivered (or at study endpoint, the teenagers expected to deliver), with no differences in these outcomes compared among the three original study groups (see Table 6.1).

We examined the same set of above-described variables in another series of stepwise discriminant analyses of the teenagers who had pregnancies after study enrollment to discriminate between the teenagers who terminated the pregnancy and those who carried it to term. For the total group, discrimination was weak, with 15% of the variance explained by negative educational change and contraceptive use. The deliverers were more likely than the aborters to have negative educational change and less likely to use contraception (see table in Appendix E).

When the pregnant teenagers were examined separately in the original study groups, distinct profiles emerged. The decision about the pregnancy had different associations in the original delivery group than in the original never-pregnant group, whereas in the original abortion group none of the 11 study variables discriminated between the teenagers who terminated or delivered a subsequent pregnancy. In the original never-pregnant group, just one variable—contraceptive use (explaining 27% of the variance)—discriminated between the teenagers who terminated or delivered the pregnancy. The delivering teenagers were less likely to use contraception. In the original delivery group, the teenagers who went on to have another child had fallen further behind in school, were less likely to have occupational goals, and had higher depression levels as measured by the SCL-90. These variables together explained 52% of the variance between the aborters and the deliverers (see table in Appendix E).

CHAPTER SUMMARY

During the 2-year study 84 teenagers (26% of the sample) became pregnant after study enrollment, and neither the incidence nor the outcome of the pregnancies differed significantly among the three original study groups. Approximately one third of the pregnancies were terminated and two thirds were carried to term.

The results in this chapter illustrate the complexity of teenage pregnancy and show that even in a sample of disadvantaged, minority-group teenagers who lived in the midst of unmarried childbearing, there was no single rationale or set of variables that described the pregnancies. The strongest factor to differentiate between the teenagers who did or did not have pregnancies after study enrollment was contraceptive use. In all three groups, teenagers who became pregnant were inconsistent contraceptive users, much more so than those who avoided pregnancy.

Other than contraceptive use, no study variables significantly differentiated the pregnant teenagers in every study group. In the original never-pregnant group, the teenagers who subsequently became pregnant were more likely to be older, to have completed high school, and to have said they "wanted" pregnancy when they enrolled in the study. They also reported more emotional distress, including depression and lower self-esteem, at the outset. Possibly these feelings were linked to not having a child in an environment where they were surrounded by early childbearing, and where having a child confirmed belonging to the group and also legitimized adulthood (Rainwater, 1970).

In the delivery group the variables that differentiated the teenagers who had a repeat pregnancy suggested another picture. Those who had another pregnancy were more likely to be younger, to be below their school grade level, to have lower educational goals, to have less belief in achieving their occupational goals, and to be closer to their boyfriends. These were teenagers who appeared to be even less ready to support a family than their peers who had one child. For them, childbearing may have been a more satisfying alternative than poor school performance and lack of economic opportunity.

In the abortion group none of the variables significantly differentiated those who had another pregnancy after study enrollment. Bolton's (1980) perspective of the "practical view" of pregnant teenagers seems most germane. He noted that the most parsimonious explanation for unmarried teenage childbearing is sexual intercourse, reminding us that "a number of adolescent pregnancies can be attributed to chance." But this does not negate the basic problem for all concerned, regardless of age, class, or background, which is the achievement of responsible sexual decision making and behavior (Bolton, 1980). Childbearing brings personal satisfactions but also has negative social and economic outcomes that young teenagers neither know nor understand. It is important to not lose sight of the many teenagers in this study who successfully avoided childbearing. Finding few differences among these teenagers can also be interpreted as a positive indication that even greater numbers of teenagers *can* become responsible decision makers before pregnancies occur.

118   EARLY CHILDBEARING

REFERENCES

Bolton, F. G., Jr. (1980). *The pregnant adolescent.* Beverly Hills, CA: Sage.

Coopersmith, S. (1967). *The antecedents of self-esteem.* San Francisco: Freeman.

Derogatis, L. R. (1977). *SCL-90* (rev. ed.). Baltimore, MD: Johns Hopkins University, School of Medicine.

Furstenberg, F. F. (1976). *Unplanned parenthood: The social consequences of teenage childbearing.* New York: Free Press.

Hardy, J. B., & Zabin, L. S. (Eds.). (1991). *Adolescent pregnancy in an urban environment.* Washington, DC: Urban Institute Press.

Hollingshead, A. B. (1975). *Four factor index of social status.* New Haven, CT: Yale University, Department of Sociology.

Koenig, M. A., & Zelnik, M. (1982). Repeat pregnancies among metropolitan-area teenagers: 1971-1979. *Family Planning Perspectives, 14*(6), 341-344.

Paulker, S. (1969). Girls pregnant out-of-wedlock. In M. LaBarre & W. LaBarre (Eds.), *The double jeopardy: The triple crisis—Illegitimacy today.* New York: National Council on Illegitimacy.

Polit, D. F., & Kahn, J. R. (1986). Early subsequent pregnancy among economically disadvantaged teenage mothers. *American Journal of Public Health, 76*(2), 167-171.

Rainwater, L. (1970). *Behind ghetto walls.* Chicago: Aldine.

Zabin, L. S., Hirsch, M. B., & Emerson, M. R. (1989). When urban adolescents choose abortion: Effects on education, psychological status, and subsequent pregnancy. *Family Planning Perspectives, 21*(6), 245-255.

SEVEN

Family Involvement:
Preventing Early Teenage Childbearing

"[I] point out the disadvantages of teen pregnancy, try to keep my daughter involved in things so that she'll want the best out of life, the most important things, and having a baby won't fit in."—Mother

"At first I was going to have a baby because I thought they were cute and I just knew I wanted a baby. But this program has changed everything and I really like that because I could have made a big mistake and then would have to regret it."—Daughter, age 12

INTRODUCTION

Based on the results of the Penn Study, we designed the Family Involvement Project, a pilot project for young teenagers and their mothers to increase family involvement in preventing early childbearing. In this project we wanted to hear what the mothers of young teenagers had to say about sexual activity, pregnancy, and childbearing in relation to their children, and wanted to encourage these mothers to become more involved in communicating their ideas about the issues in their family and community.

A major finding of the Penn Study was that large numbers of teenagers—particularly those who had babies—perceived early childbearing as acceptable in their family and community. The teenagers believed that their mothers, fathers, girlfriends, and boy-friends were (or would be) happy if they had a child, and they seldom considered the consequences or alternatives before or after pregnancy.

The Family Involvement Project was unique. We found no other reports of parent-teen communication projects in families at risk of early childbearing. Rather than focusing on communication in the family, family planning programs typically provide services to individual women (regardless of their age), whereas adolescent pregnancy programs address parenting, education, or job training for the young mothers. However, we believe programs for families at risk of early childbearing need to include ways to improve family communication so sexual behavior, contraception, and the negative effects of early teen pregnancy are discussed with children before pregnancy occurs. Frequently teenagers reported "not knowing" about these issues, which suggests they had never discussed or considered them with their families or anyone else.

We know families have considerable influence on their children's sexual pathways. Stack (1974) and others wrote that blacks in lower socioeconomic groups depended heavily on family members for economic as well as social support, and that the family's attitudes toward sexual behavior and childbearing could be expected to be important to the teenagers. This expectation was supported by the Penn Study, which found that teenagers who gave birth believed their families supported early childbearing, and that teenagers who avoided childbearing believed their families opposed early childbearing. In a survey of teenagers at their first visit to a family planning clinic, Nathanson and Becker (1986) reported that the role of family members frequently was more important than the often-cited role of peers. Furthermore, black parents were more likely than white parents to approve of contraception because they were concerned about the problems of possible offspring and were eager to prevent pregnancy. White families in the study were less likely to approve of contraception and were more concerned with the morality of sexual behavior than with its outcome—pregnancy.

In the Penn Study we found that never-pregnant teenagers were more likely than pregnant teenagers to have talked with their mothers about contraception and pregnancy. Compared to mothers and daughters in the delivery group, those in the never-pregnant and abortion groups demonstrated more agreement that they had discussed pregnancy and contraception as well as the content and quality of those discussions. In general our findings suggested that the more the family communicated about sex and contraception, the better the teenager was prepared to make responsible decisions about sexual behavior.

Despite the potential positive influence of family involvement on teenage sexual behavior, communication about sex typically is minimal or lacking. "Not many children receive much direct instruction about sexuality, or sexual intercourse, or fertility regulation from their parents" (Fox, 1981). Poor parent-adolescent communication about sexual behavior is further diminished by miscommunication. For example, the parents may think they said one thing, but the teenagers may believe they heard something else. Newcomber and Udry (1985) noted, "it is evident that what adolescents think their parents believe and say about sex does not agree with what the parents report." Another comparison of mother-daughter communication about sex-related issues showed only a modest level of correspondence (Furstenberg, Herzog-Baron, Shea, & Webb, 1984), again suggesting that comments about difficult issues are not spoken and heard in the same ways.

In spite of this apparent lack of effective communication between the generations on sexual issues, the teenage daughters were more likely to avoid pregnancy when such communication occurred (Baker, Thalberg, & Morrison, 1988). Even the Newcomber and Udry (1985) study, which found little or no agreement between mothers' and daughters' reports of sexual communication, found significantly lower levels of intercourse for girls whose mothers said they had communicated with their daughters about sexual issues.

THE FAMILY INVOLVEMENT PROJECT

The Family Involvement Project was designed to demonstrate the feasibility of helping families encourage responsible sexual behavior in young adolescents and to prevent early teenage child-bearing. It was community based and intended to foster community involvement in discussing early teenage childbearing. The project took place in the mid-1980s. Its specific goals were to:

- Help mothers identify and communicate their values about sexual behavior and pregnancy to their early adolescent children
- Demonstrate that mothers of teenagers at high risk of pregnancy can aid in preventing early teenage childbearing
- Help young teenagers recognize the negative effects of childbearing on their lives and effectively prevent unwanted pregnancies
- Demonstrate the feasibility of increasing community involvement in preventing teenage childbearing
- Demonstrate the feasibility of outreach from a medical setting to a community at risk of teenage pregnancy

Design

Project participants attended four, 2-hour group meetings, which were held once a week. We conducted brief assessments at enrollment, after the last group meeting, and after 1 year. We obtained a comparison group by having the group participants network and recruit friends of the same age, gender, social class, and race. These comparison subjects completed the initial and 1-year follow-up questionnaires, but did not participate in the group meetings.

Subjects

Participants were recruited by mothers and community leaders who were supervised by a project staff member familiar with the community. Contacts were obtained through a network of school, religious, health, and community organizations. Persons interested in organizing a group of mothers or teenagers among their friends and neighbors were the key to recruitment in this project. The only criteria for mothers was having a never-pregnant daughter from age 11 to 14 and the willingness to participate. The criteria for the teenagers were age 11 to 16 and no previous pregnancies. (The teenagers' mothers did not need to participate in the mothers' group in order for them to participate in the teenager group.)

The project enrolled 123 mothers and 305 female teenagers: Seventy-seven percent of the mothers had daughters in the project, and 33% of the teenagers had mothers in the project. All participants signed consent forms approved by the Institutional Review Board of the University of Pennsylvania. All were African-American residents in a large urban area. They were predominantly in single-parent, low-income households. At the 1-year follow-up 95% of the mothers and 92% of the teenagers were recontacted by project staff and completed brief follow-up questionnaires.

The control subjects included 67 mothers and 88 teenagers with the same ages and background characteristics as the group participants. At the 1-year follow-up 91% of control-group mothers and 77% of control-group teenagers were contacted and completed follow-up questionnaires.

Groups

Small groups of participants met in their own neighborhoods in volunteers' homes or in nearby public meetings areas, such as community centers or churches. There were 37 groups: Fifteen convened in homes, 16 in community centers, 3 in churches, and 3 in housing projects. Group membership ranged from 5 to 29, with averages of 8 in mother groups and 11 in teenager groups. In some groups, mothers and their daughters met at the same time, but in separate locations with different leaders. These mothers and teenagers usually joined together at the final session.

Trained group leaders led the groups. The principal leader had extensive experience in family therapy with low-income black families. Drawing on her family-therapy training, she focused on group interactions in discussing mother-daughter relationships to increase awareness about the problems of teen pregnancy and to improve communication about these problems. As recruitment for the project expanded, the principal leader trained and supervised seven additional group leaders. All of these leaders were black and had professional training in counseling. They maintained consistency across their groups by following a manual and by participating in regularly scheduled reviews of group process, in which they discussed videotapes and audiotapes of the group meetings.

Group Format

The project staff developed a short manual to provide consistent content for group meetings. The manual identified the theme for each session; provided behavioral, cognitive, and emotional goals; and suggested activities and handout materials. Themes included:

- Members' perceptions of family communication, particularly mother-daughter communication about sex, pregnancy, and contraception
- Family messages about sexual issues
- Effects of family messages on teenagers' sexual behavior
- Anxiety related to the group process

Discussions emphasized the relationship between sexual behavior and pregnancy, and the limitations and problems caused by early teenage childbearing.

Assessments

Project staff members developed short self-report questionnaires to obtain information from participants at the beginning and end of the group series and at the 1-year follow-up. Control subjects completed the same initial and follow-up questionnaires.

RESULTS OF THE FAMILY INVOLVEMENT PROJECT

The project provided information about mothers' and teenagers' perceptions of teen pregnancy, teenage sexual experience, and mother-daughter communication.

Mothers

All mothers who participated in the project had never-pregnant daughters from age 11 to 14 (average age 13.5 years). About 40% of the mothers lived with a spouse or male partner. Approximately 50% had technical training or education beyond high school, 30% were high school graduates, and 20% had not completed high school. Approximately 60% were employed, primarily in clerical or technical (34%), unskilled (17%), or professional (9%) jobs. About 30% reported receiving welfare.

Comparisons of these background characteristics between the mother participants and controls showed no significant differences. Furthermore, there were no differences between the mothers and controls at enrollment in any of the attitudinal variables described in the following sections.

Mothers' Perceptions of Teenage Pregnancy

Nearly all the mothers said they viewed teenage pregnancy as a major problem. When asked what they thought were major influences on teenage pregnancy, nearly 75% of the mothers cited the media—television, movies, and music. They also cited "bad families" (63%), insufficient information about birth control (62%), drugs (62%), welfare (59%), poverty and lack of jobs (55%), and racism (28%). Some mothers saw welfare, poverty, lack of jobs, and racism as so constricting to their lives that early childbearing was a wanted and satisfying option for their children.

When asked what could be done to prevent or delay teenage pregnancy, 75% of the mothers indicated "more lectures from parents and adults." Many also suggested other approaches, such as "keep kids off the streets" (55%), less welfare (47%), more jobs and career counseling (42%), more sex education in schools (28%), more availability of birth control (17%), more religious education (15%), and better family relations (12%).

It is notable that these mothers believed parenting behaviors, such as "more lectures" and "keeping kids off the streets," were more effective at preventing teen pregnancy than programs, public policies, or social changes. The mothers may have preferred these solutions because they knew and could act on them. The mothers may have viewed policy and social change approaches as less effective because they could not control or did not understand them. However, it is striking that only a few mothers (3%) thought "nothing could be done" to reduce teenage pregnancy.

Of the mothers, 20% knew their daughters had steady boyfriends, and 7% said their daughters had sex. About 25% of these mothers thought their young teenage daughters were interested in—or not opposed to—having a baby. Although nearly all the mothers said teenage pregnancy was a major problem, only one third thought their lives would be worse if their young daughter had a baby in the near future. Like the teenage participants in the Penn Study, the greatest number of mothers (46%) said they "didn't know" how their young daughters' childbearing would affect either their daughters' or their own lives.

When we asked the mothers specifically which outcome they would prefer if their daughter became pregnant, 29% indicated keeping the baby, 28% indicated abortion, 2% suggested adoption, and the greatest number (41%) said they "didn't know" what their preferred outcome would be. The majority (66%) said their daughters should use birth control to prevent pregnancy, 3% objected to its premarital use, 7% objected to its use at any time, and 24% had no opinion or did not answer.

At enrollment the most common response to many of these attitudinal questions was having no opinion about possible effects of, or choices concerning, pregnancy. The mothers may have responded this way because they did not want to reveal their lack of objection to early childbearing. Or they may never have given much thought to these questions. They may have believed that life went on much the same whether or not pregnancies occurred. Notably, most of these mothers approved of contraceptive use. However, they did not express any compelling reasons for their daughters to prevent pregnancy.

Most mothers expressed concerns about teenage pregnancy, but few could describe ways they addressed the problem in their own families or elsewhere. Most had never talked to other adults about teenage pregnancy as a problem, less than half had ever talked with their daughters about sex and dating, and even fewer had ever mentioned birth control.

In sum, communication about sexual behavior and the problems of teenage pregnancy was minimal at the outset of the project. Even though one fourth of the mothers thought their young adolescent daughters already were interested in having a baby, they provided little information or guidance about sexual behavior and the problems of early childbearing.

Teenagers

The teenage participants (average age 13) were placed in younger (ages 11 to 13) and older (ages 14 to 16) groups. Overall, 40% lived in two-parent households. About 62% of their mothers and 53% of their fathers were employed. Slightly more than 25% reported that their household received welfare. All the teenagers were in school in grades 6 to 10, and 80% said they wanted to continue their education beyond high school. The teenagers in the control group had the same background characteristics. Furthermore, the teenage participants and controls did not differ at enrollment in how much they talked with their mothers about sexual topics or in any of the attitudinal variables described in the following sections.

These teenagers were familiar with adolescent childbearing. Only 9% of the older teenagers (ages 14 to 16) said their close friends did *not* have babies. (This question was not on the younger teen questionaire.) Two thirds of the teenagers said they had talked with their friends about getting pregnant, suggesting substantial communication about the possibility of pregnancy among peers.

In contrast to their mothers (a quarter of whom thought their daughters presently were interested in having a baby), more teenagers said they were interested in having a baby in the near future. When considered together with those who were uncertain or "didn't know," half the teenagers did not have strong opposition to early childbearing. Less than half of the teenagers thought having a baby would make their lives worse. The majority indicated that early childbearing would improve or make no difference in their lives or that they "didn't know" whether a baby would affect their lives.

Although the teenagers were unmarried and too young to be employed, 41% wanted to keep the baby and 33% "didn't know" what they would do if they became pregnant in the near future. Few indicated that they would choose abortion (14%) or adoption (7%) as a pregnancy outcome. Most (68%) endorsed contraceptive use, 23% "didn't know" what they thought about contraception, and 8% said it was wrong or a health hazard. Only one third of the teenagers who had engaged in sexual intercourse had ever used contraception.

In sum, most of the teenagers had close-up views of young childbearing, and many accepted it as an option for themselves. They discussed pregnancy with friends, and the great majority of them had friends who had babies. Less than half of the teenagers viewed a baby as a detriment to their lives, and few saw themselves choosing abortion or adoption if they became pregnant in the near future. Particularly, they did not perceive conflicts between early childbearing and completing high school, obtaining higher education, or gaining occupational training. Like the mothers, most of the teenagers agreed with contraception in principle, but many did not perceive compelling reasons to prevent pregnancy.

Teenagers' Sexual Experience

At enrollment 60% of the teenagers said they had a steady boyfriend and 35% had had sex. When examined by age group, 82% of the teenagers ages 15 to 16 and 17% of those ages 11 to 14 reported having sex. Few of the sexually active teenagers in either age group said they used contraception (19% in the older group, and 3% in the younger group).

When we compared the responses of mothers who had daughters in the study with the responses of daughters who had mothers in the study, we found that many mothers did not know about their daughters' sexual involvement. Twice as many daughters said they had a steady boyfriend (46%) than reported by their

Table 7.1 Talking About Sexual Topics as Reported by Mothers and Teenagers at Project Enrollment (percentage distribution)

	Mothers[a] (*n*=123)	*Teenagers*[b] (*n*=145)
Talked with [mother/daughter] about sex (ever)	89[c]	73
Sexual topics discussed with [mother/daughter]		
Changes in adolescence	68	64
Menstrual	68	75[d]
Pregnancy, how occurs	67	79
What to say to boys who want sex	64	55[d]
Sexually transmitted diseases	53	23[e]
Dating without sex	49	37
Birth control methods	43	36[e]
Abortion	40	32
Where to obtain birth control	37	30
How to use birth control	32	28

[a]None of the mothers' responses significantly different from those of control mothers.
[b]Only teenagers ages 14-16. Younger teenagers were not asked these questions.
[c]Responses significantly different from teenagers (chi-square $p < 0.01$).
[d]Teenagers reported significantly more discussion ($p < 0.05$) than teenage controls.
[e]Teenagers reported significantly less discussion than teenage controls.

mothers (23%). Three times more teenagers reported sexual activity (24%) than mothers reported for their daughters (8%).

Mother-Daughter Communication

At enrollment we asked about communication about sex and pregnancy. Most of the mothers (89%) said they had talked with their daughters about sex and pregnancy, but only about 75% of the daughters said they had any discussion with their mothers ($p < 0.01$). However, mothers and daughters tended to agree about communication on specific topics, as shown in Table 7.1, and the number who reported such communication was notably similar to the reports of teenagers in the Penn Study (see Chapter 4). More than two thirds of the mothers and daughters were most likely to have talked about menstruation, changes of adolescence, and conception. Fewer talked about dating, how to handle sex and dating, birth control methods, sexually transmitted diseases, and abortion. Only one third reported ever discussing where to obtain or how to use birth control methods.

The mothers (71%) were much more likely than the teenagers (38%) to say that mother-daughter discussions about sexual issues were comfortable ($p < 0.0001$). Some teenagers said the discussions were positive and helpful, but others answered that their mothers avoided discussions; acted nervous, embarrassed, or angry; or ridiculed the subject.

Although the teenagers cited their mothers as the most likely source of sexual information (71%), other female family members (principally sisters, grandmothers, and aunts) were nearly as likely to provide such information (68%). Only 28% of the teenagers said their girlfriends were a source of sex *information,* which they distinguished from sex discussions. Few cited any male relatives (15%) and even fewer cited their boyfriends (5%) as sources of sex information. Only 5% said they had not obtained sex information from someone.

RESULTS OF THE GROUP MEETINGS

At the final meeting of each group participants completed a brief posttest questionnaire to report changes in their ideas and in mother-daughter communication about teenage pregnancy. These are the main results:

- The mothers were much more likely than the teenagers to indicate improvement in discussing teenage pregnancy issues ($p < 0.0001$), although both mothers and teenagers reported improvement (see Figure 7.1).
- The teenagers were much more likely than the mothers to indicate that their ideas about teenage pregnancy changed, although both groups reported change (see Figure 7.1). Many teenagers and mothers reported a greater awareness of the limitations and problems that accompany early childbearing.
- When mothers and their daughters participated in group meetings (in separate groups for mothers and teenagers), mother-daughter

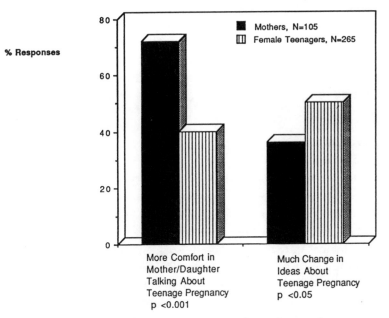

% Responses

Figure 7.1. Comparison of post-group responses by mothers and teenagers.

communication improved the most ($p < 0.001$). Mothers without participating daughters reported improved communication more than teenagers without participating mothers.

- Mothers of younger teenagers (ages 11 to 14) reported greater benefit from the group discussions than mothers of older teenagers (ages 15 to 16) ($p < 0.001$).
- The younger teenagers (ages 11 to 14) reported the most change in ideas about teenage pregnancy and more improvement in mother-daughter communication, compared to the older teenagers and the mothers ($p < 0.001$).

RESULTS AT THE 1-YEAR FOLLOW-UP

One year after the final group meeting, 95% of the mothers and 92% of the teenagers were contacted by the project staff. Ninety-one percent of the control mothers and 77% of the control teenagers also were contacted. The remainder could not be located by phone or mail. All participants who were contacted responded to a brief follow-up questionnaire in a telephone interview. The follow-up questions were about mother-daughter communication, the teenagers' sexual activity, and pregnancy during the 1-year interval after the group sessions.

Mothers

At the 1-year follow-up we found significant differences between project participants and controls in their concerns and communication about teenage pregnancy ($p < 0.001$) (see Figure 7.2). Participant mothers were more likely than control mothers to indicate changes in their ideas about teenage pregnancy, particularly the problems involved. They were also more likely to have talked with their daughters and/or friends about preventing teenage pregnancy. In addition, the participant mothers were much more likely to say their daughters were not interested in childbearing.

When we examined the mothers' follow-up responses in relation to their daughters' ages, we found no differences, except in family planning enrollment. Not many daughters (12%) in the younger group had enrolled in family planning, but 41% of the older daughters had.

At the 1-year follow-up the number of mothers who said their daughters were sexually active increased slightly from 7% to 11%. Six mothers (5%) said their daughters had become pregnant in the year after the group meetings. One pregnancy was terminated, and five were carried to term.

Compared to the post-group assessments, many mothers continued to report more understanding in the mother-daughter relationship, changed ideas about teenage pregnancy, greater involvement in trying to prevent teenage pregnancy, and more discussion with their daughters about it. Fewer said that if their daughter had a baby, their lives would be better or no different (5% compared to 22% at enrollment, $p < 0.005$).

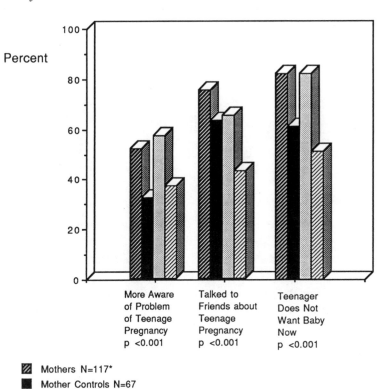

Figure 7.2. Comparison of 1-year follow-up responses: Mothers versus controls, teenagers versus controls.
*Numbers are responses at 1-year follow-up.

Teenagers

Teenage participants were much more likely than the teenage controls to report changed ideas about pregnancy ($p < 0.01$) (see Figure 7.2). They also were more likely to indicate they had talked with friends about problems of teen pregnancy ($p < 0.001$). Many more teenager participants said they did *not* want a baby compared to teenage controls ($p < 0.001$). Many more teenagers at follow-up were certain that they did not want a baby, compared to

Table 7.2 Percent of Teenagers Reporting Sex Before and 1 Year After
             Project Participation

	At Enrollment	During Follow-up Year
Had sex	35	14*
Ages 11-14	17	7
Ages 15-16	82	32

*McNamar chi-square test, $p < 0.001$.

their responses at enrollment ($p < 0.001$). Age did not affect these
responses; they were similar in the younger and older age groups.

Although 35% of the teenagers at enrollment said they had had
intercourse, only 14% indicated they had had intercourse during
the year after the group meetings ($p < 0.001$) (see Table 7.2). This
was less than the control teenagers reported (22% said they had
intercourse in the follow-up year), but the difference was not significant. Nonetheless, this reported incidence of sexual activity
was of particular interest because it suggested that many of the
teenagers chose not to be sexually active. Possibly the reported levels of sexual activity reflected the teenagers' needs to provide the
"right" answer. Possibly the answers at follow-up were accurate
because teenagers tend to have sex sporadically and many did not
have steady boyfriends during that time. Nevertheless, of those
who ever had sexual intercourse, less than half of them reported
having sex in the year after they participated in the project.

Pregnancy Among the Teenage Participants

During the follow-up year 7 participants and 2 controls (.025%
of the teenage sample at follow-up) became pregnant. Three participants and 1 control terminated the pregnancy. These very small
numbers and the follow-up period of only 1 year are insufficient to
determine which of the attitudinal and behavioral changes reported by these teenagers and mothers had an impact on delaying
pregnancies. We can provide only some general comparisons for
consideration. At enrollment the teenage participants were more

likely to report sexual experience than others their age (Hofferth, Kahn, & Baldwin, 1987). This suggested that more of the project participants were at risk of pregnancy, particularly among the younger teenagers. Four of the pregnancies occurred to teenagers from ages 12 to 14, and two were carried to term. Among the older teens (ages 15 to 16), there were three pregnancies with two carried to term, which is about half the state birthrate for black females of the same ages.

CHAPTER SUMMARY

This community-based project demonstrated a way to increase mothers' and teenagers' awareness of the limitations of early child-bearing in their lives. The project consisted of a series of group discussion meetings, conducted separately for mothers and young, never-pregnant teenagers, that highlighted problems of early childbearing and encouraged mother-daughter communication about sexual issues and behavior. Adult volunteers assembled groups of friends or neighbors, and each group then met regularly with a trained leader to talk about designated topics related to teenage pregnancy.

The backgrounds and circumstances of many of the group participants were very similar to the teens in the Penn Study. However, overall, the Family Involvement participants were more likely to be in 2-parent families, only about 30% were in welfare households, and more than half the mothers had completed high school. Although we did not find differences in the results in terms of these variables, further study is needed to know whether outcomes would be similar in samples that were drawn predominantly from single-parent, welfare households. Possibly the intermingling, rather than isolation, of the poorest groups with others who more clearly perceived disadvantage to early teenage childbearing was an important factor in the attitudinal changes of the project participants, even though we cannot assume that these results would be the same in other groups. The main outcomes of the Family Involvement Project were:

- The networking techniques used to assemble groups demonstrated the possibilities of reaching high-risk families *before* teenage pregnancies occurred.
- Mothers with younger teenagers (ages 11 to 14) reported the most change and improvement in communication with their daughters after the group meetings.
- Younger teenage participants (ages 11 to 14) were much more likely than older teenagers (ages 15 to 16) to report changed ideas about teenage pregnancy and improved communication with their mothers.
- Less than half of the teenagers who said they had sex before enrolling in the project had sex in the follow-up year, which reduced their risk of early teenage childbearing.
- The attitudinal and behavioral changes of group participants were greater than those of controls at the 1-year follow-up.
- Although the intervention was not designed to study behavioral change over time, mothers and teenagers appeared to maintain their changes in attitudes about early childbearing 1 year after the project ended.

Mother-daughter communication and recognition of the limitations of early childbearing are only two small pieces of the teenage pregnancy problem. Major factors are poor education, joblessness, and limited career opportunities, but even these determinants do not entirely explain the problem. As Vinovskis (1988) argued in *The Public Interest,* "13- and 14-year-olds are neither emotionally nor financially ready to deal with the serious consequences of early sexual activity. . . . *None of these programs will succeed . . . unless parents talk more openly with their children about sex."* If families do not view early, unmarried pregnancy and childbearing as unacceptable, these problems are not likely to change. If families do not provide guidance for their children's sexual activity, information about the problems of early childbearing, reasons for delaying childbearing, and hope for educational and occupational goals, sexually active young teenagers are unlikely to avoid pregnancy.

To change the acceptability of early childbearing, we must improve schools and job opportunities, but also help families at risk learn how to encourage their children to complete school, obtain jobs, and perceive early adolescent childbearing as a major obstacle to these goals. The relatively simple, community-based model we have described showed that helping mothers and young teenagers discuss sexual issues and articulate the problems of early childbearing can enable families and communities to gain greater control over unwanted teenage pregnancy.

REFERENCES

Baker, S. A., Thalberg, S. P., & Morrison, D. M. (1988). Parents' behavioral norms as predictors of adolescents' sexual activity and contraceptive use. *Adolescence, 23*(90), 266-282.

Fox, G. L. (1981). The family's role in adolescent sexual behavior. In T. O. Ooms (Ed.), *Teenage pregnancy in a family context.* Philadelphia: Temple University Press.

Furstenberg, F., Herzog-Baron, R., Shea, J., & Webb, D. (1984). Family communication and teenagers' contraceptive use. *Family Planning Perspectives, 16*(4), 163-170.

Hofferth, S. L., Kahn, J. R., & Baldwin, W. (1987). Premarital sexual activity among U.S. teenage women over the past three decades. *Family Planning Perspectives, 19*(2), 46-53.

Nathanson, C. A., & Becker, M. H. (1986). Family and peer influence on obtaining a method of contraception. *Journal of Marriage and Family, 48*(3), 513-525.

Newcomber, S. F., & Udry, J. R. (1985). Parent-child communication and adolescent sexual behavior. *Family Planning Perspectives, 17*(4), 169-174.

Stack, C. (1974). *All our kin: Strategies for survival in a black community.* New York: Harper & Row.

Vinovskis, M. A. (1988). Teenage pregnancy and the underclass. *The Public Interest, 93*(Fall), 87-96.

EIGHT

Male Teenagers and Contraception

INTRODUCTION

Contraceptive services for males are only a small component of the family planning system. Most contraceptive methods are for women. Even the term *family planning* implicitly links fertility management with female contraceptive methods.

The female orientation of family planning is no accident. The leaders of the birth control movement fought to enable women to control their ability to reproduce. They wanted women to be able to "decide for themselves whether [to] become mothers, under what conditions, and when" (Scrimshaw, 1981). Margaret Sanger campaigned from 1914 to 1937 to establish birth control clinics to free women from unrelenting childbirth (Reed, 1978). The development of oral contraceptives ("the pill") in the 1960s, made possible in part by the financial support of Katherine McCormick, seemed to make Sanger's vision of female control over fertility a reality. The pill gave women a highly reliable birth control method that did not require cooperation from the male partner.

More than a generation after gaining autonomy in contraception, more women are expecting men to assume equal, or shared, responsibility for preventing pregnancy. Women found that fertility control brings not only freedom, but also burdens. The pill, a medication used over a long time, can cause side effects and serious complications in some women. In addition, pregnancy prevention requires remembering to take the pill daily. It also requires the admission that sexual intercourse is likely, a rational approach to sex that is difficult for many people, particularly teenagers.

Before the 1960s and the emergence of the pill, male teenagers were held more accountable for pregnancy than they are today. Unless they planned to marry, premarital sex was perilous, particularly among middle-class and working-class teenagers (Davis & Grossbard-Schectman, 1980). If a male teenager caused a pregnancy, he typically had three choices: leave town, marry, or help his girlfriend obtain an abortion (which for most was unavailable and also risked the young woman's life or subsequent fertility). Davis and Grossbard-Schectman (1980) concluded that this social system certainly did not preclude teenage pregnancy, but it did keep it relatively low. Indeed, the birthrates of unmarried teenagers were consistent with this premise. In 1970 the birthrate among unmarried women from ages 15 to 19 was 22.4 (per 1,000), whereas in 1989 it increased to 40.6 (National Center for Health Statistics, 1991). However, the birthrates among unmarried, nonwhite teenagers were already high (90.8 in 1970 and 89.1 in 1989) and not simply explained by this premise.

Social sanctions for unmarried teenage childbearing are weakened or nonexistent. Teenage pregnancy seldom leads to marriage—or to any continued responsibility by the male partner in the pregnancy. The young women must terminate or deliver the pregnancy. If they are unmarried and have a child, permanent economic support from the father is unlikely. Abundant studies describe the sexual activity, contraceptive use, attitudes, and problems of single teenage mothers, but we know little about these same behaviors and attitudes among their male partners. Only recently has there been information on the sexual activity of male teenagers (Sonenstein, Pleck, & Leighton, 1991), and almost no studies have investigated their attitudes toward contraceptive decision making (Scales & Everly, 1977; Sonenstein, Pleck, & Ku, 1989). This situation raises several important questions:

- Are male teenagers unconcerned about pregnancy?
- Do male teenagers "want" pregnancy?

- Do they understand the risk of pregnancy from unprotected inter-course?
- What do they know about contraception?
- Where do they learn about contraception?

To help answer these questions, we studied male teenagers in three settings: (a) in high school health classes, using a self-report questionnaire; (b) in the Penn Study, through in-depth interviews with the male partners of a small subgroup of the female teenagers; (c) in the Family Involvement Project (described in Chapter 7), where several additional groups with very young male teenagers were explored. The responses of these male teenagers are not "hard" scientific data obtained in controlled study. But by responding to the same questions in the same settings as the female teenagers, the male teenagers demonstrated the similarities—and differences—between their views of contraception and pregnancy and the views of their female counterparts.

MALE TEENAGERS IN
HIGH SCHOOL CLASSES

We obtained responses about contraception and pregnancy from male teenagers who attended health classes together with female students in three large, urban high schools near the Penn Study site. In these classes, which were conducted in grades 9 through 12, staff members of the Department of Obstetrics and Gynecology presented eight sessions on family life. The sessions included discussions of pregnancy and contraception and were presented to the young men and women together in their regularly scheduled, required health class. At the end of the family life series, the students completed the Sexual Information and Attitudes Questionnaire (SIAQ), which was described in Chapter 2. The questionnaire elicited attitudes and information about contraception and pregnancy, which were analyzed and reported elsewhere (Freeman, Rickels, Huggins, Mudd, Garcia, & Dickens, 1980). Approximately 600 black students responded. Of these, 250 were male, and their answers are described in this section.

Do Male Teenagers Want a Baby?

In this sample of high school students, young men were no different from young women in the same classes in terms of "wanting" pregnancy. About 20% of male and female teenagers said they currently wanted (or had) a child. It appeared that, just as some female teenagers viewed pregnancy as the pathway to being a woman, some male teenagers viewed fatherhood as the pathway to becoming a man. However, this was not the predominant response of either the males or the females. The proportion of teenagers who stated they wanted a pregnancy was similar to the proportion found in a national survey conducted around the same time, which showed that 21% of black females from ages 15 to 19 who experienced premarital pregnancy indicated that pregnancy was wanted (Zelnik & Kantner, 1980).

Although most of the males did not "want" to be teenage fathers, many did not cite any major reason that they should avoid having a child. In response to the question of how a baby would affect their lives, the responses of the males and females were nearly identical. The largest number (43%) said they "didn't know" how a pregnancy would affect their lives. Only 35% said their lives would be "worse" if pregnancy occurred, and 22% said their lives would be no different or better.

Teenagers will use contraception—or use it effectively—only if they do not want pregnancy and its consequences. Those who have no idea of the effects of pregnancy on their lives are unlikely to be consistently motivated to prevent pregnancy. This "not knowing" or absence of fear of the consequences of pregnancy reported by the teenagers in this study was strongly associated with ideas of when they wanted to have a baby. Indeed, 90% of the teenagers who indicated that pregnancy would have negative consequences in their lives clearly indicated that they did not want pregnancy until after their teenage years. This contrasted starkly with the teenagers who said pregnancy would have no effect or make their lives better, half of whom said they wanted a pregnancy soon. Among the teenagers who "didn't know" how pregnancy would affect their lives, one fourth *said* they wanted pregnancy in their teen years. These responses reflect only intended behavior and do not incorporate the even larger group who appeared unmotivated to prevent pregnancy because they "didn't know" how it would affect their lives.

What Do Male Teenagers Know About Contraception?

The male and female teenagers attended the same classes together and participated in the same discussions of pregnancy and contraception. They almost invariably agreed that the responsibility for contraception should be shared by both partners. However, when we compared the SIAQ responses to questions about contraceptive information and attitudes, we found that the male teenagers had even less information than the female teenagers ($p < 0.01$ for the total SIAQ scores). Like their female counterparts, most males could not identify the most fertile time in the menstrual cycle. (This lack of knowledge is particularly troublesome because many of these teenagers had sex when they believed it was the "safe" time of the month. What some thought was the "safe" time was, in fact, the most fertile time. This and other timing errors might delay, but not prevent, pregnancy.) Furthermore, they thought the females *could* tell when they were "safe" ($p < 0.001$). The male teenagers relied on the female teenagers to prevent pregnancy, although more than half of both groups could not correctly identify when pregnancy was most likely to occur.

The male teenagers' contraceptive information was meager and their attitudes about needing contraception were more problematic than those of the females who were in the same classes where the issues were discussed. The concept that contraception was needed even for occasional sex was endorsed by 44% of the males, compared to 64% of the females ($p < 0.001$). The idea that pregnancy was a risk even if it did not occur after the first sex experience was endorsed by 82% of the males, compared to 91% of the females ($p < 0.01$). Only 57% of the males, compared to 64% of the females, agreed that males respect females who use birth control ($p < 0.01$). The notion of having unprotected sex because "it showed more love" was endorsed by 21% of the males, compared to 10% of the females ($p < 0.01$). Furthermore, the females' contraceptive information improved with school grade (grades 9 to 12, $p < 0.001$), but the male teenagers' scores showed no increase after grade 10.

Based on SIAQ responses the male teenagers appeared less likely than the female teenagers in the same high school classes to recognize the risk of pregnancy. The males had less contraceptive information and fewer positive attitudes about contraceptive use. Moreover, the male teenagers believed the females *did* have the correct information—a perception that they believed justified their lack of involvement. Unfortunately, many of the female teenagers had little more contraceptive information than the males, were likely to risk unprotected intercourse, and rationalized that they did not need contraception "just yet" (Zabin & Clark, 1981).

Where Did the Male Teenagers Learn About Contraception?

The male teenagers differed significantly from the females in where they learned about contraception. About 75% of the males indicated that school health classes were the primary information source. Books (29%) and friends (23%) were secondary sources. Fewer than 20% said they had obtained any contraceptive information from a parent or other family member.

The male teenagers' impersonal sources of contraceptive information contrasted with those of the females, who were likely to learn about contraception in discussions with other females. The female teenagers were much more likely to indicate they had obtained contraceptive information from their mothers (40%, $p < 0.001$), sisters (22%, $p < 0.001$), or girlfriends (23%, $p < 0.05$).

The people with whom the teenagers *talked* most about contraception differed from the people they *learned* the most from. Male and female teenagers talked primarily with their friends about sex and contraception, but they did not learn the most about these subjects from these discussions, as was found in previous studies (Scales & Everly, 1977; Thornburg, 1981). If they talked about contraception, *both* males and females talked with girlfriends (35% and 40%, respectively). Although male teenagers talked among themselves about sex, fewer than 5% said they had ever talked with their male friends about contraception.

Summary

Among the teenagers surveyed in high school health classes, the study found that:

- Male teenagers were no more likely than female teenagers to want pregnancy. About 20% of both sexes said they wanted a pregnancy or already had a child.
- Few male teenagers worried about the possibility of pregnancy. Mainly, they "didn't know" how pregnancy would affect their lives.
- Male teenagers had significantly less information about pregnancy risk and contraception than female teenagers, even after both groups had participated in a family life series in their high school health classes.
- The male teenagers communicated much less about contraception with their family and friends.

We speculated that the poorer information and attitudes of the male teenagers were due to the fact that they did not see contraception and pregnancy as their concerns. The male teenagers thought the females knew about contraception. The male teenagers believed that pregnancy would have few consequences in their lives, and that the females would know the "safe" time, take the pill, and assume the responsibility for the outcomes of sex and pregnancy. The male teenagers had low levels of contraceptive information, perhaps because it seemed irrelevant to them.

MALE PARTNERS OF TEENAGERS IN THE PENN STUDY

The Penn Study provided a second glimpse of male teenagers' attitudes about contraception and pregnancy. We conducted individual in-depth interviews with 22 male partners of teenagers in the delivery group and 8 male partners of teenagers in the abortion group. The male teenagers also completed the visual analog scales to rate their feelings about pregnancy (described in Chapter 3). Although this small number of male teenagers is not a representative sample, it provided some information about the "silent" half of the teenage couples who had pregnancies.

On the average, the 30 male teenagers were age 18.8 and about 2 years older than their partners. All were black and unmarried. About 30% had completed high school, 40% were attending high school, and 30% had dropped out of high school. Those who were not in school were working in service or unskilled labor jobs. (These were low-level jobs, such as fast-food service. However, because none of the teenagers said they were unemployed, they appeared to be not representative of poor young black males.) The average age at first intercourse was age 12.

Did These Male Teenagers "Want" Pregnancy?

The male teenagers indicated about the same degree of "wanting" pregnancy as the female teenagers reported on the visual analog scales described in Chapter 3. In the abortion group the average "wanted" scores were 42 for the males and 41 for the females; in the delivery group the "wanted" scores were 59 for the males whose girlfriends were still pregnant and 73 for those whose babies had been born. These compared to the female delivery group's scores of 51 early in pregnancy and 91 after the baby was born.

Pregnancy was not a new experience to most of these young men: Twenty-seven percent had been involved in at least one earlier pregnancy, 90% said they had friends who had children, and 60% had siblings who were pregnant before marriage. In spite of their experience, about 75% of the young men initially expressed surprise when the pregnancy occurred, although few (13%) doubted their paternity. "I was shocked" was the most frequent response to learning of the pregnancy, mixed with feelings of being "happy" and "sad." Most of the young men said they had discussed their future as a couple with their partners, but few talked specifically about pregnancy or marriage. Moreover, once their partners were pregnant, there was little discussion of options. About 33% of those whose partners chose delivery had thought about abortion, but not mentioned it to their partners; 75% of the men whose partners had abortions had expected that the pregnancy would be carried to term. In spite of little discussion, 80% indicated that the couple agreed on the outcome.

When asked who made the decision about the pregnancy outcome, 30% (all in the delivery group) said the decision was a mutual one with their partner; the remainder were equally likely to say that they, their partner, or her mother made the decision. Most (80%) of the male partners said they agreed with the decision that was made. More than 50% had given no thought to marriage, although 65% wanted to marry the partner "someday."

When these young men considered future parenthood, they were similar to many other Americans. They wanted an average of three children. They thought the best age to marry was between age 22 and 25. They imagined themselves at age 25 "being married, working, and a homeowner," "trying to get a career together," and "being financially stable." However, only one third named a specific occupation in which they would work at that time, and most of those qualified it with a "maybe." They had goals, but no clear idea of the pathways to the goals, and 70% had not yet completed high school.

What Did the Male Partners
Know About Contraception?

We asked the young men to name all contraceptive methods they had heard about and then asked whether they recognized methods they had not mentioned. All had heard of condoms, and all but one knew about the pill. More than 75% either mentioned or recognized all eight methods discussed. Their assessments of method effectiveness were fairly knowledgeable: Most rated sterilization, the pill, and condoms as effective. But the young men also held myths and attitudes that undermined effective contraceptive use:

- 40% had told a sexual partner they could not get her pregnant.
- 67% believed withdrawal (coitus interruptus) was effective.
- 70% did not know when in the menstrual cycle the woman was most likely to become pregnant.
- 40% believed contraception was solely the woman's responsibility.
- 42% agreed that preventing pregnancy was "too much hassle to do all the time."
- 67% did not know that their teenage partners could obtain free contraception at the family planning clinic.

These responses suggested that, although the young men knew about contraceptive methods, their attitudes and information hindered consistent contraceptive use. In fact, none of the young men claimed they used contraception consistently, and two had never used contraception. About 60% had never discussed contraception with their partners before they became pregnant.

Summary

These interviews with male teenagers whose partners became pregnant gave some sense of their attitudes about contraception and pregnancy. These male teenagers were not a representative sample, even of the male partners in the Penn Study. Those who agreed to be interviewed had good relationships with their partners and were willing to be involved in an interview where they were asked questions about contraception and pregnancy. Nonetheless, their responses give a voice to the male half of every teenage pregnancy.

- The young men did not think about the likelihood of pregnancy. Most expressed surprise when it occurred, even though pregnancy was a common event among their friends and siblings and 27% had previously had a partner become pregnant.
- The young men said they "wanted" pregnancy at levels similar to those of their partners. Pregnancy was more wanted than unwanted

in the delivery group, but more unwanted than wanted in the abortion group.

- Nearly all of the young men knew about contraceptive methods. However, they had misinformation and attitudes that were inconsistent with effective contraceptive use.
- The young men reported almost no discussion with their partners about contraception, pregnancy, or the outcome of pregnancy after it occurred.
- They were involved with their partners and wanted to be good fathers, although they were vague about the exact nature of their parental responsibilities.
- Most of them had no economic means to support a family and no specific educational or occupational goals. They did not know how they would reach their goals of "being married, working, and a homeowner." Programs and policies to prevent teenage pregnancy must address these socioeconomic issues together with family planning and contraceptive responsibility.

MALE TEENAGERS IN THE FAMILY INVOLVEMENT PROJECT

In the Family Involvement Project described in Chapter 7, 32 male teenagers participated in all-male groups. These teenagers attended four group sessions, conducted by trained leaders, to discuss sexual issues and behavior. They received the same brief questionnaires as the female teenagers at enrollment, after the last group session, and at the 1-year follow-up. Their background characteristics were similar or identical to those of the female teenagers. Their average age was 14.

Like the female teenagers, most of the male teenagers said they were close to their mothers and had supportive extended families. Only 63% were close to their fathers or stepfathers—the same proportion as their female counterparts. Less than half were active in school or community activities, and only a few were involved in church activities or part-time jobs. Two thirds said they wanted education beyond high school and cited college or job training as goals.

Of these male teenagers, 72% said they had a steady girlfriend, 69% had had intercourse, 16% had used contraception, and 3% (1 teenager) had produced a pregnancy. The male teenagers were more likely than female teenage participants to say they had had intercourse (69% and 35%, respectively; $p < 0.001$).

Did These Male Teenagers "Want" Pregnancy?

When asked whether they "wanted" a baby, the male teenagers' responses echoed those of the female teenagers. About 50% of the males and females said they were "interested," "uncertain," or "didn't know" whether they wanted a baby now. The other 50% were clear they did not want a baby. When asked what effect a baby would have in their lives, 41% said they didn't know, 37% said their lives would be better or no different, and 22% said their lives would be worse. The male teenagers were even less likely than the females to think that a baby would have a negative effect at this point in their lives (22% and 46%, respectively; $p < 0.05$). Only 44% thought it was important to use contraception if they had sex.

Where Did the Male Teenagers Learn About Contraception?

These male teenagers obtained their sexual information largely from male family members—fathers, brothers, cousins, and uncles (91%). This did not usually include contraceptive information, which was not examined in greater detail in the Family Involvement Project. The male teenagers were less likely than the female teenagers to have talked with their mothers about sexual issues (56% and 73%, respectively). When mothers and sons did discuss sexual topics, the most common topic was sexually transmitted disease (28%), and the *least* common topic was contraceptive use, which only one male teenager (3%) had discussed with his mother. In contrast, mothers and daughters tended to discuss sexually transmitted disease least (although the percent who reported discussing it [23%] was similar to the mother-son numbers) and menstruation most (75%). Mothers and daughters (30%) were more than three times more likely than mothers and sons (9%) to have discussed obtaining contraception ($p < 0.05$).

Less than half of the male teenagers (44%) said their mothers responded positively to talking about sexual topics, which was similar to the numbers reported by the female teenagers (38%). Nevertheless, mothers, other family members, and friends were the sources of sexual information for the male teenagers. None of these teenagers said they had obtained sex information from teachers or other professionals.

Summary

Most of these male teenagers said they had had sexual intercourse, but only 16% had ever used contraception when they enrolled in the Family Involvement Project. They were less likely than their female peers to think that teenage pregnancy was a problem, and few described any strong motivation to avoid pregnancy. Less than one quarter thought that having a baby would have a negative impact on their lives. Their families rarely discussed pregnancy and contraception.

The Family Involvement Project suggested the potential for changing attitudes and behavior of young male teenagers. Young teens, primarily junior high school age, participated in group discussion sessions, which focused on mother-son communication and attitudes about early teenage childbearing. At the 1-year follow-up 48% of the male teenagers reported improved mother-son communication and 37% reported more discussion of sex and pregnancy with their mothers. Whereas few male teenagers at the outset had thought pregnancy would have negative effects in their lives, 78% recognized much more about the problems of early childbearing after their group participation, and 85% clearly indicated they did not want a baby. Whereas nearly all the male teenagers said they had sexual experience prior to the project, only four (15%) said they had sex in the interval between the group series and the 1-year follow-up; all of these said they used contraception.

It is important to underscore that the changes that occurred—particularly in improved information about pregnancy and contraception and increased family communication—were significantly greater among younger teenagers (ages 11 to 14) than older teenagers (ages 15 to 16), as also was found for the female teenagers and the mothers who participated in the project. The younger teenagers appeared more responsive to learning about the issues discussed and wanted to communicate with their parents. They learned more about the problems of early childbearing and were more likely to think about the consequences. "I've changed about not getting a girl pregnant," wrote a 14-year-old male, who used contraception at the 1-year follow-up.

CHAPTER SUMMARY

Some of these male teenagers were from high school classes where they attended a family life course, some were the partners of teenagers who became pregnant, and some were participants in a community-based pregnancy prevention project, but the themes were similar throughout. The male teenagers did not know much about contraception, or if they did, they had other sexual attitudes that hindered consistent contraceptive use. Even the high school students, who attended with their female counterparts the same family life classes, had less information than the females at the end of the course. We speculated that this was because the male teenagers did not think contraception or childbearing issues were important for them.

Only a small number of these teenagers thought pregnancy would have any negative effects on their lives. Possibly this was true, but it also has major implications for pregnancy prevention programs. Young male, as well as female, teenagers need sex education that engages them personally. They need to hear about and talk about responsible sexual behavior and what parenting means for them and their children. The communities that make up our society must expect men, whether married or not, to have responsibility for their children. Male teenagers need to know about condom use, not only for contraception but also for prevention of

AIDS and other diseases that risk their fertility. Pregnancy prevention programs must reach adolescents sooner—before they have the first pregnancy, and even before they begin sexual activity, which was around puberty for many of these teenagers. Sex education is an ongoing learning process that reflects our values, not a single course in the school curriculum or a single lecture at home, which for too many teenagers offers too little, too late. The many medical and social programs that help pregnant or parenting female teenagers must be extended to help young male teenagers avoid fatherhood.

REFERENCES

Davis, K., & Grossbard-Schectman, A. (1980). *Study on how mother's age and circumstances affect children* (Final report to National Institute for Child Health and Human Development). Los Angeles: University of Southern California Press.

Freeman, E. W., Rickels, K., Huggins, G., Mudd, E. H., Garcia, C.-R., & Dickens, H. O. (1980). Adolescent contraceptive use: Comparisons of male and female attitudes and information. *American Journal of Public Health, 70*(8), 790-797.

National Center for Health Statistics. (1991). Advance report of final natality statistics, 1989. *Monthly Vital Statistics Report, 40*(8 Suppl.). Hyattsville, MD: Public Health Service.

Reed, J. (1978). *From vice to public virtue: The birth control movement and American society since 1830.* New York: Basic Books.

Scales, P., & Everly, K. (1977, January). A community sex education program for parents. *The Family Coordinator, 26,* 37-45.

Scrimshaw, S. C. M. (1981). Women and the pill: From panacea to catalyst. *Family Planning Perspectives, 13*(6), 254-256, 260-262.

Sonenstein, F. L., Pleck, J. H., & Ku, L. C. (1989). Sexual activity, condom use, and AIDS awareness among adolescent males. *Family Planning Perspectives, 21*(4), 152-158.

Sonenstein, F. L., Pleck, J. H., & Leighton, C. K. (1991). Levels of sexual activity among adolescent males in the United States. *Family Planning Perspectives, 23*(4), 162-167.

Thornburg, H. D. (1981). Adolescent sources of information on sex. *Journal of School Health, 51*(4), 274-277.

Zabin, L. S., & Clark, S. D. (1981). Why they delay: A study of teenage family planning clinic patients. *Family Planning Perspectives, 13*(5), 205-217.

Zelnik, M., & Kantner, J. F. (1980). Sexual activity, contraceptive use, and pregnancy among metropolitan-area teenagers. *Family Planning Perspectives, 12*(5), 230-237.

NINE

Conclusions and Recommendations

A GLIMPSE 10 YEARS LATER

Nearly 10 years after we first interviewed the Penn Study teenagers, we reinterviewed 95 of them to examine the relationship of childbearing to their educational, occupational, and income status at this later time (Iverson, 1990). These young women represented about one third of the original sample. They were randomly selected and placed in approximately equal-size groups based on their pregnancy status at the end of the Penn Study: never pregnant, pregnancy terminated by abortion, or one child. The follow-up sample did not include the small group of teenagers who had two or more babies at the end of the study, because the research aim was to examine the effects on income of one child compared to no children in the teen years. The interviewed teenagers were no different from the remaining sample on the basis of statistical comparisons of all variables at the end of the study.

Two points stood out dramatically from these interviews. One was that these young women had relatively few children. The other was that those who did not have any children had much higher incomes than those who had children.

A remarkable number (35%) of the teenagers who had no child at the end of the Penn Study still had no children nearly 10 years later, when they were in their mid-twenties. At the follow-up interviews the never-pregnant teenagers and abortion-group teenagers were equally successful at delaying motherhood, and the proportion of childlessness was the same in each of these two groups. For those who had become mothers, the average number of children was 1.7, with a range of 1 to 4 children. Most (86%) of the teenagers were still unmarried. Overall, 83% had completed high school. Of those who had not finished high school, all but one had a child during the Penn Study.

The women without children had much higher incomes than those with children (averaging $18,000 and $12,000, respectively). This relationship between childbearing and income was not altered by the timing of the child's birth (before or after the teenager completed high school), the teenager's age at first childbirth, the age of the youngest child, or the total number of children. For these teenagers, of whom few had married, having even one child before their mid-twenties had a detrimental effect on their income. Those who delayed childbearing—nearly half of whom lived in welfare households as teenagers—had incomes above the poverty level and appeared to be moving out of the poverty of their childhood.

Among the women with children, those who had not completed high school had the lowest incomes, those who had training beyond high school had the highest incomes (which were lower on average than the incomes of the women who had no children), and the high school graduates with no further training had incomes between the other two groups. The timing of the first child's birth (before or after completing high school), the number of children, the woman's age at first birth, and the age of the youngest child had no direct effects on income. Once childbearing was begun, it did not further affect income levels of the women in their mid-twenties (Iverson, 1990).

Possibly these negative effects of early childbearing on income will lessen in later years when the young mothers gain longer employment experience. It is also possible that the women with no children will have insufficient incomes to support them above the poverty level when they have families. However, the results are similar to findings in a more extensive follow-up study of teenage mothers in later life (Furstenberg, Brooks-Gunn, & Morgan, 1987).

The researchers concluded that lasting economic disadvantage was related to early teenage childbearing, although clearly it did not apply to all teenage mothers. Although many teenage mothers were not in poverty in later years, "the majority did not fare as well as they probably would have had they been able to postpone parenthood" (Furstenberg, Brooks-Gunn, & Morgan, 1987).

Childbearing alone did not cause failure to complete high school. In the Penn Study some teenagers dropped out of school before they had a child. For these and others who perceived no future benefits from their school experience, childbearing may have been a more satisfying choice in their lives. Nonetheless, the only way for these women to achieve above-poverty-level income in their mid-twenties was to finish high school.

For those who had dropped out of high school, had children, and had little or no employment, the prospects of completing high school—and increasing their earnings—appeared bleak. For the single mothers who finished high school, the timing of the child's birth (before or after completing high school) had little effect on income in their mid-twenties. For those who had delayed all childbearing, income was significantly higher. The teenagers with no children were more likely to have post-high-school education or longer work experience that prepared them for higher earning jobs. Although we cannot predict whether those who were childless in their mid-twenties will earn sufficient income to sustain a family above the poverty level, we can say that their chances appeared better than those who were young single parents.

CONCLUSIONS

The Penn Study was based on the experiences of young black teenagers from a poor urban area where early childbearing was common, although family planning programs and abortion services were available at little or no cost in nearby public health and university medical centers. These were young teenagers, who ranged in age from 13 to 17 and had not finished high school when they enrolled in the study. Divided into three groups based on their pregnancy status at enrollment (never-pregnant teenagers who were using family planning services, teenagers who terminated a first pregnancy, and teenagers pregnant for the first time and intending to deliver), they talked about their perceptions, feelings, and behaviors during the 2-year study. Among the three groups, we examined and compared variables, such as the "wantedness" of pregnancy; factors that affected the decision to terminate or deliver a pregnancy; the influence of family members, boyfriends, and girlfriends; and subsequent pregnancies during the study. We then conducted a community-based project to improve family communication about sexual activity and childbearing, and we explored the attitudes and perceptions of contraception and childbearing in small groups of young male teenagers.

What Did We Learn?

These teenagers came from similar backgrounds and disadvantaged circumstances. Yet many successfully avoided childbearing while others did not. Educational goals and social supports made the difference. Teenagers who avoided childbearing were much more likely to have educational goals beyond high school, believe that their families supported these goals, have occupational goals they believed they could achieve, and believe that their families (particularly their mothers) did not support early childbearing.

Many teenagers used contraception effectively for an extended length of time. The never-pregnant teenagers used family planning services for at least 1 year before they entered the study, and more than three fourths remained nonpregnant during the 2-year study. Nearly 10 years later a sizeable number still were childless.

Teenagers who terminated their first pregnancy were indistinguishable in all major study variables from the never-pregnant teenagers. They had educational goals beyond high school, families who were less likely to support early childbearing, and mothers who encouraged pregnancy termination. After the abortion, they used contraception effectively and had no higher incidence of pregnancy during the next 2 years than teenagers in the other study groups. In the 2 years after the abortion, the group overall fared well in school, gained more part-time work experience, increased their self-esteem, had no deterioration in the measured emotional distress factors, and many clearly indicated that their lives were better compared to the study entry point 2 years earlier.

The delivery-group teenagers, who were pregnant at study enrollment, were no more disadvantaged than the other two groups as indicated by race, residence, schools attended, parents in the household, family size, social class, mother's education, or school grade level. However, the delivery-group teenagers were more likely to live in welfare households, have mothers who started bearing children even earlier in the teen years than the mothers in the never-pregnant and abortion groups, and drop out of school or do poorly in school. Compared to teenagers in the other groups, delivery-group teenagers were less likely to intend to graduate from high school or to have occupational goals. Also, they were more likely to have never worked for pay and to believe they could not achieve their occupational goals. They thought a baby would not affect their education or occupational goals, and they perceived social support for early childbearing, particularly from their mothers.

At the end of the study we found that teenagers who avoided further pregnancy during the study were more alike than not. Delivery-group teenagers *who did not have another pregnancy* typically continued school and had occupational goals. However, teenagers who had more than one pregnancy during the study fell further behind in school and were even less likely to have work experience or goals. These teenagers had even fewer expectations for the future and perceived strong social support for childbearing.

Did These Teenagers Want Pregnancy?

For many of them, the motivation to avoid childbearing derived from believing in future opportunities more than from perceiving early childbearing as undesirable or unwanted. Very few teenagers *intended* pregnancy, but many were ambivalent about wanting pregnancy. Clearly, some teenagers wanted pregnancy more than they wanted to prevent it. The delivery-group teenagers overall were more likely to say they wanted the pregnancy compared to the teenagers in the abortion and never-pregnant groups. Those who became pregnant *after* enrolling in the study were more likely to have indicated at the outset that they wanted pregnancy, compared to the teenagers who did not have pregnancies. Teenagers who had babies clearly indicated that they did *not* want another pregnancy for about 1 year after the birth.

But the majority of the teenagers—pregnant and nonpregnant alike—did not have strong feelings either way. Even in the delivery group the teenagers' indications of how much they "wanted" pregnancy hovered around the midpoint of the scale. All the teenagers in this study lived in communities where early childbearing was widespread and generally accepted, and where many did not value education beyond high school or believe that educational and occupational opportunities were available to them. The teenagers who believed they had opportunities were the ones who did not start childbearing in their early and midteen years.

The three study groups had different perceptions of whether early teenage childbearing would diminish their future lives. Teenagers who delayed childbearing through contraception or abortion clearly believed their opportunities would be curtailed by early motherhood. Even many teenagers who had a child were determined to finish high school and obtain employment, suggesting that they might have delayed childbearing if they had understood the implications of pregnancy before it occurred or could have avoided the "mistakes" that led to pregnancy. However, other teenagers did *not* believe childbearing affected their future, which offered few options as they saw it. For them, school offered little, and they often had no occupational goals that they thought they could achieve.

What Did We Learn About
Changing Attitudes and Behaviors?

When we went into the communities with the Family Involvement Project, we found that mothers of very young teenagers were concerned but guarded about revealing their thoughts on sexual issues and early teenage childbearing. They wondered what they could do or what they would be expected to do about teenage pregnancy. Most had experienced early childbearing themselves, and many had not completed high school and had low-paying jobs or were welfare recipients. Some thought postponing childbearing held no advantages, others had never thought or talked about it, and most (in spite of their concerns) had no idea what they could do about it. Many had not talked with their young daughters about sexual behavior, educational goals, or occupational goals—or about the conflicts between these goals and early childbearing.

In the Family Involvement Project, the mothers engaged in discussions that they felt empowered them to communicate about sexual issues and childbearing with each other and with their children. Some articulated previously unspoken attitudes, and others gained new information that altered their perceptions about early childbearing and sexual behavior. After participating in the group series, both mothers and daughters reported significant changes in the content and amount of communication with each other about these issues. Moreover, in the year after the project, many young, sexually experienced teenagers (from ages 12 to 14) who had prior sexual experience refrained from sex, and the "older" teenagers (ages 15 and 16) were more likely to obtain family planning services if they were sexually active.

We do not suggest that this brief program solved the problems of teenage pregnancy. However, we believe it is one approach that could be incorporated into other program interventions and institutional contexts to help very young teenagers learn more about how early childbearing affects their lives and how to manage sexual behavior. Young teenagers need guidance to learn that they can control their own bodies and that it is appropriate to postpone sex until they are older and better prepared to deal with its consequences.

Unanswered Questions

No study answers all questions, and clinical samples cannot be generalized to all teenagers. Nevertheless, the observed differences within this population at high risk of teenage pregnancy illustrate that it is not a monolithic problem, but one with different causes and consequences for different groups of teenagers. Although these teenagers were black, the common denominator of early childbearing is economic disadvantage. (Pregnancies among middle-class teenagers are more often terminated by abortion.) In the Penn Study the teenagers who gave birth were even poorer than those who avoided childbearing and were more likely to perceive early motherhood as accepted by their families and friends. Whether these or different factors are important in other populations at risk of teenage pregnancy needs further study.

The effects of age on teenage pregnancy also need further study, particularly the differences between young teenagers, who are economically and emotionally unable to support a family, and older teenagers, who have unintended pregnancies. The enormous developmental differences between the early and late teen years must be recognized. Older teenagers need to learn about contraception and obtain contraceptive services *before* they have sex. They need family planning services that are supportive and accessible. Very young teenagers need to know unequivocally that delaying sex is appropriate. They need supportive programs that help them learn about their opportunities and goals in addition to childbearing, and show them how to manage their behavior in all kinds of sexual situations. Young teenagers who become mothers need not only contraceptive services, but also extensive support services to help them complete high school, obtain job training, and value stable relationships as the basis for childbearing.

How different populations view the costs and benefits of early childbearing is an important topic for further study. In the most disadvantaged groups, where poor education may lead to school dropout and young teenagers do not perceive occupational opportunities, the effect of childbearing on later income may not be any greater than the effects of poor education and unskilled jobs or unemployment. Therefore, the purported "costs" of early childbearing may hold no meaning for these young people. We need more information on the actual costs of early childbearing in other populations that have high teenage pregnancy rates.

Further development of community-based programs could add an important element to pregnancy prevention. We have largely ignored the role of families as a resource in preventing teenage childbearing, although most young teenagers are more influenced by their families than by any other factor. Our Family Involvement

Project showed that mothers who participated had hope for their children, but they had little personal experience and no community leaders who spoke out about early teenage pregnancy and its effects on their lives.

RECOMMENDATIONS

What can be done to reduce teenage pregnancies? First, it is essential to recognize that teenage pregnancy is a complex problem that goes far beyond a single solution of contraception (or abstinence). The desirability of pregnancy is embedded in attitudes about sexuality, in social conditions, and in economic opportunities, and is further complicated by the general cognitive and emotional immaturity of young teenagers.

Based on our findings in the Penn Study, the Family Involvement Project, and our study of male teenagers and contraception, we submit the following recommendations for helping to reduce teenage pregnancy.

Family planning programs must reach teenagers before pregnancy occurs. In addition to making convenient, low-cost, supportive services available to teenagers, contraceptive programs must reach out, not just be available. Many teenagers postpone obtaining contraceptive services because they believe pregnancy "won't happen to them." Had the abortion-group teenagers used contraception sooner, many might have prevented pregnancy in the first place. Recently developed school-based programs are one effort to be more accessible to teenagers, but many more community-based programs are needed.

Family planning and sex education for teenagers need to become gender-free. Pregnancy prevention programs need to provide education and services for male teenagers as equally important participants, not simply adjuncts to the process of female contraception. All males, as well as females, must learn about condom use, both for contraception and for the prevention of acquired immunodeficiency syndrome (AIDS) and other sexually transmitted diseases.

Subsidized abortion and follow-up contraceptive services must be available. Terminating unintended pregnancy gave young teenag-

ers a chance to avoid becoming child-mothers and grow into responsible young adults. The number of abortions can be reduced
by reaching teenagers sooner, before pregnancy occurs, with education and contraceptive services.

*The diversity of circumstances of pregnant teenagers must be recog-
nized and met with appropriate assistance for decision making.* In the
Penn Study the abortion-group teenagers almost always were encouraged to terminate the pregnancy by their mothers, whereas
delivery-group teenagers typically gave birth without considering
the decision or discussing it extensively with their families. Family
counseling sessions that discuss *both* options (abortion and delivery), for teenagers who want to deliver the pregnancy as well as
for those who want to terminate it, would benefit many young
teenagers. Older teenagers, who legally are adults, may require
only supportive, accessible services for the pregnancy decision
they have made for themselves. Still other teenagers need confi-
dentiality or protection from harmful or abusive relationships and
skilled clinicians to help them with pregnancy decisions.

*Both male and female teenagers must be taught about responsible sex-
ual behavior and contraception.* Males largely have been ignored in
teenage contraception and childbearing, and many are ignorant of
the issues and feel little or no responsibility for pregnancy or children. Our Family Involvement Project showed that much could be
done by helping mothers talk about sexual issues with their male
and female children. Both males and females need sex education
that starts before sexual activity begins (*junior* high school or
sooner) and includes contraceptive information and discussion of
sexual behavior. Media messages about responsible behavior
might contribute to changing the attitudes of young male teenagers.

*Leaders at all levels must say clearly that sexual activity and childbear-
ing are inappropriate* for very young teenagers, who do not know
how to be good parents because they are children themselves.
Contraceptive and abortion services are needed, but so are messages that help young people understand that they control their
own behavior.

*Community members with leadership abilities should be funded to
work in their communities,* providing services and support. Caring
individuals who know and understand the community can help

others change their attitudes and behaviors. As demonstrated by the Family Involvement Project, the involvement of mothers and young teenagers in discussions about early childbearing changed their communication and made a difference in the teenagers' subsequent sexual behavior.

Our society has to grapple with its acceptance of young teenage pregnancy, whether through encouragement or indifference to social conditions that support it. If the social surroundings discourage pregnancy among young teenagers because it limits their opportunities and makes upward mobility more difficult, young adolescents would have clearer motivation to postpone sexual involvement or use contraception to prevent unintended pregnancy.

Poor education, joblessness, and restricted opportunities also are undeniable forces in early unmarried childbearing. For many disadvantaged teenagers, childbearing reflects—rather than causes—the limitations of their lives. But if we recognize that teenage pregnancy is a complex problem, we then acknowledge that changes are needed on many levels. We need not only programs and services, but also families to talk with their children and communities to care about what their young people do. The major lesson we learned from these teenagers was that those who saw a future for themselves, which they learned in their families, were the ones who avoided teenage childbearing.

REFERENCES

Furstenberg, F. F., Brooks-Gunn, J., & Morgan, S. P. (1987). Adolescent mothers and their children in later life. *Family Planning Perspectives, 19*(4), 142-151.

Iverson, R. R. (1990, December). *Income and employment consequences for African American participants of a family planning clinic.* Unpublished doctoral dissertation, Bryn Mawr College, Bryn Mawr, Pennsylvania.

Measurement Instruments and Assessment Points in the Study

Measure	Time 1 (Enrollment)	Time 2 (6 months)	Time 3 (1 year)	Time 4 (2 years)
Interview questionnaire	X	X	X	X
Analog scales (wanted, planned pregnancy)	X	X	X	X
Sexual Information and Attitudes Questionnaire (SIAQ)	X		X	X
Symptom Checklist (SCL-90) (Derogatis, 1977)	X	X	X	X
Self-esteem scales (Coopersmith, 1967; Rosenberg, 1965)	X	X	X	X
Sex Role Questionnaire (SRQ) (Cvetkovich & Grote, 1980)	X		X	X
Sex Attitude Questionnaire (SAQ) (Cvetkovich & Grote, 1980)	X		X	X
Eysenck Personality Inventory, Junior Version (Eysenck, 1975)				X

APPENDIX B

Statistical Procedures Used

Data analysis used the SAS statistical program procedures (SAS Institute, 1989). Statistical tests were considered significant at the $p < 0.05$ level, with conservative two-tailed interpretation. The categorical interview data were tested for the null hypothesis of no association between the study groups using chi-square tests. Yates's correction for continuity was used with cell sizes less than 5. The equality of means was tested using t statistics. General linear model (GLM) analyses of variance and covariance were conducted for scores from rating scales (e.g., visual analog scales, SCL-90, self-esteem scales) with the pregnancy status groups as the classification variable. When main effects were significant, comparisons among groups were made using the Tukey method. Repeated measures analysis of variance (PROC GLM) was used to study rating scale scores over time (at study enrollment, 1-year, and 2-year follow-up), with the pregnancy status groups as the classification variable.

To assess the independent contributions of significant study variables in classifying pregnancy status groups, the stepwise regression method was used. The stepwise method begins with no variables in the model. F statistics are calculated for each of the independent variables, reflecting the variable's contribution to the model if it is added. At each step the variable with the largest F statistic is added to the model. After the variable is added, any variable already in the model that does not produce a significant F statistic is deleted. The procedure ends when no variable outside the model has a significant F value to enter and all variables in the model have significant F values to remain.

APPENDIX C

Summary of Theoretical Framework With Main Variables for Analysis

1. Background
   a. 2-parent, female-headed household
   b. Welfare household
   c. No. of siblings who are teenage parents
   d. Age
   e. Social class index (education, occupation of parents)
   f. Mother's age at first birth
   g. No. of times moved
   h. Frequency of church attendance
2. Feelings about pregnancy
   a. Wanted
   b. Planned
   c. Happy
3. School and work experience
   a. Attending school/graduated high school/dropout
   b. At school grade level/repeated grades
   c. Any paid work experience
4. Opportunities and goals
   a. Educational goals
   b. Occupational goals
   c. Likelihood of reaching goals
   d. Perceived effect of baby on goals
5. Support of family and friends for early childbearing (individual and summed ratings of mother, father, grandmother, sister, brother, boyfriend, girlfriend)
   a. Happy about baby

    b. Supportive of early childbearing
    c. Support for abortion
    d. Educational goals of family for teen
    e. Closeness to each of the above persons in social network
    f. Mother's role in pregnancy outcome decision
6. Relationships with boyfriend, best girlfriend
    a. Closeness of relationship
    b. Length of relationship
    c. No. of friends with babies
7. Sex information
    a. Sex Information and Attitude Questionnaire (SIAQ) scores
    b. Contraceptive use, "always" vs. other
    c. Information on contraceptive methods
8. Cognitive status
    a. Evaluation of pregnancy risk
    b. Understanding of contraceptive method (self-role in use)
    c. Future orientation (interviewer rating)
    d. See self as mother
9. Psychological status
    a. Self-esteem scores (self-acceptance, assertiveness, family relations)
    b. Symptom Checklist (SCL-90): total and 9 factor scores of emotional distress
    c. Eysenck Personality Inventory (Junior Version)

CLASSIFICATIONS OF PREGNANCY STATUS GROUPS

1. At study enrollment
    a. Delivery, abortion, never-pregnant (and between-group comparisons)
2. At 2-year follow-up
    a. Delivery, abortion, never-pregnant: original status
    b. Pregnancy after enrollment (termed subsequent pregnancy) compared to no subsequent pregnancy, within and between the original status groups

Background Characteristics of the Sample at Enrollment (Percent Distribution)

	Never-Pregnant Group	Abortion Group	Delivery Group	Total
Age				
13	7	5	3	5
14	11	9	17	13
15	33	30	25	28
16	22	30	26	26
17	26	26	30	28
Family structure				
Mother & father	23	19	21	21
Mother & stepfather	18	8	12	13
Mother only	48	60	52	53
Father only	3	2	2	2
Other relatives	7	8	10	8
Other, boyfriend	2	2	4	3
2-parent household				
Yes	23	19	21	21
Female-headed household				
Yes	48	60	52	53
2-adult household	45	36	38	40

	Never-Pregnant Group	Abortion Group	Delivery Group	Total
Contact with father				
In HH	23	19	21	21
Out of household/with contact	58	60	54	57
No contact	8	10	13	11
No father	10	10	12	11
Household size				
Mean ± SD	4.9 ± 2.1	5.0 ± 2.5	5.2 ± 2.3	5.1 ± 2.3
No. of siblings				
Mean ± SD	2.9 ± 1.7	3.0 ± 1.8	3.3 ± 1.8	3.1 ± 1.7
Sister teenage mother				
Yes	26	30	28	28
Welfare status[a]				
Yes	47	58	72	60
No	49	42	22	36
Don't know	5	0	6	4
Medicaid[a]	53	53	76	63
Ratio working adults to all household[b]	.21	.17	.17	.18
Ratio working adults to adults in household[c]	.50	.43	.46	.46
Hollingshead social class[d] **(2 factor index)**				
1	3	1	3	2
2	2	5	3	3
3	13	14	10	12
4	41	32	28	33
5 (low)	42	49	55	49
Mother's age 1st child[a]				
≤ 14-15	11	17	33	21
16-17	43	35	33	37
18-19	24	16	14	18
20-24	13	23	16	17
≥ 25	10	9	4	7
$X \pm SD$[b]	18.9 ± 4.7	18.6 ± 3.8	17.4 ± 3.3	18.2 ± 3.96

	Never-Pregnant Group	Abortion Group	Delivery Group	Total
Mother's education				
< HS	54	45	47	49
HS	36	39	47	41
> HS	10	16	6	10
Mother's occupation[b]				
Unskilled, unemployed	40	48	59	49
Technical, clerical	39	32	27	32
Managerial, professional	10	14	5	10
No information	10	7	9	10
Moved in last 5 years				
0	58	44	56	53
1-2	16	45	30	36
≥ 3	7	10	15	10
Birthplace				
Phila.	92	88	88	90
Phila. area	2	8	4	4
Other	7	3	8	6
In school[a]				
Yes	88	95	81	87
Graduated HS	10	3	2	5
No, dropped	2	1	17	8
School grade				
≤ 9	30	21	30	27
10	21	33	33	29
11	18	22	21	20
12	32	24	16	23
Grade level[c]				
At level	79	68	61	69
Below level	16	28	36	28
Above level	6	2	3	4
School marks[b]				
A	6	6	5	6
B	39	35	23	32
C	41	50	45	45
D	9	7	11	9
F	4	2	15	8

	Never-Pregnant Group	*Abortion Group*	*Delivery Group*	*Total*
Religion				
Protestant	68	66	64	66
Catholic	11	15	10	12
Other (incl. Muslim)	10	4	11	9
None	10	15	15	13

Significant differences between groups (chi-square test):

[a]$p < 0.001$

[b]$p < 0.01$

[c]$p < 0.05$

[d]Based on mother or the higher of 2-parent households

Additional Statistical Tables

Table E.1 Self-Esteem Scores for the Three Main Study Groups at Enrollment and 1-Year and 2-Year Follow-ups

| | *Time 1 Status* | | | |
	NP	*TA*	*DEL*	*P Value (ANOVA)*
Self-Acceptance (Rosenberg)				
Enrollment	8.1 (1.97)	7.88 (1.9)	7.88 (1.9)	NS
1 year	8.42 (1.72)	8.59 (1.4)	8.18 (1.7)	NS
2 years	8.48 (1.89)	8.68 (1.7)	7.98 (1.7)	.03

NOTES: Higher scores = more esteem, score range 0-10
Time effect: NS
Time * group: NS
Tukey tests: NS
NS = not significant

| | *Time 1 Status* | | | |
	NP	TA	DEL	P Value (ANOVA)
Family Scale (Coopersmith)				
Enrollment	3.99 (2.1)	3.83 (2.2)	4.43 (1.8)	NS
1 year	4.53 (1.9)	4.18 (2.1)	3.94 (2.1)	.02
2 years	4.62 (.19)	4.53 (2.1)	3.85 (2.0)	.01

NOTES: Higher scores = more esteem, score range 0-7
Time effect: $p = 0.06$
Time * group: $p = 0.0001$
Tukey tests: T4, NP versus DEL, $p < 0.05$
NS = not significant

| | *Time 1 Status* | | | |
	NP	TA	DEL	P Value (ANOVA)
Assertiveness (Coopersmith)				
Enrollment	3.63 (1.2)	3.47 (1.3)	3.44 (1.2)	NS
1 year	3.85 (1.0)	3.78 (1.1)	3.63 (1.2)	NS
2 years	3.83 (1.2)	3.98 (1.0)	3.56 (1.2)	.05

NOTES: Values are mean scores with standard deviations.
Higher scores = more esteem, score range 0-5
Time effect: NS
Time * group: NS
Tukey tests: NS
NS = not significant

Table E.2 SCL Factors at Enrollment, 1 Year, and Endpoint for the Total Sample, $N = 326$

Factor	Enrollment	1 Year	2 Years
Somatization	.71 (.58)	.56 (.50)	.62 (.61)
Obsessive-compulsive	.84 (.67)	.80 (.61)	.72 (.67)
Initial sensitivity	.94 (.69)	.84 (.65)	.72 (.63)
Depression	.88 (.60)	.80 (.55)	.76 (.59)
Anxiety	.64 (.59)	.56 (.56)	.53 (.59)
Hostility	.92 (.78)	.79 (.76)	.71 (.74)
Phobic anxiety	.59 (.67)	.46 (.53)	.41 (.55)
Paranoid ideation	1.03 (.78)	.96 (.72)	.87 (.77)
Psychoticism	.60 (.59)	.53 (.54)	.48 (.55)
Total (GSI)	.80 (.53)	.70 (.48)	.66 (.54)

NOTES: Values are mean scores with standard deviations.
3-group ANOVA at each timepoint showed no significant differences.
Repeated measures ANOVA: time effect significant for all factors.
Pairwise comparisons of factors between groups (Tukey) not significant at any timepoint.

Table E.3 Eysenck Personality Inventory Scores

	Time 1 Status		
Endpoint	NP ($N = 107$)	TA ($N = 88$)	DEL ($N = 107$)
Extroversion	15.74 (3.8)	14.97 (3.6)	14.75 (3.3)
Neuroticism	14.94 (15.3)	12.88 (5.4)	13.90 (8.99)

NOTES: Values are mean scores with standard deviations.
Higher scores indicate greater extroversion, neuroticism.
3-group ANOVA showed no significant differences.
Normative data collected from a black school student sample showed the mean (SD) for extroversion was 15.99 (3.68) and for neuroticism was 13.33 (5.01) (Eysenck & Eysenck, 1975).

Table E.4 Sex Information and Attitude Questionnaire (SIAQ)

	Status at Enrollment			
Time				
Enrollment	22.39 (4.23)	22.09 (3.58)	20.71 (3.81)	.02
1 year	23.01 (3.44)	22.47 (3.49)	21.43 (4.44)	.05
2 years	23.31 (3.81)	23.29 (3.30)	22.44 (3.94)	NS

NOTES: Tukey tests: T1, NP versus DEL, $p < 0.05$; no others significant.
Time effect: $p = 0.0001$
Time * group: NS

Table E.5 Effects of Selected Study Variables on Pregnancy Outcome Decision to Abort or Deliver at Study Enrollment (in stepwise discriminant analysis)

Variable[a]	*Abortion Versus Delivery*
Mother happy about baby	.25[b]
Number of friends with baby	.03
Model R^2	.27

[a]Other Time 1 variables entered in the analysis: pregnancy "wanted," mother supports childbearing, total support for childbearing, attending school, closeness to boyfriend, length of relationship with boyfriend, siblings having teenage pregnancies.
[b]Partial R^2

Table E.6 Effects of Significant Study Variables on Subsequent Pregnancy That Occurred in the 2-Year Study Period for the Total Sample and in Each Study Group (in stepwise discriminant analysis)

| | | Enrollment Group | | |
| | Total Sample | Never Pregnant | Abortion | Delivery |
Variable[a]				
Contraceptive use in year 2 (T4)[b]	.12[c]		.22[c]	.15[c]
SCL depression factor (T1)	.03	.11[c]		
Pregnancy "wanted" (T1)	.02	.05		
Closeness to boyfriend (T1)	.03			
Negative educational change (T4)	.02			
Age (T1)		.06		
Social class index (T1)		.05		
Model R^2	.19	.24	.22	.15

[a]Other variables entered in the analysis: age (T4), below school grade (T4), school dropout (T4), self-esteem (T4).

[b]T4 is the 2-year follow-up assessment; T1 is at enrollment.

[c]Partial R^2

Table E.7 Effects of Significant Study Variables on Abortion or Delivery of Pregnancies That Occurred in the 2-Year Study Period, for the Total Subsequent Pregnancy Group and in Each Study Group (in stepwise discriminant analysis)

	Enrollment Group			
Variable[a]	*All Subsequent Pregnancies* (*n* = 84)	*Never Pregnant* (*n* = 23)	*Abortion* (*n* = 25)	*Delivery* (*n* = 36)
Negative educational change (T4)[b]	.09[c]			.28[c]
Contraceptive use year 2 (T4)	.07	.27[c]		
Likelihood of occupational goals				.20
SCL depression factor				.18
Model R^2	.15	.27		.52

[a]Other variables entered in the analysis: age (T4); below school grade (T4); school dropout (T4); social class index (T1); closeness to boyfriend (T1); pregnancy "wanted" (T1); self-esteem (T4).
[b]T4 is the 2-year follow-up assessment; T1 is at enrollment.
[c]Partial R^2

APPENDIX F

1	2	3		6	7	8	9	10	11	12	13	14	15	16

| 0 | 1 | | | | | | | | | | | | | |

Card Number / Visit No. / Patient Number / Group No. / Age / Day of Year / Year

Name _____

Group _____ Age _____

Date _____ Study # _____

Interviewer _____

Social Security # _____

I. LIVING SITUATION

1. How many people live in your household? (include subject) _____ (18–19)

*2. List the relationship to you and age of each person in your household now:

Relationship	Age
(20–21)	(22–23)
(24–25)	(26–27)
(28–29)	(30–31)
(32–33)	(34–35)
(36–37)	(38–39)
(40–41)	(42–43)
(44–45)	(46–47)
(48–49)	(50–51)
(52–53)	(54–55)
(56–57)	(58–59)

*3. List any parents, siblings or children not listed above:

Relationship	Age	Residence (City)	Length of time since last contacted
(60)	(61–62)	(63)	(64)
(65)	(66–67)	(68)	(69)
(70)	(71–72)	(73)	(74)
(75)	(76–77)	(78)	(79)

1	2		6	7	8
0	2				

Card Number / Patient Number

*4. Where were you born?
City & State: _____ (10)

5. Date of birth: (month, day, year)_____
Day of year _____ Year _____
(11–13) (14–15)

6. How many times have you moved in the past 5 years? (Code 0–7, 8 = ≥ 8) _____ (16)

II. SCHOOL

7. Are you attending school now?
   1 ☐ yes
   2 ☐ no, dropped
   3 ☐ no, graduated
   17 _

8. What is your present school grade (If dropped school, record last grade attended) _____
   18 _
   19 _

9. a) Age/Grade relationship (If not in school, indicate situation when last attended school):
   at grade level ☐1
   repeated grade(s) ☐2
   skipped grade(s) ☐3
   b) Repeated grade(s), number of times _____
   Skipped grade(s), number of times _____
   20 _
   21 _
   22 _

10. Do you plan to graduate from high school?
    Certain .... ☐1
    Probably .... ☐2
    About 50/50 chance .... ☐3
    Small chance .... ☐4
    No .... ☐5
    23 _

11. What grades have you usually had in school during the past year?
    High (A average) ...... ☐1
    Good (B average) ...... ☐2
    Average (C average) .... ☐3
    Poor (D average) ...... ☐4
    Failing .... ☐5
    24 _

12. What education do you want to have? (Highest grade, type of training beyond high school)
    Partial High School .... ☐1
    High School diploma .... ☐2
    College .... ☐3
    Professional degree (M.A., Ph.D., etc.) ...... ☐4
    Technical training (nurse, secretarial school, computer training, mechanical training army, etc.) .... ☐5
    "Whatever I want" .... ☐6
    "Parents don't care" .... ☐7
    Other .... ☐8
    "Don't know, can't say" .... ☐0
    25 _

13. What education do your parents want you to have? (Highest grade, type of training beyond high school)
    _____ (Same List as #12)
    26 _

14. How much would having a baby while you are in high school change your educational plans?
    Very much .... ☐1
    Much .... ☐2
    Somewhat .... ☐3
    A little .... ☐4
    Not at all .... ☐5
    27 _

page 2

WORK

How many paying jobs have you had?
(Code 0–7, 8 = ≥ 8) _____ 28 _____

What were they and how long did you work at each?

Job	Length of time job held	(Job)	(Time)
_____	_____	29 ___	33 ___
_____	_____	30 ___	34 ___
_____	_____	31 ___	35 ___
_____	_____	32 ___	36 ___

What kind of work do you want to do when you finish school (include homemaker)? _____ 37 ___

Who/what was important to you in choosing this work? (Probe for why you chose it; influenced by what persons, experiences?)

38 ___

ne, can't say . . . □0	Teacher . . . . . . □4
ol . . . . □1	Work experience . □5
st . . . . □2	Friend . . . . . . □6
r relative . . . . . □3	Other . . . . □7

What do you think chances are you will actually do this job?

	About 50/50 □3
mely likely □1	Not very likely □4
what likely □2	Not at all likely □5

39 ___

ECONOMIC FACTORS

20. After your first child is born, do you expect to:
   Be a full time homemaker . . . □1
   Attend school . . . . □2
   Work full time . . . . □3
   Work part time . . . . □4
   Other . . . . □5

40 ___

* 21. What do you expect to be your *main* occupation when you are 30?

_____ 41 ___

22. What do you see yourself doing two years from now?
   Homemaker . . . . . □1   Working + Baby . . . □5
   School . . . . □2   Baby . . . . □6
   School + Baby . . . □3   Nothing . . . . □7
   Working . . . . . . □4   Other . . . . □8
                              Don't know . . . . . . □0

42 ___

23. What is the most important thing in your life?

43 ___

Don't know, can't say . □0   Family . . . . □4
Baby . . . . □1   Health . . . . □5
Baby + Boyfriend . . . □2   Money . . . . □6
Education . . . . □3   Other . . . . □7

Where would you go for each of the following services or items? Would you have to pay?

Service/Item	Where Obtained	Payment (1) Yes	(2) No	(0) No info. or Incorrect info.	Obtained	Payment
eral health ck-up	_____	□	□	□	44 ___	61 ___
up for birth control methods	_____	□	□	□	45 ___	62 ___
gnancy test	_____	□	□	□	46 ___	63 ___
h control pills	_____	□	□	□	47 ___	64 ___
doms	_____	□	□	□	48 ___	65 ___
(IUD)	_____	□	□	□	49 ___	66 ___
m	_____	□	□	□	50 ___	67 ___
pital & doctor care for gnancy & delivery	_____	□	□	□	51 ___	68 ___
lth ck-ups for your baby	_____	□	□	□	52 ___	69 ___
t trimester abortion	_____	□	□	□	53 ___	70 ___
Program (food for baby)	_____	□	□	□	54 ___	71 ___
care for baby	_____	□	□	□	55 ___	72 ___
ond trimester abortion	_____	□	□	□	56 ___	73 ___
nseling for a pregnancy did not want	_____	□	□	□	57 ___	74 ___
treatments	_____	□	□	□	58 ___	75 ___
training	_____	□	□	□	59 ___	76 ___
t money for yourself & baby	_____	□	□	□	60 ___	77 ___

25. This is a list of the ways in which medical bills are paid. When you had your *last* medical visit, in which of these ways was your bill paid?
   Your (or your boyfriend's) own money ..... ☐1
   Parents or other relatives .... ☐2
   Medical card (Welfare) .... ☐3
   Insurance .... ☐4
   Other govt. (state, local, military) .... ☐5
   Some other way (describe) .... ☐6

   78 ___

26. Give purpose of last medical visit:
   Gynecological .... ☐1
   FPS (BC) .... ☐2
   FPS (TA) .... ☐3
   Private M.D. (Exam) ...... ☐4
   Other .... ☐5

   79 ___

	1	2		6	7	8
	0	3				

Card Number ... Patient Number

27. Which of these pay for food or rent in your household at this time? (check all that apply)
   (*Note:* Code up to 6 answers)
   Self .... ☐01   Other family members
   Mother .... ☐02   or friends ..... ☐08
   Father .... ☐03   Social Security ... ☐09
   DPA (Welfare) .. ☐04   Other disability ... ☐10
   Stepparent(s) ... ☐05   Other sources
   Grandparent(s) .. ☐06   (Describe) ..... ☐11
   Your boyfriend .. ☐07   _____
                           Don't know ..... ☐12

   {10 ___
   {11 ___
   {12 ___
   {13 ___
   {14 ___
   {15 ___
   {16 ___
   {17 ___
   {18 ___
   {19 ___
   {20 ___
   {21 ___

28. Does anyone in your household receive money from DPA (welfare) now?
   Yes ☐1   No ☐2   Don't know ☐3

   22 ___

29. Do you expect you (or your mother) will get money from DPA for the baby when your first baby is born?
   Yes ☐1   No ☐2   Don't know ☐3

   23 ___

V. RELATIONSHIPS

*30. How would you describe yourself? (Tell me something about who and what you are):

   24 ___

31. Are both your natural parents living?
   ☐1 Yes
   ☐2 No (Mother: year deceased _____)
   ☐3 No (Father: year deceased _____)
   ☐4 (Mother living; unsure about father)

   25 ___

*32. How do you rate the following relationships at this time? (*Subject places a mark on each line*)

   Not Close

   L_____ (Mother)   (26-28)
   L_____ (Father)   (29-31)
   L_____ (Boyfriend)   (32-34)
   L_____ (Best girlfriend)   (35-37)
   L_____ (The most important person not already listed. (38-40)
   Who?)
        (Person)

*33. Describe as much as you can about the person you would like to be most like: _____
                                    (Person)

	All the time	A Lot	Mod. amt.	Once in a while	Never	NA
*34. Do you feel your mother understands you?	☐	☐	☐	☐	☐	☐
*35. Do you argue with your mother?	☐	☐	☐	☐	☐	☐
*36. Does your mother like your girlfriends?	☐	☐	☐	☐	☐	☐
*37. Does she like your present boyfriend?	☐	☐	☐	☐	☐	☐
*38. Do you talk about sensitive subjects with your mother?	☐	☐	☐	☐	☐	☐
*39. Do you talk about sex with your mother?	☐	☐	☐	☐	☐	☐
*40. Do you want to be like your mother?	☐	☐	☐	☐	☐	☐

*41. How would you describe living with your family?

If you found out you were pregnant now (when you found out you were pregnant), who is the first person you would tell (told)?
Boyfriend .... □1 Sister....... □5
Girlfriend .... □2 No one ...... □6
Mother...... □3 Other; .... □7
Father ...... □4 (who) _____

52 __

Who came with you the first time you came here for your (pregnancy, abortion, birth control) services?
Boyfriend .... □1 Sister....... □5
Girlfriend .... □2 No one ...... □6
Mother...... □3 Other; .... □7
Father ...... □4 (who) _____

53 __

How old were you when you started going out with boys? {54 __ {55 __

How long have you been going with your present boyfriend?
Several times .. □1 1-2 years ..... □5
1-3 months ... □2 > 2 years ..... □6
4-6 months ... □3 No boyfriend now □7
7-12 months .. □4

56 __

If respondent has no boyfriend now, ASK: "Why did you break up with your boyfriend?"

NO BOYFRIEND, SKIP TO QUESTION 57.
NO BOYFRIEND, Code Cols. 58-71 0's.

Do you expect that your present boyfriend is the person you will marry?
Almost certain . □1 Unlikely ...... □4
Fairly likely ... □2 No chance ..... □5
50/50 chance .. □3

58 __

What is your boyfriend like as a person?

*49. Describe for me what your boyfriend means to you:

60 __

50. How old is your present boyfriend? (in years) _____ {61 __ {62 __

51. Is he attending school now?
1 □yes
2 □no; dropped
3 □no; graduated

63 __

57 __

52. What is his present (last attended) school grade? _____ {64 __ {65 __

53. What further education or training does he want to have?
Nothing further.................... □1
Graduate from H.S. .... □2
College (describe) .... □3

66 __

Other training (technical, skills) .... □4

Boyfriend doesn't know.............. □5
Respondent doesn't know his plans .... □6

*54. Does he have a job now?
Yes, full time .... □1
(describe) _____

67 __

Yes, part time...................... □2
(describe) _____

(Descrip.)
68 __

No .... □3

*55. What job does he want to have at age 25?
_____

69 __

59 __

He doesn't know .... □9
Respondent doesn't know............... □0

56. At what age does your boyfriend want to marry? (in years) _____ {70 __ {71 __
He doesn't know .... □85
Married now .... □86
Never .... □87
Respondent doesn't know............. □00

```
        1  2   6  7  8
       ┌──┬──┬──┬──┬──┐
       │0 │4 │  │  │  │
       └──┴──┴──┴──┴──┘
        Card        Patient
        Number      Number
```

VI. FAMILY FORMATION

57. At what age do you want to marry? (in years) _____
  Never   ☐ 87
  Married now ☐ 88   {10
  (date of marriage) _____   {11
  Don't know ☐ 00

58. At what age do you intend to have your first child?
  (in years) _____
  Never   ☐ 87   {12
  Pregnant now ☐ 88   {13
  Don't know ☐ 00

59. How likely is it that you would have a child before you marry?
  Certain . . . . ☐ 1
  Fairly likely . . . . ☐ 2
  About 50/50 chance . . . . ☐ 3   14 __
  < 50/50 chance . . . . ☐ 4
  Almost no chance . . . . ☐ 5

60. What do you see as the advantages and disadvantages of getting married if you become pregnant?
  (Interviewer: INDICATE RANK ORDER)

          (Advant.)
          15 __
          16 __
          17 __

          (Disadvant.)
          18 __
          19 __
          20 __

          Advantages   Disadvantages
(Code first 3 responses in each category)
Social reasons   __ 1   Not ready, too young __ 1
More adult   __ 2   No love   __ 2
Better for baby __ 3   Parents opposed   __ 3
Money   __ 4   Money   __ 4
Independence   __ 5   Loss of freedom   __ 5
Sense of family __ 6   Other   __ 6
Other   __ 7   Can't say, none   __ 0
Can't say, none __ 0

61. What are your reasons for having a child before getting married?
  (Interviewer: INDICATE RANK ORDER)

(Code first 3 responses)
  Can't say, none . . . . __ 0
  Don't need to be married . . . . __ 1
  Boyfriend opposed . . . . __ 2   21 __
  Parents opposed . . . . __ 3
  No love . . . . __ 4   22 __
  Can't (e.g., boyfriend away) . . . __ 5
  No boyfriend . . . . __ 6   23 __
  Other . . . . __ 7

62. What age was your mother when her *first* child was born?   {24
  (in years) _____   {25

63. How many of your sisters and brothers have children?

Relationship	Age now	Age at birth of first child
(26)	(27–28)	
(29)	(30–31)	
(32)	(33–34)	
(35)	(36–37)	

1 – Sister
2 – Brother

64. Has anyone in your family had an abortion?
  No ☐ 0   Yes ☐ (Code number, 8 ≥ 8)

Relationship	Age at abortion
		38 __

65. How many of your close friends have a baby? _____   39 __
  (Code number, 8 ≥ 8)

66. How many of your close friends do *not* have a baby? _____   40 __
  (Code number, 8 ≥ 8)

67. How many of your friends do you know have had an abortion?   41 __
  _____ (Code number, 8 ≥ 8)

68. How do you think each of the following persons would feel about your having a baby *now*?

	(5) Very happy	(4) Somewhat happy	(3) Neutral	(2) Somewhat unhappy	(1) Very unhappy	
Mother	☐	☐	☐	☐	☐	42
Father	☐	☐	☐	☐	☐	43
Boyfriend	☐	☐	☐	☐	☐	44
Best girlfriend	☐	☐	☐	☐	☐	45
Yourself	☐	☐	☐	☐	☐	46

(Note: If answer is "Don't know," leave blank and code 0)

69. When you have your baby (if you had a baby now) what kinds of help do you think each of these people would actually give? (Check all that apply)

	Place to live	Money	Child Care	Advice	Nothing
Mother	(47)	(48)	(49)	(50)	
Father	(51)	(52)	(53)	(54)	
Boyfriend	(55)	(56)	(57)	(58)	
Boyfriend's parents	(59)	(60)	(61)	(62)	

(Code Blank = 0, Check = 1)

page 6

When you have your baby (if you had a baby now), who will pay rent and food money for you and the baby? (Check all that apply)
____DPA (welfare)   ____Boyfriend
____Mother   ____Boyfriend's parent
____Father   ____Other (describe)
____Self

63 ____

What advantages and problems do you see in having a baby now? (List as many as possible. INTERVIEWER: INDICATE RANK ORDER)

(Advant.)
64 ____
65 ____
66 ____

(Problems)
67 ____
68 ____
69 ____

Advantages	Problems
de first 3 responses in each category)

nt baby . . . . ____1   Education . . . . ___1
rfriend wants baby . ____2   Money . . . . ___2
n family . . . . ____3   Not ready, too young . ___3
apendence . . . . . . ____4   Tied down . . . . . . ___4
re adult . . . . ____5   Education & money . ___5
inst abortion . . . . ____6   All the above . . . . ___6
er . . . . ____7   Other . . . . ___7
't say . . . . ____0   Can't say . . . . . . ___0

Tell me something about how you see yourself as a mother:

70 ____

't say   ☐0 All negative ☐
ue, few things   ☐1 Limited mix ☐
eotypically feminine ☐2 Overview, objective, realistic ☐

SEXUAL AND CONTRACEPTIVE

Menstrual

At what age did you have your first menstrual period?

Have not had one ☐00

71 ____
72 ____

---

*74. What do you remember, what were your feelings about your first period? (Record as much detail as possible):

73 ____

75. After your periods began, did your relationship with your mother change?
   Yes ☐1   No ☐2   Not certain ☐0
If yes, how?

74 ____

Closer ☐1   Farther ☐2   N.A. ☐0

75 ____

76. During the past *year*, how often did your period come? (count first day to first day):
  Less than 21 days . . . . . . ☐1
  21-35 days . . . . ☐2
  35-60 days . . . . ☐3
  2-5 months . . . . ☐4
  6 months or more . . . . . . ☐5
  No regular pattern . . . . . . ☐6
  No periods in past year . . . ☐7
  Other . . . . ☐8
  (describe) _____

76 ____

1	2	6	7	8
0	5			

Card Number   Patient Number

77. During the past year, have you regularly experienced any of these symptoms at or around the time of your period?

	(1) Usually	(2) Sometimes	(0) Never	
Mild discomfort or cramps	☐	☐	☐	10 ____
Severe discomfort or cramps	☐	☐	☐	11 ____
Increased tiredness	☐	☐	☐	12 ____
Nausea	☐	☐	☐	13 ____
Headaches	☐	☐	☐	14 ____
Increased irritability	☐	☐	☐	15 ____
Depression (feeling blue or unhappy) . . .	☐	☐	☐	16 ____
Increased pimples	☐	☐	☐	17 ____
Weight gain/fluid retention	☐	☐	☐	18 ____
Breast tenderness	☐	☐	☐	19 ____
Other (describe) _____	☐	☐	☐	20 ____

78. What medications do you take to relieve any discomforts or symptoms of your menstrual period? (describe)

21 ___

N/A .... □0   Non-prescription
Aspirin, Tylenol . □1   (Midol, Pamprin) ... □3
Prescription .... □2   Folk remedy
                         (hot tea, etc.) ..... □4

79. How often do you stay in bed because of these menstrual symptoms?
Every month ...... □1
Most months ...... □2
Few times a year .... □3
Never .... □4

22 ___

80. Did your mother have discomforts or symptoms with her menstrual period?
No .... □1
Yes .... □2
(describe):

23 ___

Don't know .... □0
Other .... □3

81. Did you ever talk with your parents about:

	Yes (1)	No (2)	*Age when first talked about it
How your body changes during adolescence	□	□	24 ___ 25-26 ___
The menstrual cycle	□	□	27 ___ 28-29 ___
How pregnancy occurs	□	□	30 ___ 31-32 ___
Methods of birth control	□	□	33 ___ 34-35 ___
Where to get birth control methods	□	□	36 ___ 37-38 ___
How to use birth control methods	□	□	39 ___ 40-41 ___
Venereal disease (VD)	□	□	42 ___ 43-44 ___
The subject of abortion	□	□	45 ___ 46-47 ___

*If no, code 00
If yes, code age

82. Did you talk about these subjects
Only with your mother .... □1
Only with your father .... □2
With both of them, but always at different times .... □3
With both of them together, at least some times .... □4
Other (describe) .... □5

48 ___

Never talked about this subject with parents .. □0

83. Would you say the average female is *most* likely to become pregnant if she has intercourse:
Right before her period begins .... □1
During her period .... □2
About 2 weeks before her period begins..... □3
Right after her period .... □4
Don't know .... □0

4 ___

84. If you have sex about once a week without using any birth control, what are the chances of getting pregnant in one year?
Extremely likely .... □1
Fairly likely .... □2
A little likely .... □3
Not at all likely .... □4

5 ___

85. Do you intend to have a child sometime in the next two years?
Pregnant now .... □1
Yes (not pregnant now). ..... □2
No .... □3
Uncertain .... □0

5 ___

86. When you have sex, how much do you worry about getting pregnant?
Not at all .... □1
Somewhat .... □2
A lot .... □3
All the time .... □4

5 ___

87. What did (do) you think you would do if you got pregnant?
Didn't know .... □0
Get an abortion .... □1
Have a baby .... □2
Never thought about it ...... □3
Other (describe) .... □4

5 ___

88. How old were you when you first used a contraceptive method? (Include using a condom, if partner used condoms).
Age ___
(If used contraceptive, code age, if not, code reason)
If respondent never used a method, ask why she never started using birth control (*PROBE*)
Don't know, no reason .... □31
Fear health, side effects .... □32
Didn't know where to obtain ...... □33
Didn't plan sex .... □34
Other .... □38
IF RESPONDENT NEVER USED A METHOD, SKIP TO
QUESTION #104 (Code Cols. 54-73 0's)

5 ___
5 ___

89. What was the first method you used?
None, N/A .... □0   IUD .... □4
Pill .... □1   Diaphragm .... □5
Foam .... □2   Withdrawal ...... □6
Condom ...... □3   Suppositories ...... □7
                     Other .... □8

5 ___

How long was this after your first intercourse experience? (months) _____ — 57. / 58.

What happened to make you start using a birth control method when you did? (record all reasons given)

59. ____

96. Have you had (did you have) any other worries about this method?

No worries .... □0	Pregnancy ... □5
Cancer .... □1	Sterilization .. □6
Heart problems ...... □2	Smoking .... □7
Weight gain .... □3	Other ..... □8
Effects on unborn child .. □4	

65 ____

97. Do these worries affect how you use your method?

NA, no worries .... □0	Stopped .... □4
No .... □1	New method . □5
More careful .... □2	Other ..... □6
Afraid to use, don't take regularly .... □3	

66 ____

98. Are you using a birth control method now?
No; pregnant .... □0
No; not having sex .... □1
*No; because: .... □2

67 ____

From what person or where did you learn about the first birth control method that you used? (1 answer only)

Books .... □01	HUP outreach in school
Girlfriend ..... □02	(if named specifically) □06
Boyfriend .... □03	Counselor, social worker,
TV .... □04	nurse in clinic ..... □07
Classes in school . □05	Doctor .... □08
	Mother .... □10
	Other relative ...... □11
	(who) _____

60. / 61.

Yes; same method .... □3
**Yes; another method, because: .. □4

How hard/easy is it for you to get supplies of this method when you need to?
Very hard .... □1
Somewhat hard .... □2
Somewhat easy .... □3
Very easy .... □4
Name the things that make it hard or easy.

62 ____

*NA □0	**Name of method
Side effects □1	NA .... □0
Dr. medical □2	Pill .... □1
Mother □3	Foam .... □2
	Condom ...... □3
	IUD .... □4
	Diaphragm ..... □5
	Withdrawal .... □6
	Suppositories ... □7
	Other .... □8

* 68 ____

** 69 ____

Did you have (have you had) any side effects with this method?

None .... □0	Bleeding ..... □4
Cramps .... □1	Headaches ..... □5
Nausea .... □2	Other .... □6
Weight gain ..... □3	

63 ____

99. Did you or your boyfriend use any form of birth control the last time you had sex?

No (respondent is pregnant) ..... □0
No (respondent is not pregnant) ... □1
Yes, pill .... □2
Yes, foam .... □3
Yes, condom .... □4
Yes, IUD .... □5
Yes, diaphragm .... □6
Yes, withdrawal .... □7
Yes, suppositories .... □8

70 ____

What did you do about these side effects?

NA, none .... □0
Nothing .... □1
Dr., prof. help .... □2
Mother .... □3
Girlfriend .... □4
Stopped method ...... □5
New method .... □6
Other .... □7

64 ____

100. When you have used birth control, did your boyfriend know about it?
Not certain .... □0
Yes .... □1
No .... □2
Other (describe) .... □3

71 ____

101. How likely do you think the birth control method you are (were) using will keep you from getting pregnant?

Extremely likely .... □1
Fairly likely .... □2
A little likely ...... □3
Not at all likely ..... □4

Reasons for answer:

72 —

102. What do you have to do to have your method work properly?

Don't
know □0
Take/use
properly □1
Nothing □2

1	2		6	7	8
0	6				

Card
Number

Patient
Number

103. When you are (were) using the pill, how often each month would you forget to take a pill?

Never .... □1   5 or >times.......... □4
1-2 times.. □2   NA, never used the pill ... □0
3-4 times.. □3

10 —

104. Do you know how to use any of the following:

	(1) No	(2) Uncertain	(3) Yes, but have never used	(4) Yes, have used	
Condom	□	□	□	□	11 —
Foam	□	□	□	□	12 —
Diaphragm	□	□	□	□	13 —
Coil (IUD)	□	□	□	□	14 —

105. Did you ever become pregnant while using a birth control method?

No; became pregnant, but not using a method ... □1
No; never pregnant .... □2
Yes; what do you think happened?
(explain top of next column)
Missed pill .... □3
Method failed ...... □4
Don't know .... □5

15 —

106. Would you ever have (have you had) an abortion?

Uncertain .... □0
No; why not? .... □1

Yes; have had an abortion .... □2
Yes; have not had an abortion, but would have one if . □3

16

107. If you did not want a child and knew you could not get an abortion, would you do anything differently to avoid pregnancy?

Uncertain □0   No □1

If yes; what?

Better contraceptive use,
more careful .... □2   Different method ... □4
No sex .... □3   Get sterilized ..... □5

17

108. How much does (did) your boyfriend encourage using birth control?

Always (he asks about it when having sex or uses it) .... □1
Sometimes .... □2
Rarely .... □3
Never (he never mentions using birth control) .... □4
He opposes using birth control .... □5

18

109. How old were you when you first had sex with a boyfriend?

___

What did this mean to you?

Can't say .... □0
Felt more grown up .. □1
Felt closer .... □2
Didn't like, negative .. □3

{19
{20

21

How many times have you ever had sex?
- Never .... □0
- 1 only .... □1
- 2–5 times .... □2
- 6–10 times ...... □3
- >10 times .... □4

How many times did you have sex during the past *month*?
- NA/none .... □0
- 1–5 times ...... □1
- 6–10 times ..... □2
- >10 times ...... □3

How would you describe sex with your present (last) boyfriend?
- NA .... □0
- Very pleasurable .... □1
- Somewhat pleasurable ...... □2
- OK .... □3
- Somewhat unpleasant ...... □4
- Very unpleasant .... □5

What was the main reason you started having sex when you did?

Could you describe for me in your own words what you *like* and what you *dislike* about having sex? (INTERVIEWER: INDICATE RANK ORDER)

first 2 responses in each category)

Like		Dislike	
t say 0		Can't say 0
e description 1		Vague description ... 1
tional feeling 2		Physical 2
cal feeling ... 3		Feeling used 3
se 4		It's not much fun ... 4
free will ... 5		Being forced 5
r 6		Other 6

22 ___
23 ___
24 ___
25 ___
26 ___
27 ___
28 ___ (Dislike)
29 ___

VIII. FAMILY BACKGROUND

115. List the present occupational status and last school grade *completed* for *all* members of the present household. (Record all information, code six oldest only).

Relationship	Present occupation	Last school grade completed
(30–31)	(32)	(33)
(34–35)	(36)	(37)
(38–39)	(40)	(41)
(42–43)	(44)	(45)
(46–47)	(48)	(49)
(50–51)	(52)	(53)

116. List the present occupational status and last school grade *completed* for parent(s) not listed in household.

*Relationship	Present occupation	Last school grade completed
(54)	(55)	(56)
(57)	(58)	(59)

*mother = 1, father = 2

117. What is your religion?
- Protestant .... □1
  - (denomination) _____
- Catholic .... □2
- Muslim .... □3
- Other .... □4
  - (specify) _____
- None .... □5

60 ___

118. How often do you usually attend religious services or functions?
- Never .... □0
- >once a week ..... □1
- Once a week ..... □2
- 2–3 times a month ... □3
- Once a month ...... □4
- Several times a year .. □5
- Once a year or less ... □6

61 ___

IX. PREGNANCY OR ABORTION EXPERIENCE

119. How often had you thought you might get pregnant after you first had sex?
- Never .... □0
- Once in a while .... □1
- Often .... □2
- Always thought about it ...... □3

62 ___

120. How supportive are each of the following persons about your having a baby *now*?

	(5) Very supportive	(4) A little supportive	(3) Indifferent	(2) Somewhat opposed	(1) Very opposed	(0) Do not know	
Mother	☐	☐	☐	☐	☐	☐	63 ___
Father	☐	☐	☐	☐	☐	☐	64 ___
Boyfriend (father of baby)	☐	☐	☐	☐	☐	☐	65 ___
Best girlfriend	☐	☐	☐	☐	☐	☐	66 ___
Sister	☐	☐	☐	☐	☐	☐	67 ___
Grandmother	☐	☐	☐	☐	☐	☐	68 ___
Other (person listed in #32)	☐	☐	☐	☐	☐	☐	69 ___

121. How supportive are each of these persons about your having an abortion if you want one?

	(5) Very supportive	(4) A little supportive	(3) Indifferent	(2) Somewhat opposed	(1) Very opposed	(0) Do not know Would not tell	
Mother	☐	☐	☐	☐	☐	☐	70 ___
Father	☐	☐	☐	☐	☐	☐	71 ___
Boyfriend (father of baby)	☐	☐	☐	☐	☐	☐	72 ___
Best girlfriend	☐	☐	☐	☐	☐	☐	73 ___
Sister	☐	☐	☐	☐	☐	☐	74 ___
Grandmother	☐	☐	☐	☐	☐	☐	75 ___
Other (person listed in #32)	☐	☐	☐	☐	☐	☐	76 ___

122. If you got pregnant again during the next two years, how likely is it you would have an abortion?

Very likely . . . . ☐1
Somewhat likely . . . . ☐2
A little likely . . . . . . ☐3
Not at all likely . . . . . ☐4
Can't say . . . . ☐0

1	2		6	7	8
0	7				

Card Number   Patient Number

NOTE: THE FOLLOWING QUESTIONS ARE FOR DELIVERERS & POST TA'S ONLY. IF NEVER PREGNANT, CODE COLS. 10–43 0'S.

123. Check whether respondent will deliver or had an abortion.
If *delivery*, due date:
Day of year _____ Year _____
If *abortion*, number weeks pregnant at TA: _____

124. When did you first suspect that you were pregnant?
Before period was due . . . . ☐1
When period was late . . . . ☐2
When missed 2 periods . . . . ☐3
When missed 3 periods . . . . . . ☐4
Other (describe) . . . . ☐5   17 ___

_____

125. What were your reasons for deciding to have (the baby/abortion)?
(INTERVIEWER: INDICATE RANK ORDER)

(Code first 3 responses)
___ 00 Can't say
___ 01 Wanted to
___ 02 Boyfriend wanted me to
___ 03 Mother wanted me to
___ 04 Other pressure (family, medical)
___ 05 Dislikes abortion (murder, religion)
___ 06 Dislikes abortion (fear, pain, procedure)
___ 07 No other option recognized or available
___ 08 Education
___ 10 Money
___ 11 Didn't want baby
___ 12 Not ready, too young
___ 13 "It was the responsible thing to do"

{18 {19
{20 {21
{22 {23

126. How much did you think about getting an abortion?
A lot . . . . ☐1
Moderate amount . . . ☐2
A little . . . . ☐3
Not at all . . . . ☐4   24 ___

127. Who was the person you talked with *MOST* about your plans for this pregnancy?
No one . . . . . . ☐0   Other family member . . ☐4
Mother . . . . . . ☐1   Professional . . . . ☐5
Boyfriend . . . . ☐2   Other . . . . ☐6
Girlfriend . . . . ☐3   25 ___

128. What other persons did you talk with about your plans for this pregnancy? (PROBE FOR: relatives, friends, professionals; list all)

26 (M
27 (Boy
28 (Girl
29 (Re
30
(Cou
31 (D
32 (

Code in each column the number of persons in that category.
No . . . . ☐0
Yes (1 person . . . . . . ☐1
Yes ▷1 person) . . . . ☐2

29. Who mainly made the decision to have the (abortion/baby)?
Self ...... □1   Boyfriend ... □3
Mother .... □2   Father ..... □4
Other ... □5
(describe) _____   33 ___

30. Who would you say this abortion/baby is mainly for?
Self ...... □1   Boyfriend ... □3
Mother .... □2   Father ..... □4
Other .... □5
(describe) _____   34 ___

31. Is your present boyfriend the one who made you pregnant?
Yes □1   No □2
Other □3 (describe) _____   35 ___

32. How would you describe your relationship with your boyfriend since your pregnancy?

                                                       36 ___

Can't say .. □0   Broke up, no boyfriend . □5
Fantastic .. □1   He doesn't know,
Better .... □2   didn't tell .... □6
No change .. □3   Other .... □7
Worse .... □4

33. What was your boyfriend's reaction when you got pregnant?

Happy .... □1
Surprised .... □2
Upset .... □3
Won't tell him .... □4
Indifferent, doesn't care .... □5
He doesn't know yet ...... □6

---

134. When you found out you were pregnant how much did you think about getting married?
Not at all .... □1
A little .... □2
Moderate amount ... □3
A lot .... □4   38 ___

135. What are your reasons for not getting married?
(INTERVIEWER: INDICATE RANK ORDER)

                                                       39 ___

                                                       40 ___

(Code first 2 responses)
Can't say .... ___0
Not ready .... ___1
Parents object ...... ___2
Don't need to ...... ___3
Boyfriend away ..... ___4
Boyfriend objects ... ___5
Don't want to ...... ___6
(no other reason)

NOTE: THE FOLLOWING QUESTIONS ARE FOR DELIVERERS ONLY. IF TA'S OR NEVER PREGNANT, CODE COLS. 41-44 0'S.

136. Where do you and the baby plan to live?
With both parents of subject ..... □1
With both parents of boyfriend .... □2
With mother of subject .... □3
With mother of boyfriend .... □4
With boyfriend (father of baby) ... □5
With girlfriend .... □6
Alone with baby .... □7
Other (describe) _____ □8   41 ___

137. How long do you plan to live in this arrangement?
Don't know .... □0
Until financially ready ... □1
Until graduate .... □2
Forever .... □3   42 ___

138. Who will care for the baby most of the time?
Self .... □1
Subject's grandmother ... □2
Subject's mother ...... □3
Partner's mother ...... □4
Boyfriend .... □5
Other .... □6
(describe) _____   43 ___

139. Describe all the ways you think the father of the baby will contribute to its care.

Materially . . . . □1
Physically . . . . □2
Emotionally . . . . □3
Materially & physically . . . □4
All . . . . □5
Nothing . . . . □6
Other . . . . □7

44

INTERVIEWER RATING SHEET
GLOBAL ASSESSMENTS

	LOW (1)	(2)	(3)	(4)	HIGH (5)	
1. COPING SKILLS (performance competence)	□	□	□	□	□	51
2. FUTURE ORIENTATION (conceptualizes future behavior, goals and outcomes realistically)	□	□	□	□	□	52
3. AFFECT (flat, dull/energetic, alert)	□	□	□	□	□	53
4. RELATIONSHIPS (dependent/independent)	□	□	□	□	□	54
5. SEXUALITY (degree of comfort discussing)	□	□	□	□	□	55

6. Indicate any areas of the interview where you thought the answers were questionable. (If none, write "none.")

56

Write 1–2 paragraphs describing what struck you most about this girl as a person.

RATING SCALE FOR STAGES OF ADOLESCENCE

(CHECK ONE CATEGORY—EARLY, MIDDLE OR LATE—UNDER EACH ITEM)

Scale Item	Source	Adolescent Stage	
Who accompanied to clinic?	43	1 ☐ **EARLY** Girlfriend to GYN; parent to FPS 2 ☐ **MIDDLE** Parent to GYN; girlfriend to FPS 3 ☐ **LATE** Boyfriend, no one	58 ___
Whom would/did she first tell about her pregnancy?	42	1 ☐ **EARLY** Girlfriend, unaware of pregnancy. 2 ☐ **MIDDLE** Parents 3 ☐ **LATE** Boyfriend, no one with abortion	59 ___

Scale Item	Source	Adolescent Stage
3. What is relationship with boyfriend like?	48, 49; 32, 42, 45, 47, 52–56, 100, 108, 112, 129, 134, 139	1 ☐ **EARLY** · Transitory relationship; Irrelevant to pregnancy; Girl does not know him well 2 ☐ **MIDDLE** Narcissistic extension of self; feels need for him, but cannot describe him well. Parents may object to him. 3 ☐ **LATE** Some stable, realistic relationship to boyfriend. History of knowing him; some degree of intimacy.
4. What is sexual experience?	114; 108, 112	1 ☐ **EARLY** Feels it to be depersonalized experience; cannot describe sex; irrelevant to relationship. Does not seem to actively enjoy sex, except perhaps cuddling. 2 ☐ **MIDDLE** Uses sex to hold onto boyfriend, but no real sense of mutuality. Need to be loved, recognized is most important. 3 ☐ **LATE** More enjoyment of sexual expression; indicates pleasure from sexual activity; real feelings about boyfriend as boyfriend.
5. How does girl describe her family?	32, 41; 33–40	1 ☐ **EARLY** Isolated from family; does not express closeness except to mother; may seem to be fighting closeness to mother/ internally. Also undifferentiated closeness. 2 ☐ **MIDDLE** Actively fighting parent(s); rivalrous and rebellious. 3 ☐ **LATE** Can objectify relationship to and feelings about family even if in conflict with them. Some distance and understanding of them as people.
6. How does girl describe herself?	30; 33–72	1 ☐ **EARLY** Little self-concept; describes other people's response to her or cannot answer question. 2 ☐ **MIDDLE** Describes self in self-absorbed manner, either aggrandized or self-deprecating. 3 ☐ **LATE** More self-representation, perhaps with identity confusion, but some insight into changing self.

page 16

Scale Item	Source	Adolescent Stage	
		1 ☐ **EARLY** Concerned for self: cannot describe self in mothering role. Competes with baby for her own mother's attention.	
How does girl describe herself as a mother?	72; 71	2 ☐ **MIDDLE** Motherhood idealized. Emphasis on baby as a thing that is hers, but variable in taking responsibility for it. Little concept of problems of mothering, but some concern about problems for self.	64 ___
		3 ☐ **LATE** Able to talk about loving and having a child with less ambivalence about responsibility for care of child. Recognizes problems.	
		1 ☐ **EARLY** Unfocused; vague; little realistic concept of future.	
What are girl's future plans and interest?	12-14, 17-23, 71	2 ☐ **MIDDLE** Some sense of future but not yet actively working toward a goal.	65 ___
		3 ☐ **LATE** More goal oriented; more plan about future; may be working towards goals.	

TOTAL SCORES

___ EARLY (0-8)	66 ___
___ MIDDLE (0-8)	67 ___
___ LATE (0-8)	68 ___

Stage of Adolescence
Predominantly early ..... ☐1
Early-middle .... ☐2
Early-late .... ☐3   69 ___
Predominantly middle .... ☐4
Middle-late .... ☐5
Predominantly late ...... ☐6

Bibliography

Abrahamse, A. F., Morrison, P. A., & Waite, L. J. (1988). *Beyond stereotypes: Who becomes a single teenage mother?* Santa Monica, CA: Rand.

Abrams, M. (1985). Birth control use by teenagers. *Journal of Adolescent Health Care, 6*(3), 196-200.

Adler, N. E. (1975). Emotional responses of women following therapeutic abortion. *American Journal of Orthopsychiatry, 45*(3), 446-456.

Adler, N. E., David, H. P., Major, B. N., Roth, S. H., Russo, N. F., & Wyatt, G. E. (1990). Psychological responses after abortion. *Science, 248*(4951), 41-44.

Adler, N. E., & Dolcini, P. (1986). Psychological issues in abortion for adolescents. In G. B. Melton (Ed.), *Adolescent abortion: Psychological and legal issues.* Lincoln: University of Nebraska Press.

Alan Guttmacher Institute. (1981, April). *Teenage pregnancy: The problem which has not gone away.* New York: Planned Parenthood Federation of America.

Alan Guttmacher Institute. (1989). *Teenage pregnancy in the United States: The scope of the problem and state responses.* New York: Author.

Alan Guttmacher Institute. (1992). *Abortion factbook, 1992 edition: Readings, trends, and state and local data to 1988.* New York: Author.

American Psychological Association (APA), Public Interest Directorate. (1987). *Psychological sequelae of abortion.* Report to the Surgeon General. Washington, DC: Author.

An, C. B., Haverman, R., & Wolfe, B. (1991). Teen out-of-wedlock births and welfare receipt: The role of childhood events and economic circumstances. *Review of Economics and Statistics.* Manuscript submitted for publication.

Armstrong, E., & Pascale, A. (1990). *Fact sheet: Adolescent sexuality, pregnancy, and parenthood.* Washington, DC: Center for Population Options.

Bachrach, C. A. (1984). Contraceptive practice among American women, 1973-1982. *Family Planning Perspectives, 16*(1), 253-259.

Baker, S. A., Thalberg, S. P., & Morrison, D. M. (1988). Parents' behavioral norms as predictors of adolescents' sexual activity and contraceptive use. *Adolescence, 23*(90), 266-282.

Baldwin, W. (1983). Trends in adolescent contraception, pregnancy, and childbearing. In E. R. McAnarney (Ed.), *Premature adolescent pregnancy and parenthood.* New York: Grune & Stratton.

Baldwin, W., & Cain, V. S. (1980). The children of teenage parents. *Family Planning Perspectives, 12*(1), 34-43.

Baumann, K. E., & Udry, J. R. (1981). Subjective expected utility and adolescent sexual behavior. *Adolescence, 16*(63), 527-534.

Billy, J. O. G., & Udry, J. R. (1981). The influence of male and female best friends on adolescent sexual behavior. *Adolescence, 20*(77), 21-32.

Blum, R. W., & Resnick, M. D. (1982). Adolescent sexual decision-making: Contraception, pregnancy, abortion, motherhood. *Pediatric Annals, 11*(10), 797-805.

Bolton, F. G., Jr. (1980). *The pregnant adolescent.* Beverly Hills, CA: Sage.

Bracken, M., Hachamovitch, M., & Grossman, A. (1974). The decision to abort and psychological sequelae. *Journal of Nervous and Mental Disorders, 158*(2), 154-162.

Bracken, M. B., Klerman, L. B., & Bracken, M. (1978). Abortion, adoption, or motherhood: An empirical study of decision-making during pregnancy. *American Journal of Obstetrics and Gynecology, 130*(3), 251-262.

Bracken, M. B., & Swigar, M. E. (1972). Factors associated with delay in seeking induced abortions. *American Journal of Obstetrics and Gynecology, 113*(6), 301-309.

Brandt, C. L., Kane, F. J., & Moan, C. A. (1978). Pregnant adolescents: Some psychosocial factors. *Psychosomatics, 19*(12), 790-793.

Brooks-Gunn, J., & Furstenberg, F. F., Jr. (1986). The children of adolescent mothers: Physical, academic, and psychological outcomes. *Developmental Review, 6*(3), 224-251.

Burden, D. S., & Klerman, L. V. (1984). Teenage parenthood: Factors that lessen economic dependence. *Social Work, 29*(1), 11-16.

Burt, M. R. (1986). *Estimates of public costs for teenage childbearing.* Washington, DC: Center for Population Options.

Burt, M. R., & Levy, F. (1987). Estimates of public costs for teenage childbearing: A review of recent studies and estimates of 1985 public costs. In S. L. Hofferth & C. D. Hayes (Eds.), *Risking the future: Adolescent sexuality, pregnancy, and childbearing* (Vol. 2, pp. 264-293). Washington, DC: National Academy Press.

Card, J. J., & Wise, L. L. (1978). Teenage mothers and teenage fathers: The impact of early childbearing on parents' personal and professional lives. *Family Planning Perspectives, 10*(4), 199-205.

Casper, L. M. (1990). Does family interaction prevent adolescent pregnancy? *Family Planning Perspectives, 22*(3), 109-114.

Cates, W., Jr. (1980). Adolescent abortion in the U.S. *Journal of Adolescent Health Care, 1*(1), 18-25.

Cates, W., Jr., Schultz, K. F., & Grimes, D. A. (1983). The risks associated with teenage abortion. *New England Journal of Medicine, 309*(11), 621-624.

Center for Population Options. (1989, September). *Teenage pregnancy and too early childbearing: Public costs, personal consequences.* Washington, DC: Author.

Center for Population Options. (1990a, July). *Adolescents and abortion: Choice in crisis.* Washington, DC: Author.

Center for Population Options. (1990b). *Teenage pregnancy and too early childbearing: Public costs, personal consequences* (5th ed.). Washington, DC: Author.

Center for Population Options. (1992). *Teenage pregnancy and too early childbearing: Public costs, personal consequences* (6th ed.). Washington, DC: Author.

Centers for Disease Control. (1987, August). *Teenage pregnancy and fertility in the U.S.: 1970, 1974, 1980. Regional and state variations and unintended fertility.* Atlanta, GA: Department of Health and Human Services.

Centers for Disease Control. (1991a, July). Abortion surveillance, United States, 1988. *Morbidity and Mortality Weekly Report, 40*(SS-2), 15-42.

Centers for Disease Control. (1991b). Premarital sexual experience among adolescent women, United States, 1970-1988. *Morbidity and Mortality Weekly Report, 39*(51-52), 929.

Centers for Disease Control. (1992). Sexual behavior amongst high school students, United States 1990. *Morbidity and Mortality Weekly Report, 40*(51-52), 1-8.

Children's Defense Fund. (1985, May). *Adolescent and young adult fathers: Problems and solutions.* Washington, DC: Author.

Children's Defense Fund's Adolescent Prevention Clearinghouse. (1988). *Teenage pregnancy: An advocate's guide to the numbers.* Washington, DC: Children's Defense Fund.

Chilman, C. (1979). Teenage pregnancy: A research review. *Social Work, 24*(6), 492-498.

Chilman, C. (Ed.). (1980a). *Adolescent pregnancy and childbearing: Findings from research* (NIH Publication No. 81-2077). Washington, DC: Department of Health and Human Services.

Chilman, C. (1980b). *Adolescent sexuality in a changing society* (GPO Publication No. 10-1426). Washington, DC: Department of Health, Education, and Welfare.

Chilman, C. (1980c). Toward a reconceptualization of adolescent sexuality. In C. Chilman (Ed.), *Adolescent pregnancy and childbearing: Findings from research* (pp. 101-127). Washington, DC: Department of Health and Human Services.

Clark, S. D., Jr., Zabin, L. S., & Hardy, J. B. (1984). Sex, contraception, and parenthood: Experience and attitudes among urban black young men. *Family Planning Perspectives, 16*(2), 77-82.

Cobliner, W. G. (1974). Pregnancy in the single adolescent girl: The role of cognitive functions. *Journal of Youth and Adolescence, 3*(1), 17-29.

Cobliner, W. G. (1981). Prevention of adolescent pregnancy: A developmental perspective. In E. R. McAnarney & G. Stickle (Eds.), *Pregnancy and childbearing during adolescence: Research priorities for the 1980s.* New York: Alan R. Liss.

Coopersmith, S. (1967). *The antecedents of self-esteem.* San Francisco: Freeman.

Cutright, P. (1972). The teenage sexual revolution and the myth of an abstinent past. *Family Planning Perspectives, 4*(1), 24-31.

Cvejic, H., Lipper, I., Kinch, R. A., & Benjamin, P. (1977). Follow-up of 50 adolescent girls two years after abortion. *Canadian Medical Association Journal, 116*(1), 44-46.

Cvetkovich, G., & Grote, B. (1980). Psychological development and the social problem of teenage illegitimacy. In C. Chilman (Ed.), *Adolescent pregnancy and childbearing: Findings from research* (pp. 15-41) (NIH Publication No. 81-2077). Washington, DC: Department of Health and Human Services.

Dale, L. G. (1970). The growth of systematic thinking: Replication and analysis of Piaget's first chemical experiment. *Australian Journal of Psychology, 22*(3), 277-286.

Davis, K., & Grossbard-Schectman, A. (1980). *Study on how mother's age and circumstances affect children.* Final report to National Institute for Child Health and Human Development. Los Angeles: University of Southern California Press.

Derogatis, L. R. (1977). *SCL-90* (rev. ed.). Baltimore, MD: Johns Hopkins University School of Medicine.

Dickens, H. O., Mudd, E. H., Garcia, C.-R., Tomar, K., & Wright, D. (1973). One hundred pregnant adolescents: Treatment approaches in a university hospital. *American Journal of Public Health, 63*(9), 794-800.

Dickens, H. O., Mudd, E. H., & Huggins, G. R. (1975). Teenagers, contraception, and pregnancy. *Journal of Marriage and Family Counseling, 1*(2), 175-181.

Dryfoos, J. G. (1984a). A new strategy for preventing unintended teenage childbearing. *Family Planning Perspectives, 16*(4), 193-195.

Dryfoos, J. G. (1984b). A time for new thinking about teenage pregnancy. *American Journal of Public Health, 75*(1), 13-14.

Duncan, G. J., & Hoffman, S. D. (1990). Teenage welfare receipt and subsequent dependence among black adolescent mothers. *Family Planning Perspectives, 22*(1), 16-20.

East, P. L., & Felice, M. E. (1990). Outcomes and parent-child relationships of former adolescent mothers and their 12-year-old children. *Developmental and Behavioral Pediatrics, 11*(4), 175-183.

Edelman, M. W. (1987). *Families in peril: An agenda for social change.* Cambridge, MA: Harvard University Press.

Edwards, L., Steinman, M., Arnold, K., & Hakanson, E. (1980). Adolescent pregnancy prevention services in high school clinics. *Family Planning Perspectives, 12*(1), 6-14.

Elster, A. B., & Lamb, M. E. (1986). *Adolescent fatherhood.* Hillsdale, NJ: Lawrence Erlbaum.

Elster, A. B., & Panzarine, S. (1980). Unwed teenage fathers: Emotional and health educational needs. *Journal of Adolescent Health Care, 1*(2), 116-120.

Emans, S. J., Grace, E., Woods, E. R., Smith, D. E., Klein, K., & Merola, J. (1987). Adolescents' compliance with the use of oral contraceptives. *Journal of the American Medical Association, 257*(24), 3377-3381.

Evans, J. R., Selstad, G., & Welcher, W. H. (1976). Teenagers: Fertility control behavior and attitudes before and after abortion, childbearing, or negative pregnancy test. *Family Planning Perspectives, 8*(4), 192-200.

Eysenck, S. B. G. (1975). *Manual for the Junior Eysenck Personality Inventory.* San Diego, CA: Educational and Industrial Testing Service.

Ezzard, N. V., Cates, W., Jr., Kramer, D. G., & Tietze, C. (1982). Race-specific patterns of abortion use by American teenagers. *American Journal of Public Health, 72*(8), 809-814.

Finkel, M. L., & Finkel, D. J. (1975). Sexual and contraceptive knowledge, attitudes, and behavior of male adolescents. *Family Planning Perspectives, 7*(6), 256-260.

Fischman, S. H. (1977). Delivery or abortion in inner-city adolescents. *American Journal of Orthopsychiatry, 47*(1), 127-133.

Forrest, J. D. (1988a). The delivery of family planning services in the United States. *Family Planning Perspectives, 20*(2), 88-95, 98.

Forrest, J. D. (1988b). Unintended pregnancy among American women. In S. K. Henshaw & J. Van Vort (Eds.), *Abortion services in the United States, each state & metropolitan area, 1984-1985.* New York: Alan Guttmacher Institute.

Forrest, J. D., Hermalin, A., & Henshaw, S. (1981). The impact of family planning clinic programs on adolescent pregnancy. *Family Planning Pregnancy, 13*(3), 109-116.

Fox, G. L. (1980). *Mother-daughter communications re sexuality.* Final report to the National Institute of Child Health and Human Development. Detroit, MI: Merrill Palmer Institute.

Fox, G. L. (1981). The family's role in adolescent sexual behavior. In T. O. Ooms (Ed.), *Teenage pregnancy in a family context.* Philadelphia: Temple University Press.

Fox, G. L. (1982). *The childbearing decision: Fertility attitudes and behavior.* Beverly Hills, CA: Sage.

Freeman, E. W. (1977). Influence of personality attributes on abortion experience. *American Journal of Orthopsychiatry, 47*(3), 503-513.

Freeman, E. W. (1978). Abortion: Subjective attitudes and feelings. *Family Planning Perspectives, 10*(3), 150-155.

Freeman, E. W., Rickels, K., Huggins, G. R., & Garcia, C.-R. (1984). Urban black adolescents who obtain contraceptive services before or after first pregnancy. *Journal of Adolescent Health Care, 5*(3), 183-190.

Freeman, E. W., Rickels, K., Huggins, G. R., Garcia, C.-R., & Polin, J. (1980). Emotional distress patterns among women having first or repeat abortions. *Obstetrics and Gynecology, 55*(5), 630-636.

Freeman, E. W., Rickels, K., Huggins, G., Mudd, E. H., Garcia, C.-R., & Dickens, H. O. (1980). Adolescent contraceptive use: Comparisons of male and female attitudes and information. *American Journal of Public Health, 70*(8), 790-797.

Freeman, E. W., Rickels, K., Mudd, E. H., & Huggins, G. R. (1982). Never-pregnant adolescents and family planning programs: Contraception continuation and pregnancy risk. *American Journal of Public Health, 72*(8), 815-822.

Freeman, E. W., Rickels, K., Mudd, E. B. H., Huggins, G. R., & Garcia, C.-R. (1982). Self-reports of emotional distress in a sample of urban black high school students. *Psychological Medicine, 12,* 809-817.

Freeman, E. W., Sondheimer, S. J., & Rickels, K. (1985). Influence of maternal attitudes on urban black teens' decisions about abortion vs. delivery. *Journal of Reproductive Medicine, 30*(10 suppl.), 731-735.

Friede, A., Hogue, C. J. R., Doyle, L. L., Hammerslough, C. R., Sniezek, J. E., & Arrighi, H. (1986). Do the sisters of childbearing teenagers have increased rates of childbearing? *American Journal of Public Health, 76*(10), 1221-1224.

Furstenberg, F. F. (1976). *Unplanned parenthood: The social consequences of teenage childbearing.* New York: Free Press.

Furstenberg, F. F., Jr., & Brooks-Gunn, J. (1986). The children of adolescent mothers: Physical, academic, and psychological outcomes. *Developmental Review, 6*(3), 224-251.

Furstenberg, F. F., Brooks-Gunn, J., & Morgan, S. P. (1987). Adolescent mothers and their children in later life. *Family Planning Perspectives, 19*(4), 142-151.

Furstenberg, F. F., Jr., Brooks-Gunn, J., & Morgan, S. P. (1987). *Adolescent mothers in later life.* New York: Cambridge University Press.

Furstenberg, F. F., Jr., & Crawford, A. G. (1978). Family support: Helping teenage mothers to cope. *Family Planning Perspectives, 10*(6), 322-333.

Furstenberg, F. F., Herzog-Baron, R., Shea, J., & Webb, D. (1984). Family communication and teenagers' contraceptive use. *Family Planning Perspectives, 16*(4), 163-170.

Furstenberg, F. F., Jr., Moore, K. A., & Peterson, J. L. (1985). Sex education and sexual experience among adolescents. *American Journal of Public Health, 75*(11), 1331-1332.

Gabrielson, I. W., Klerman, L. V., Currie, J. B., Tyler, N. C., & Jekel, J. F. (1970). Suicide attempts in a population pregnant as teenagers. *American Journal of Public Health, 60*(12), 2289-2301.

Garcia, C.-R., & Rosenfeld, D. L. (1977). *Human fertility: The regulation of reproduction.* Philadelphia: F. A. Davis.

Geronimus, A. T. (1991, October). Teenage childbearing and social and reproductive disadvantage: The evolution of complex questions and the demise of simple answers. *Family Relations, 40,* 463-471.

Gispert, M., Brinich, P., Wheeler, K., & Krieger, L. (1984). Predictors of repeat pregnancies among low-income adolescents. *Hospital and Community Psychiatry, 35*(7), 719-723.

Gispert, M., & Falk, R. (1976). Sexual experimentation and pregnancy in young black adolescents. *American Journal of Obstetrics and Gynecology, 126*(4), 459-466.

Hanson, S. L., Morrison, D. R., & Ginsberg, A. L. (1989). The antecedents of teenage fatherhood. *Demography, 26*(4), 579-596.

Hanson, S. L., Myers, D. E., & Ginsberg, A. L. (1987). The role of responsibility and knowledge in reducing teenage out-of-wedlock childbearing. *Journal of Marriage and Family, 49*(2), 241-256.

Hardy, J. B., & Duggan, A. K. (1988). Teenage fathers and the fathers of infants of urban, teenage mothers. *American Journal of Public Health, 78*(8), 919-922.

Hardy, J. B., Duggan, A. K., Masnyk, K., & Pearson, C. (1989). Fathers of children born to young urban mothers. *Family Planning Perspectives, 21*(4), 159-163.

Hardy, J. B., King, T. M., & Repke, J. (1987). The Johns Hopkins adolescent pregnancy program: An evaluation. *Obstetrics and Gynecology, 69*(3, Pt. 1), 300-306.

Hardy, J. B., & Zabin, L. S. (Eds.). (1991). *Adolescent pregnancy in an urban environment.* Washington, DC: Urban Institute Press.

Hayes, C. (Ed.). (1987). *Risking the future: Adolescent sexuality, pregnancy, and childbearing* (Vol. 1). Report by the National Research Council. Washington, DC: National Academy Press.

Hendricks, L. E., Howard, C. S., & Caesar, P. P. (1981). Help-seeking behavior among selected populations of black, unmarried adolescent fathers. *American Journal of Public Health, 71*(7), 733-735.

Henshaw, S. K., Binkin, N. J., Blaine, E., & Smith, J. C. (1985). A portrait of American women who obtain abortions. *Family Planning Perspectives, 17*(2), 90-96.

Henshaw, S. K., Kenney, A. M., Somberg, D., & Van Vort, K. (1989). *Teenage pregnancy in the United States: The scope of the problem and state responses.* New York: Alan Guttmacher Institute.

Henshaw, S. K., & Van Vort, J. (1989). Teenage abortion, birth, and pregnancy statistics: An update. *Family Planning Perspectives, 21*(2), 85-88.

Henshaw, S. K., & Van Vort, J. (Eds.). (1992). *Abortion factbook 1992 edition: Readings, trends, and state and local data to 1988.* New York: Alan Guttmacher Institute.

Hofferth, S. L., Kahn, J. R., & Baldwin, W. (1987). Premarital sexual activity among U.S. teenage women over the past three decades. *Family Planning Perspectives, 19*(2), 46-53.

Hogan, D. P., Astone, N. M., & Kitagawa, E. M. (1985). Social and environmental factors influencing contraceptive use among black adolescents. *Family Planning Perspectives, 17*(4), 165-169.

Hogan, D. P., & Kitagawa, E. M. (1985). The impact of social status, family structure, and neighborhood on the fertility of black adolescents. *American Journal of Sociology, 90*(4), 825-855.

Hogue, C. J. R., Cates, W., & Tietze, C. (1982). The effects of induced abortion on subsequent reproduction. *Epidemiologic Reviews, 4,* 66-94.

Hogue, C. J. R., Cates, W., Jr., & Tietze, C. (1983). Impact of vacuum aspiration abortion on future childbearing: A review. *Family Planning Perspectives, 15*(3), 119-126.

Hollingshead, A. B. (1975). *Four factor index of social status.* New Haven, CT: Yale University, Department of Sociology.

Horn, M. C., & Mosher, M. D. (1984). Use of services for family planning and infertility, United States, 1982. *Advance data from vital and health statistics,* No. 102 (DHHS Publication No. [PHS] 85-1250). Hyattsville, MD: National Center for Health Statistics.

Inamdar, S. C., Siomopoulos, G., Osborn, M., & Bianchi, E. C. (1979). Phenomenology associated with depressed moods in adolescents. *American Journal of Psychiatry, 136*(2), 156-159.

Inazu, J. K., & Fox, G. L. (1980). Maternal influence on the sexual behavior of teenage daughters. *Journal of Family Issues, 1*(1), 81-102.

Iverson, R. R. (1990, December). *Income and employment consequences for African American participants of a family planning clinic.* Unpublished doctoral dissertation, Bryn Mawr College, Bryn Mawr, Pennsylvania.

Jencks, C. (1991). Is the American underclass growing? In C. Jencks & P. E. Peterson (Eds.), *The urban underclass* (pp. 28-100). Washington, DC: Brookings Institution.

Jencks, C., & Peterson, P. E. (Eds.). (1991). *The urban underclass.* Washington, DC: Brookings Institution.

Jessor, R., Costa, F., Jessor, S. L., & Donovan, J. E. (1983). The time of first intercourse: A prospective study. *Journal of Personality and Social Psychology, 44*(3), 608-626.

Jessor, S. L., & Jessor, R. (1975). Transition from virginity to non-virginity among youth: A social-psychological study over time. *Developmental Psychology, 11*(4), 473-484.

Jones, D. J., & Battle, S. F. (Eds.). (1990). *Teenage pregnancy: Developing strategies for change in the twenty-first century.* New Brunswick, NJ: Transaction Books.

Jones, E. F., Forrest, J. D., Goldman, N., Henshaw, S. K., Lincoln, R., Rosoff, J. I., Westoff, C. F., & Wulf, D. (1985). Teenage pregnancy in developed countries: Determinants and policy implications. *Family Planning Perspectives, 17*(2), 53-63.

Jones, E. F., Forrest, J. D., Goldman, N., Henshaw, S. K., Lincoln, R., Rosoff, J., Westoff, C. F., & Wulf, D. (1986). *Teenage pregnancy in industrialized countries.* New Haven, CT: Yale University Press.

Kahn, J., Smith, K., & Roberts, E. (1984). *Familial communication and adolescent sexual behavior.* Final report to the Office of Adolescent Pregnancy Programs. Cambridge, MA: American Institutes for Research.

Kane, F. J., Moan, C. A., & Bolling, B. (1974). Motivational factors in pregnant adolescents. *Diseases of the Nervous System, 35*(3), 131-134.

Keller, R., Sims, J., Henry, W. K., & Crawford, T. J. (1970). Psychological sources of resistance to family planning. *Merrill-Palmer Quarterly, 16*(3), 286-302.

Kisker, E. (1985). Clinic effectiveness in serving adolescents: Teenagers talk about sex, pregnancy, and contraception. *Family Planning Perspectives, 17*(2), 83-90.

Koenig, M. A., & Zelnik, M. (1982). Repeat pregnancies among metropolitan-area teenagers: 1971-1979. *Family Planning Perspectives, 14*(6), 341-344.

Koop, E. (1989). Health impact of abortion. *Congressional Record, 135*(33), E906.

Kreipe, R. E., Roghmann, K. J., & McAnarney, E. R. (1981). Early adolescent childbearing: A changing morbidity. *Journal of Adolescent Health Care, 2*(2), 127-131.

Ladner, J. A. (1971). *Tomorrow's tomorrow: The black woman.* Garden City, NY: Doubleday.

Lazarus, A. (1985). Psychiatric sequelae of legalized elective first trimester abortion. *Journal of Psychosomatic Obstetrics and Gynecology, 4*(3), 141-150.

Leibowitz, A., Eisen, M., & Chow, W. (1980). *Decision-making in teenage pregnancy: An analysis of choice.* Santa Monica, CA: Rand Corporation.

Litt, I. F., & Glader, L. (1987). Follow-up of adolescents previously studied for contraceptive compliance. *Journal of Adolescent Health Care, 8*(4), 349-351.

Luker, K. (1975). *Taking chances: Abortion and decision not to contracept.* Berkeley: University of California Press.

MacDonald, A. P. (1970). Internal-external locus of control and the practice of birth control. *Psychological Reports, 27*(1), 206.

Marsiglio, W. (1987). Adolescent fathers in the United States: Their initial living arrangements, marital status, and educational outcome. *Family Planning Perspectives, 19*(6), 240-251.

Marsiglio, W. K., & Mott, F. L. (1986). The impact of sex education on sexual activity, contraceptive use, and premarital pregnancy among American teenagers. *Family Planning Perspectives, 18*(4), 151-162.

McAdoo, H. P. (Ed.). (1981). *Black families.* Beverly Hills, CA: Sage.

McAnarney, E. R. (1985). Adolescent pregnancy and childbearing: New data, new challenges. *Pediatrics, 75*(5), 973-975.

McAnarney, E. R., & Hendee, W. R. (1989). Adolescent pregnancy and its consequences. *Journal of the American Medical Association, 262*(1), 74-77.

McAnarney, E. R., Roghmann, K. J., Adams, B. N., Tatelbaum, R. C., Kash, C., Coulter, M., Plume, M., & Charney, E. (1978). Obstetric, neonatal, and psychosocial outcome of pregnant adolescents. *Pediatrics, 61*(2), 199-205.

McCarthy, J., & Radish, E. (1982). Education and childbearing among teenagers. In E. R. McAnarney (Ed.), *Premature adolescent pregnancy and parenthood* (pp. 279-292). New York: Grune & Stratton.

McCormick, M. C., Brooks-Gunn, J., Shorter, T., Wallace, C. Y., Holmes, J. H., & Heagarty, M. C. (1987). The planning of pregnancy among low-income women in central Harlem. *American Journal of Obstetrics and Gynecology, 156*(1), 145-149.

McLaughlin, S. D., Grady, W. R., Billy, J. O. G., Landale, N. S., & Winges, L. D. (1986). The effects of the sequencing of marriage and first birth during adolescence. *Family Planning Perspectives, 18*(1), 12-18.

Menken, J. (1980). The health and demographic consequences of adolescent pregnancy and childbearing. In C. Chilman (Ed.), *Adolescent pregnancy and childbearing: Findings from research* (pp. 157-205). Washington, DC: Department of Health and Human Services.

Miller, S. H. (1983). *Children and parents: A final report.* New York: Child Welfare League of America.

Miller, W. B. (1974). Relationships between the intendedness of conception and the wantedness of pregnancy. *Journal of Nervous and Mental Disease, 159*(6), 396-406.

Mindick, B., Oskamp, S., & Berger, D. E. (1977). Prediction of success or failure in birth planning: An approach to prevention of individual and family stress. *American Journal of Community Psychology, 5*(4), 447-459.

Moore, K. A. (1978). Teenage childbirth and welfare dependency. *Family Planning Perspectives, 10*(4), 233-235.

Moore, K. A. (1986). *Children of teen parents: Heterogeneity of outcomes.* Final report to the National Institute of Child Health and Human Development. Washington, DC: Child Trends.

Moore, K. A., & Burt, M. R. (1982). *Private crisis, public cost.* Washington, DC: Urban Institute Press.

Moore, K. A., & Caldwell, S. (1977). The effect of government policies on out-of-wedlock sex and pregnancy. *Family Planning Perspectives, 9*(4), 164-169.

Moore, K. A., & Hofferth, S. L. (1980). Factors affecting early formation: A path model. *Population and Environment, 3*(1), 73-98.

Moore, K. A., Simms, M. C., & Betsey, C. L. (1986). *Choice and circumstance.* New Brunswick, NJ: Transaction Books.

Morin-Gunthier, M., & Lortie, G. (1984). The significance of pregnancy among adolescents choosing abortion as compared to those continuing pregnancy. *The Journal of Reproductive Medicine, 29*(4), 255-259.

Mosher, W. D., & Horn, M. C. (1988). First family planning visits by young women. *Family Planning Perspectives, 20*(1), 33-40.

Mott, F. L. (1986). The pace of repeated childbearing among young American mothers. *Family Planning Perspectives, 18*(1), 5-12.

Mott, F. L., & Marsiglio, W. (1985). Early childbearing and completion of high school. *Family Planning Perspectives, 17*(5), 234-237.

Mott, F. L., & Maxwell, N. L. (1981). School-age mothers: 1968 and 1979. *Family Planning Perspectives, 13*(6), 287-292.

Mudd, E. H., Dickens, H. O., Garcia, C.-R., Rickels, K., Freeman, E., Huggins, G. R., & Logan, J. J. (1978). Adolescent health services and contraceptive use. *American Journal of Orthopsychiatry, 48*(3), 495-504.

Namerow, P., & Philliber, S. (1982). The effectiveness of contraceptive programs for teenagers. *Journal of Adolescent Health Care, 2*(3), 189-198.

Nathanson, C. A., & Becker, M. H. (1986). Family and peer influence on obtaining a method of contraception. *Journal of Marriage and Family, 48*(3), 513-525.

National Academy of Sciences. (1987). *Risking the future: Adolescent sexuality, pregnancy, and childbearing* (Vols. 1-2). Washington, DC: National Academy Press.

National Center for Health Statistics. (1989, June). Advance report of final natality statistics, 1987. *Monthly Vital Statistics Report, 38*(3 Suppl.). Hyattsville, MD: Public Health Service.

National Center for Health Statistics. (1991). Advance report of final natality statistics, 1989. *Monthly Vital Statistics Report, 40*(8 Suppl.). Hyattsville, MD: Public Health Service.

Newcomber, S. F., & Udry, J. R. (1985). Parent-child communication and adolescent sexual behavior. *Family Planning Perspectives, 17*(4), 169-174.

Olson, L. (1980). Social and psychological correlates of pregnancy resolution among women: A review. *American Journal of Orthopsychiatry, 50*(3), 48-60.

Ooms, T. (Ed.). (1981). *Teenage pregnancy in a family context.* Philadelphia: Temple University Press.

Orr, M. (1982). Sex education and contraceptive education in U.S. public high schools. *Family Planning Perspectives, 14*(6), 304-313.

Orr, M. (1984). Private physicians and the provision of contraceptives to adolescents. *Family Planning Perspectives, 16*(2), 83-86.

Osofsky, J. D., & Osofsky, H. J. (1972). The psychological reaction of patients to legalized abortion. *American Journal of Orthopsychiatry, 42*(1), 48-60.

Paulker, S. (1969). Girls pregnant out-of-wedlock. In M. LaBarre & W. Labarre (Eds.), *The double jeopardy: The triple crisis—Illegitimacy today.* New York: National Council on Illegitimacy.

Piaget, J. (1972). Intellectual evolution from adolescence to adulthood. *Human Development, 15*(1), 1-12.

Pohlman, E. H. (1969). *The psychology of birth planning.* Cambridge, MA: Schenkman.

Polit, D. F., & Kahn, J. R. (1986). Early subsequent pregnancy among economically disadvantaged teenage mothers. *American Journal of Public Health, 76*(2), 167-171.

Radecki, S. E., & Beckman, L. J. (1992). Determinants of childbearing intentions of low-income women: Attitudes versus life circumstances. *Journal of Biosocial Science, 24*(2), 157-166.

Rader, G. E., Bekker, D., Brown, L., & Richard, T. C. (1978). Psychological correlates of unwanted pregnancy. *Journal of Abnormal Psychology, 87*(3), 373-376.

Rainwater, L. (1970). *Behind ghetto walls.* Chicago: Aldine.

Reed, J. (1978). *From vice to public virtue: The birth control movement and American society since 1830.* New York: Basic Books.

Reid, J. (1982). Black America in the 1980s. *Population Bulletin, 37*(4), 137.

Rosen, R. H. (1980). Adolescent pregnancy decision-making: Are parents important? *Adolescence, 15*(57), 43-54.

Rosenberg, M. (1965). *Society and the adolescent self-image.* Princeton, NJ: Princeton University Press.

Ross, H., & Sawhill, I. (1975). *Time of transition: The growth of families headed by women.* Washington, DC: Urban Institute.

Rothenberg, P. B., & Varga, P. E. (1981). The relationship between age of mother and child health and development. *American Journal of Public Health, 71*(8), 810-817.

Rovinsky, J. J. (1972). Abortion recidivism. *Obstetrical Gynecology, 39*(5), 649-659.

Sander, J. (1991). *Before their time: Four generations of teenage mothers.* New York: Harcourt Brace Jovanovich.

SAS Institute. (1989). *SAS/STAT guide for personal computers, version 6* (4th ed.). Cary, NC: Author.

Scales, P., & Everly, K. (1977, January). A community sex education program for parents. *The Family Coordinator, 26,* 37-45.

Schinke, S. P., Blythe, B., & Gilchrist, L. (1981). Cognitive behavioral prevention of adolescent pregnancy. *Journal of Counseling Psychology, 28*(5), 451-454.

Schorr, L. B. (1988). *Within our reach: Breaking the cycle of disadvantage.* New York: Anchor Press.

Schorr, L. B. (1991). Children, families and the cycle of disadvantage. *Canadian Journal of Psychiatry, 36*(6), 437-440.

Scrimshaw, S. C. M. (1981). Women and the pill: From panacea to catalyst. *Family Planning Perspectives, 13*(6), 254-256, 260-262.

Shea, J., Herceg-Baron, R., & Furstenberg, F. F., Jr. (1984). Factors associated with adolescent use of family planning clinics. *American Journal of Public Health, 74*(11), 1227-1230.

Singh, S. (1986). Adolescent pregnancy in the United States: An interstate analysis. *Family Planning Perspectives, 18*(5), 210-220.

Smith, E., & Udry, R. (1985). Coital and non-coital sexual behavior of white and black adolescents. *American Journal of Public Health, 75*(10), 1200-1203.

Sonenstein, F. L., Pleck, J. H., & Ku, L. C. (1989). Sexual activity, condom use, and AIDS awareness among adolescent males. *Family Planning Perspectives, 21*(4), 152-158.

Sonenstein, F. L., Pleck, J. H., & Leighton, C. K. (1991). Levels of sexual activity among adolescent males in the United States. *Family Planning Perspectives, 23*(4), 162-167.

Stack, C. (1974). *All our kin: Strategies for survival in a black community.* New York: Harper & Row.

Streetman, L. G. (1987). Contrasts in the self-esteem of unwed teenage mothers. *Adolescence, 22*(86), 459-464.

Teachman, J. D., & Polonko, K. A. (1984, September). Out of sequence: The timing of marriage following a premarital birth. *Social Forces, 63,* 245-260.

Teichmann, A. T. (1984). The meanings of the notion "desire for a child." Some considerations based on an empirical study of 400 patients applying for legal abortion. *Journal of Psychosomatic Obstetrics and Gynecology, 3,* 215-222.

Thornburg, H. D. (1978). Adolescent sources of initial sex information. *Psychiatric Annals, 8*(8), 419-423.

Thornburg, H. D. (1981). Adolescent sources of information on sex. *Journal of School Health, 51*(4), 274-277.

Thornton, A., & Camburn, D. (1987). The influence of the family on premarital sexual attitudes and behavior. *Demography, 24*(3), 323-340.

Tietze, C. (1978). Teenage pregnancies: Looking ahead to 1984. *Family Planning Perspectives, 10*(4), 205-207.

Tietze, C., & Henshaw, S. K. (1986). *Induced abortion: A world review 1986* (6th ed.). New York: Alan Guttmacher Institute.

Trussell, J. (1988). Teenage pregnancy in the U.S. *Family Planning Perspectives, 20*(6), 262-272.

Udry, J. R., Talbert, L. M., & Morris, N. M. (1986). Biosocial foundations for adolescent female sexuality. *Demography, 23*(2), 217-230.

Upchurch, D. M., & McCarthy, J. (1989). Adolescent childbearing and high school completion in the 1980s: Have things changed? *Family Planning Perspectives, 21*(5), 199-202.

Upchurch, D. M., & McCarthy, J. (1990, April). The timing of a first birth and high school completion. *American Sociological Review, 55,* 224-234.

U.S. Bureau of the Census. (1985). *Statistical abstracts of the United States: 1986* (106th ed.). Washington, DC: Government Printing Office.

U.S. Bureau of the Census. (1989). *Studies in marriage and the family* (Current Population Reports, Series P-23, No. 162). Washington, DC: Government Printing Office.

Vener, A. M., & Stewart, C. S. (1974). Adolescent sexual behavior in middle America revisited: 1970-1973. *Journal of Marriage and the Family, 36,* 728-735.

Vinovskis, M. A. (1988). Teenage pregnancy and the underclass. *The Public Interest, 93*(Fall), 87-96.

Watters, W. W. (1980). Mental health consequences of abortion and refused abortion. *Canadian Journal of Psychiatry, 25*(1), 68-73.

Westoff, C. F. (1988). Contraceptive paths toward the reduction of unintended pregnancy and abortion. *Family Planning Perspectives, 20*(1), 413.

Westoff, C. F., Calot, G., & Foster, A. D. (1983). Teenage fertility in developed nations. *Family Planning Perspectives, 15*(3), 105-108.

Whitley, B. E., & Schofield, J. W. (1986). A meta-analysis of research on adolescent contraceptive use. *Population and Environment, 8*(3-4), 173-203.

Williams, L. B., & Pratt, W. F. (1990). Wanted and unwanted childbearing in the United States: 1973-1988. *Advance Data From Vital and Health Statistics,* No. 189. Hyattsville, MD: National Center for Health Statistics.

Wilson, W. J. (1981, March). The black community in the 1980s: Questions of race, class, and public policy. *Annals of the American Academy of Political and Social Sciences, 454,* 26-41.

Wilson, W. J. (1987). *The truly disadvantaged: The inner city, the underclass, and public policy.* Chicago: University of Chicago Press.

Youngs, D. D., Niebyl, J. R., Blake, D. A., Shipp, D. A., Stanley, J., & King, T. M. (1977). Experience with an adolescent pregnancy program. *Obstetrics and Gynecology, 50*(2), 212-216.

Zabin, L. S. (1981). The impact of early use of prescription contraceptives on reducing premarital teenage pregnancies. *Family Planning Perspectives, 13*(2), 72-74.

Zabin, L. S., & Clark, S. D. (1981). Why they delay: A study of teenage family planning clinic patients. *Family Planning Perspectives, 13*(5), 205-217.

Zabin, L. S., & Clark, S. D., Jr. (1983). Institutional factors affect teenagers' choice and reasons for delay in attending a family planning clinic. *Family Planning Perspectives, 15*(1), 25-29.

Zabin, L. S., Hardy, J. B., Streett, R., & King, T. M. (1984). A school, hospital, and university-based adolescent pregnancy prevention program: A cooperative design for service and research. *Journal of Reproductive Medicine, 29*(6), 421-426.

Zabin, L. S., & Hirsch, M. B. (1987). *Evaluation of pregnancy prevention programs in the school context.* Lexington, MA: D.C. Heath.

Zabin, L. S., Hirsch, M. B., & Boscia, J. A. (1990). Differential characteristics of adolescent pregnancy test patients: Abortion, childbearing, and negative-test groups. *Journal of Adolescent Health Care, 11*(2), 107-113.

Zabin, L. S., Hirsch, M. B., & Emerson, M. R. (1989). When urban adolescents choose abortion: Effects on education, psychological status, and subsequent pregnancy. *Family Planning Perspectives, 21*(6), 245-255.

Zabin, L. S., Hirsch, M. B., Emerson, E. R., & Raymond, E. (1992). To whom do inner city minors talk about their pregnancies? Adolescents' communication with parents and parent surrogates. *Family Planning Perspectives, 24*(4), 148-154.

Zabin, L. S., Hirsch, M. B., Smith, E. A., Smith, M., Emerson, M. R., King, T., Streett, R., & Hardy, J. B. (1988). The Baltimore pregnancy prevention program for urban teenagers: What did it cost? *Family Planning Perspectives, 20*(4), 188-192.

Zabin, L. S., Hirsch, M. B., Smith, E. A., Streett, R., & Hardy, J. B. (1986). Evaluation of a pregnancy prevention program for urban teenagers. *Family Planning Perspectives, 18*(3), 119-126.

Zabin, L. S., Kantner, J. F., & Zelnik, M. (1979). The risk of adolescent pregnancy in the first months after intercourse. *Family Planning Perspectives, 11*(4), 215-222.

Zealley, A. K., & Aitken, R. C. B. (1969). Measurement of mood. *Proceedings of the Royal Society of Medicine, 62*(10), 993-996.

Zellman, G. L. (1982). Public school programs for adolescent pregnancy and parenthood: An assessment. *Family Planning Perspectives, 14*(1), 15-21.

Zelnik, M., & Kantner, J. (1977). Sexual and contraceptive experience of young unmarried women in the United States, 1976 and 1971. *Family Planning Perspectives, 9*(2), 55-71.

Zelnik, M., & Kantner, J. F. (1979). Reasons for nonuse of contraception by sexually active women aged 15-19. *Family Planning Perspectives, 11*(5), 289-296.

Zelnik, M., & Kantner, J. F. (1980). Sexual activity, contraceptive use and pregnancy among metropolitan-area teenagers. *Family Planning Perspectives, 12*(5), 230-237.

Zelnik, M., Kantner, J. F., & Ford, K. (1981). *Sex and pregnancy in adolescence.* Beverly Hills, CA: Sage.

Zelnik, M., & Kim, Y. J. (1982). Sex education and its association with sexual activity, pregnancy, and contraceptive use. *Family Planning Perspectives, 14*(3), 117-126.

Zelnik, M., & Shah, F. K. (1983). First intercourse among young Americans. *Family Planning Perspectives, 15*(2), 64-70.

Index

Abortion, 6-7, 8, 128
  availability of, 40, 161-162
  boyfriend's support for, 56, 71, 75
  choice of, 60-62
  discussed with mother, 27-28
  family and peer support for, 56, 68
  influences on, 62-72
  knowledge of where to obtain, 26, 70
  middle-class teenagers and, 160
  mothers' support for, 93, 126
  negative sequelae of, 87
  numbers of, 60
  outcomes, 60-84
  psychosocial effects, 61-62
  regrets about, 81-82
  subsidized, 161-162
Abortion study group, 7
  abortion information and, 26
  attitudes toward pregnancy, 90, 96
  background characteristics, 88-94
  boyfriend's influence on pregnancy decision and, 71
  characteristics at study enrollment, 88-94
  characteristics 2 years later, 94-99
  contraceptive information and, 25, 28-29, 91-92, 97
  contraceptive use and, 24, 105
  discussions with mothers and, 121
  economic status, 74-75, 89, 94-95
  educational goals, 52, 74, 89-90, 96
  educational status, 63-64, 72-73, 89, 95, 108
  employment and, 63
  expectations of motherhood and, 48-49

  family relations and, 71, 76-77
  family support for childbearing and, 93
  feelings about pregnancy, 64-65
  follow-up, 156-157
  marriage and, 72
  mothers' support and, 69, 93
  occupational goals, 74, 89-90, 96
  psychological status, 92, 98, 112
  regrets about decision and, 81
  relationships and, 71, 76-77, 92, 97-98
  satisfaction with pregnancy decision, 79-81
  self-esteem, 33-34, 76-77
  sexual attitudes, 31
  subsequent pregnancy and, 83, 99, 115-116
  support for childbearing and, 65-68, 93
  10 year follow-up, 154
  wantedness of pregnancy and, 44, 47, 157
  worry about pregnancy, 32
Abrahamse, A. F., 42, 89
Abstractions, ability to understand, 22, 35
Adler, N. E., 61, 87
Adults in household, ratio of working adults to, 13, 14, 63, 110
Affect, assessment of, 11
Age:
  at initial intercourse, 4, 24
  of dating, 23
  of marriage, 2
  of mothers at first childbearing, 63, 88

sample, 12
subsequent pregnancy and, 106-107, 115
Aid to Families With Dependent Children, 2, 61
Aitken, R. C. B., 44
Alan Guttmacher Institute, 4, 60
Alcohol, 32
Alternatives of pregnancy, ability to weigh, 5
Ambivalence:
    about contraceptive use, 21, 29
    wantedness of pregnancy and, 8-9, 42, 44, 157
An, C. B., 57
Armstrong, E., 61
Assertiveness, self-esteem and, 33, 37, 76
Assessment points, 10-11, 164

Babies:
    effects of having, 66, 141
    happiness to have, 48-49
    income and, 153-155
Baby boomers, 1
Background characteristics, 88-94, 169-172
Baker, S. A., 121
Baldwin, W., 135
Becker, M. H., 6, 120
Bekker, D., 22
Benjamin, P., 61
Berger, D. E., 22
Bianchi, E. C., 23
Black family, approval of contraceptive use and, 6
Black teenagers:
    birthrate, 5
    births to single parent, 2, 3
    mother's support for abortion and, 70
    Penn Study and, 6
    self-esteem and, 23
    unwanted births, 43
Blacks:
    intercourse experience, 4
    poverty and, 5
Blum, R. W., 70

Bolling, B., 22
Bolton, F. G., Jr., 102, 117
Boyfriends:
    abortion support, 56, 71, 75
    acceptance of pregnancy, 54-55
    attitudes about contraception, 29
    child care and, 56
    influence on pregnancy decision, 71-72
    lack of responsibility, 31
    mothers' knowledge of, 126, 128-129
    relations with, 75-76, 92, 97-98
    repeat pregnancy and, 115
    support for childbearing, 54, 65-66, 94, 111
    wanting to please, 31, 71.
    See also Male teenagers
Bracken, M., 70
Bracken, M. B., 70
Brandt, C. L., 22
Brooks-Gunn, J., 154, 155
Brown, L., 22
Burt, M. R., 61

Canada, teenage pregnancy in, 4
Career counseling, 125
Casper, L. M., 37
Cates, W. Jr., 61
Childbearing:
    acceptability of, 42, 54-57, 110-111, 119-120
    ambivalence of, 42
    avoiding, 86-101
    effects of, 66, 141
    family and friend support for, 65-68, 93-94, 110-111
    income and, 153-155
    outcomes, 60-84
    preventing early teenage, 119-137
    regrets about, 81-82
    social support for, 65-68
    teenagers' expectations of, 48-49
    See also Delivery study group
Child care, male sharing in, 56
Children, income and, 153-155
Chilman, C., 23, 36
Clark, S. D., 20, 21
Cobliner, W. G., 21

Cognitive development, 22
College, goals for, 50, 64
Community leaders, 162-163
Concrete thought, 22
Condoms, 26, 91, 146, 151-152
Contraception:
    access to, 26
    availability of, 41, 125
    boyfriends' attitudes about, 29
    delay in using, 20-21, 91-92
    male partners knowledge of, 146-147, 149-150
    mothers' opinion of, 126
    risk-taking behavior and, 20-37
Contraceptive effectiveness, 86
Contraceptive failure, 24, 92
Contraceptive information, 25-28, 36, 91-92, 97, 160
Contraceptive use, 24, 91, 97, 128, 141
    consistent, 9
    cultural milieu and, 5
    delivery group and, 114-115
    family and, 5-6
    maintaining, 105
    U.S. teenagers, 4
Coopersmith, S., 11, 33, 76, 111
Coopersmith (1967) Inventory, 33
Coping skills, 11
Counseling, Family Involvement Project and, 123-124
Crawford, T. J., 22
Currie, J. B., 22
Cutright, P., 2
Cvejic, H., 61
Cvetkovich, G., 11, 22, 30

Dale, L. G., 22
Data collection, 10-11
Dating, age of, 23
David, H. P., 61
Davis, K., 139
Delivery:
    choice of, 60-62
    influences on, 62-72
Delivery study group, 6-7
    abortion information and, 26
    backgrounds, 63

boyfriend's influence on pregnancy decision and, 71
contraceptive information and, 25, 28-29
contraceptive use and, 24, 105, 114-115
discussions with mothers and, 121
economic status, 74-75
educational goals, 52, 74, 107, 157
educational status, 63-64, 73, 107
expectations of motherhood and, 48-49
family relations and, 76-77
feelings about another pregnancy, 45-46
feelings about pregnancy, 64-65
follow-up, 157
marriage and, 72, 75
mothers' support and, 69
occupational goals, 74, 110, 114, 157
psychological factors, 112
regrets about decision and, 81
relationship with mothers, 71
satisfaction with pregnancy decision, 79-80
self-esteem and, 33-34, 76-77
sexual attitudes, 31
subsequent pregnancy and, 45, 83, 114-116
support for childbearing and, 65-68
wantedness of pregnancy and, 44, 157
worry about pregnancy, 32
Demographic factors, subsequent pregnancy and, 113
Depression, 22-23, 112
    postabortion, 87
Derogatis, L. R., 11, 34, 77, 111
Developed countries, age at intercourse and, 4
Dickens, H. O., 11, 25, 28, 140
Drugs, 32

Economic costs, 2
Economic factors, avoiding childbearing and, 89, 94-95
Economic status, 3, 13

pregnancy decision and, 74-75
subsequent pregnancy and, 109-110
10 year follow-up, 153-155
Education, interrupted, 2
Educational achievement, 13
Educational goals, 50-52, 58, 63, 156
abortion group, 52, 74, 89-90, 96
avoiding childbearing and, 89-90,
96, 107
delivery group and, 52, 74, 207, 157
never-pregnant group, 52, 89-90, 96
repeat pregnancy and, 115
Educational status, 154
avoiding childbearing and, 89, 95
pregnancy decision and, 72-73
subsequent pregnancy and, 107-109
Education level, 14
Emerson, E. R., 61, 80, 87, 88, 104
Emily B. H. Mudd Research Fund, 7
Emotional distress, 77-78, 98, 111-112
Emotional factors, 22, 34, 37
Employment, 52, 89, 90, 95
abortion group and, 63
male teenagers, 145
pregnancy decision and, 74
England, teenage pregnancy in, 4
Everly, K., 139
Eysenck, H. J., 11, 34, 35, 78, 98
Eysenck, S. B. G., 11, 34, 35, 78, 98
Eysenck Personality Inventory, 11, 34,
78, 98

Falk, R., 22
Family:
abortion support and, 56, 68
acceptance by, 54-57
communication in, 119-137, 158-159
contraceptive information from, 27-
28
contraceptive use and, 5-6
educational expectations and, 50,
64, 90
extended, 5-6
father in, 92
income status, 3, 13
mother and grandmother in, 12
preventing early teenage childbearing and, 119-137

relations with, 75-77, 92, 97-98, 125
self-esteem and, 33
sexual behavior influences, 5-6
sexual information from, 149-150
support for childbearing, 65-68, 93-
94, 110-111
two-adult, 12
welfare recipients, 89, 95, 109
working adults in, 13, 14, 63, 110
See also Mothers
Family Involvement Project, 119-137,
148-151, 158-159
Family life, high school classes on, 140
Family planning services, 20
female orientation of, 138
preventive efforts, 9
recommendations for, 161-162
teenagers enrolled in, 7
Fathers:
acceptance of teenage pregnancy, 54
in households, 92
Females, intercourse experience, 4
Fertile time, identification of, 25, 29,
91, 147
Fischman, S. H., 70
Food stamps, 2
Forrest, J. D., 4, 41, 43
Fox, G. L., 6, 121
France, teenage pregnancy in, 4
Freeman, E. W., 11, 25, 28, 61, 77, 87,
140
Friends, see Peers
Furstenberg, F. F., 104, 121, 154, 155
Future orientation, 11, 22, 35, 37

Gabrielson, I. W., 22
Garcia, C.-R., 11, 25, 28, 61, 77, 140
Gispert, M., 22
Goals, competing with maternity, 50-53
Goldman, N., 4, 41
Grandmothers:
abortion support and, 56
in household, 12
Grandparents, paternal, 56
Grossbard-Schectman, A., 139
Grote, B., 11, 22, 30
Groups, Family Involvement Project
and, 123-124

Guilt, 21, 79, 87

Hardy, J. B., 104
Haverman, R., 57
Health-care services, availability of, 41
Henry, W. K., 22
Henshaw, S. K., 4, 41, 60
Herzog-Baron, R., 121
Hirsch, M. B., 61, 80, 87, 88, 104
Hispanics, unmarried teenage child-
     bearing, 3
Hofferth, S. L., 135
Hogan, D. P., 12, 42
Hogue, C. J. R., 61
Horn, M. C., 20, 21
Hospital of the University of Pennsyl-
     vania, 9
Household composition, 12-13
Huggins, G., 11, 25, 28, 61, 77, 140

Inamdar, S. C., 23
Income, 3
     children and, 153-155
     parents and, 13
Infant mortality, 61
Interview questionnaire, 10-11, 179-194
Intrauterine devices, 26, 92
Iverson, R. R., 153, 154

Jekel, J. F., 22
Jessor, R., 23
Jessor, S. L., 23
Job potential, 2
Job skills, lack of, 2, 3
Jones, E. F., 4, 41

Kahn, J. R., 104, 135
Kane, F. J., 22
Kantner, J., 20
Kantner, J. F., 3, 25, 41, 141
Keller, R., 22
Kinch, R. A., 61
Kitagawa, E. M., 12
Klerman, L. B., 70
Klerman, L. V., 22

Koenig, M. A., 104
Kreipe, R. E., 22
Ku, L. C., 139

Ladner, J. A., 23
Leighton, C. K., 139
Lincoln, R., 4, 41
Lipper, I., 61
Loneliness, 32
Lortie, G., 70
Low-birth-weight infants, 2, 61
Luker, K., 21

MacDonald, A. P., 22
Major, B. N., 61
Male partner, *see* Boyfriends
Male teenagers:
     contraception and, 138-152
     family planning and, 161
     self-esteem of sexually experienced,
        23
Males, intercourse experience, 4.
        See also Boyfriends; Fathers
Marriage:
     age of, 2
     as condition for childbearing, 90
     delivery group and, 75
     lack of plans for, 72
     pregnancy leading to, 139
     social pressure and, 2
Marsiglio, W. K., 36
McAnarney, E. R., 22
McCarthy, J., 61
Measurement instruments, 164
Media:
     contraceptive information from, 27
     effects on teenage pregnancy, 3
     glorification of sexuality and, 4
     influence of, 125
Medicaid, 2, 13
Medical complications, 61
Middle-class teenagers, abortion and,
     160
Miller, S. H., 23
Miller, W. B., 42
Mindick, B., 22
Moan, C. A., 22

Morgan, S. P., 154, 155
Morin-Gunthier, M., 70
Morrison, D. M., 121
Morrison, P. A., 42, 89
Mosher, W. D., 20, 21
Mother-daughter relationships, 123, 129-130
Motherhood, teenagers' expectations of, 48-49
Mothers:
    abortion decision made by, 70
    abortion discussed with, 27-28
    abortion support and, 56, 93, 126
    acceptance of teenage pregnancy, 54
    age at first childbirth, 63
    as teen childbearers, 13, 157
    average age of childbearing, 88
    communication with, 36-37
    contraceptive information from, 27-28
    contraceptive use and, 126
    head of household, 12
    influence on pregnancy decision, 68-70
    knowledge of sexual activity, 128-129
    perceptions of teenage pregnancy, 125-127
    preventing early teenage childbearing and, 119-137
    relations with, 71, 75
    support for childbearing, 65, 67, 75, 156
Mott, F. L., 36, 83
Mudd, E. H., 11, 25, 28, 77, 140

Nathanson, C. A., 6, 120
National Institute of Child Health and Human Development, 7
National Research Council, 3
National Surveys of Family Growth, 43
Netherlands, teenage pregnancy in, 4
Never-pregnant study group, 7
    abortion information and, 26
    age/pregnancy relationship, 106-107
    attitudes toward pregnancy, 90, 96
    background characteristics, 88-94

characteristics at study enrollment, 88-94
characteristics two years later, 94-99
contraceptive information and, 25, 28-29, 91-92, 97
contraceptive use, 24, 105
discussions with mothers and, 121
economic factors, 89, 94-95
educational goals, 52, 89-90, 96
educational status, 89, 95, 108
expectations of motherhood and, 48-49
family support for childbearing and, 93
follow-up, 156-157
future pregnancy, 99
occupational goals, 89-90, 96
psychological factors, 112
psychological status, 92, 98
relationships and, 92, 97-98
self-esteem, 33-34
sexual attitudes, 31
social class index, 113
10 year follow-up, 153-154
wantedness of pregnancy and, 44, 47, 157
worry about pregnancy, 32
Newcomber, S. F., 121

Occupational goals, 52-53, 58, 63, 156
    abortion group, 74, 89-90, 96
    avoiding childbearing and, 89-90, 96
    delivery group, 74, 110, 114, 157
    follow-up and, 109
    never-pregnant group, 89-90, 96
    repeat pregnancy and, 115
Occupational opportunities, 61, 163
Oral contraceptives, 26, 91, 92, 97, 138-139, 146
Osborn, M., 23
Oskamp, S., 22
Osofsky, H. J., 87
Osofsky, J. D., 87

Parenthood, as abstraction, 35
Parenthood risk factor, 89
Parenting, realistic perceptions of, 66

Parents, relations with, 75-76. *See also* Fathers; Mothers
Participant characteristics, 12-15, 63
Pascale, A., 61
Paulker, S., 102
Peers:
  abortion support, 68
  acceptance by, 54-57
  contraceptive information from, 27
  pregnancy among, 127
  relations with, 75-76, 97
  support for childbearing, 65-68, 93-94, 110-111
  supportive, 55
Penn Study of Teenage Pregnancy, 6-15
  data collection, 10-11
  participant characteristics, 12-15
  pregnancy after enrollment in, 102-117
  premises and assumptions of, 7-9
  sample attrition and, 11-12
  sample characteristics, 88-94
  sample selection, 9-10
  ten years later, 153-155
Personality dimensions, 34-35
Pill, 26, 91, 92, 97, 138-139, 146
Planning:
  for future goals, 35
  lack of, 5, 22
Pleck, J. H., 139
Pohlman, E. H., 8, 42, 44, 57
Polin, J., 61
Polit, D. F., 104
Poverty, 2, 5, 125, 155
Pratt, W. F., 43
Pregnancy:
  acceptance of, 54-57
  after study enrollment, 102-117
  ambivalence of, 42
  as abstraction, 35
  attitudes toward, 44-50, 90-91, 96
  consequences of, 141
  feelings about, 64-65
  future incidence of, 99
  male teenagers and, 138-152
  motivation to prevent, 41
  opposition to, 68
  outcomes, 103-104
  planning, 43, 46-47, 96

  prevention of, 9, 119-137
  risking, 20-37
  subsequent, 83, 134-135
  wantedness of, 7-8, 40-58, 64-65, 80, 90, 96, 110, 141, 145-146, 149, 157
Pregnancy decision:
  boyfriend's influence on, 71-72
  effects of, 81-82
  influences on, 62-72
  mother's influence on, 68-70
  outcomes of, 72-83
  psychological assessment, 76-79
  satisfaction with, 79-81
Pregnancy risk, 20-37
  contraceptive information and, 25-28, 36
  contraceptive use and, 24
  psychological factors and, 33-35, 37
  sexual behavior and, 23-24, 36
  understanding of, 41
Pregnancy scare, 7
Prenatal care, 61
Prevention, of early teenage childbearing, 9, 119-137
Procrastination, 21
Psychological assessment, pregnancy decision and, 76-79
Psychological factors, 33-35, 37
  subsequent pregnancy and, 111-113
Psychological status, avoiding childbearing and, 92-93, 98
Psychosexual maturity, 5
Psychosocial effects, abortion and, 61-62
Public Health Service, 4

Racism, 125
Rader, G. E., 22
Rainwater, L., 117
Raymond, E., 80
Reasoning ability, 22
Reed, J., 138
Relationships:
  assessment of, 11
  avoiding childbearing and, 92, 97-98
  pregnancy decision and, 75-76
Religion, 14
Religious education, 125

Residence, changes of, 13-14
Resnick, M. D., 70
Richard, T. C., 22
Rickels, K., 11, 25, 28, 61, 77, 140
Risk-taking behavior, 20-37
Roghmann, K. J., 22
Romantic notions of sex, 21
Rosen, R. H., 70
Rosenberg, M., 76
Rosenberg (1965) Scale, 33
Rosenfeld, D. L., 25
Rosoff, J. I., 4, 41
Roth, S. H., 61
Rovinsky, J. J., 22
Russo, N. F., 61

Sample attrition, 11-12
Sample characteristics, 88-94
Sample selection, 9-10
Scales, P., 139
Schofield, J. W., 5
School dropout, 15, 60-61, 73, 95, 108, 154, 155
School performance, 14, 15, 115
Scrimshaw, S. C. M., 138
Self-acceptance, 33, 37, 76
Self-esteem, 23, 33-34
    assertiveness and, 33, 37, 76
    subsequent pregnancy and, 111-113
Sex education, 27, 41, 125, 160, 161
Sexual activity:
    acceptability of, 31
    age of, 4
    choosing, 134
    sporadic, 24, 25, 91
Sexual attitudes and feelings, 30-33, 37
Sexual behavior:
    family influences on, 5-6
    pregnancy risk and, 23-24, 36
    responsible, 121-122, 162
    self-esteem and, 23
Sexual experience, 22, 128-129
    male teenagers, 23, 148-149
Sexual information and attitudes, 28-33, 91, 97, 140
Sexual intercourse:
    age at initial, 4, 24
    delay after initial, 24

    satisfaction with, 32
Sexuality, glorified, 4
Sexually transmitted diseases, 28, 161
Sexual maturity, 32
Sexual situations, unplanned, 5
Shea, J., 121
Siblings:
    number of, 88
    support for pregnancy, 66
    with babies, 54, 88
Sims, J., 22
Single motherhood, 12
    acceptance of, 1, 42, 49, 54, 70
    social sanctions for, 139
Siomopoulos, G., 23
Sisters:
    as teenage mothers, 88
    support for pregnancy, 66
Social class index, 113
Social status, 13
Social support, 55-56, 75-76
    extended family and, 5-6
    family and, 120
Socioeconomic status, 2, 3, 5, 88-89
Sonenstein, F. L., 139
Spermicidal foam, 26
Stack, C., 5, 120
Statistical procedures, 165-166
Statistical tables, 173-178
Streetman, L. G., 23
Suicide, 22
Sweden, teenage pregnancy in, 4
Symptom Checklist (SCL-90), 11, 34, 77, 111

Technical training, 50, 64
Teenage childbearing, 12
    acceptance of, 1, 42, 49, 54, 70
    factors associated with, 2-3
    preventing, 119-137
    social sanctions for, 139
Teenage pregnancy:
    as social problem, 1
    changes in ideas about, 130-135
    developed countries and, 4
    mothers having, 13
    mothers' perceptions of, 125-127
    studying, 1-17

See also Pregnancy
Teichmann, A. T., 40
Thalberg, S. P., 121
Tietze, C., 61
Trussell, J., 41
Tyler, N. C., 22

Udry, J. R., 121
Unemployment, 60, 163
United States, teenage pregnancy in, 4, 8
Unwantedness, feelings of, 8
Upchurch, D. M., 61

Van Vort, J., 60
Vinovskis, M. A., 136

Waite, L. J., 42, 89
Webb, D., 121
Welfare, 13, 60, 61, 63, 74-75, 89, 95, 109, 125, 157
Welfare budget, 2
Westoff, C. F., 4, 6, 41
Whites, intercourse experience, 4

White teenagers:
  birthrate, 5
  births to single parent, 2, 3
  self-esteem and, 23
  unwanted births, 43
Whitley, B. E., 5
Williams, L. B., 43
William T. Grant Foundation, 7
Wilson, W. J., 42
Withdrawal method, 26, 147
Wolfe, B., 57
Work experience, 52, 89, 90, 95
Working adults, ratio to adults in household, 13, 14, 63, 110
Wulf, D., 4, 41
Wyatt, G. E., 61

Youth Risk Behavior Survey (1990), 4

Zabin, L., 20
Zabin, L. S., 20, 21, 61, 80, 87, 88, 104
Zealley, A. K., 44
Zelnick, M., 3, 25, 41, 141
Zelnik, M., 20, 104

About the Authors

Ellen W. Freeman, Ph.D., is Research Professor in the Departments of Obstetrics/Gynecology and Psychiatry at the University of Pennsylvania School of Medicine. Her research centers on women's health issues, particularly as they intersect with the reproductive system. In addition to teenage pregnancy, contraception, and abortion, she conducts studies in infertility and premenstrual syndrome and directs the Premenstrual Syndrome Program in the Department of Obstetrics and Gynecology. She has published numerous reports of her research in leading medical journals.

Karl Rickels, M.D., is the Stuart and Emily B. H. Mudd Professor of Human Behavior and Professor of Psychiatry at the University of Pennsylvania School of Medicine. He has devoted his entire professional career to the study of the interface between emotional illness, its behavioral manifestations, and its treatment. His research interests range from the study of women's health issues, such as teenage pregnancy, infertility, and premenstrual symptomatology, to the study and treatment of anxiety, panic disorder, and depression. He conducts a large research group concerned with tranquilizer dependency. He has published nearly 500 articles in leading medical journals based on the findings of his research activities and has edited several books.

216